CRUEL TRUTH

CRUEL TRUTH

K.A. LINDE

ALSO BY K. A. LINDE

CRUEL PROMISE

A CRUEL PREQUEL

K.A. LINDE

WINTER

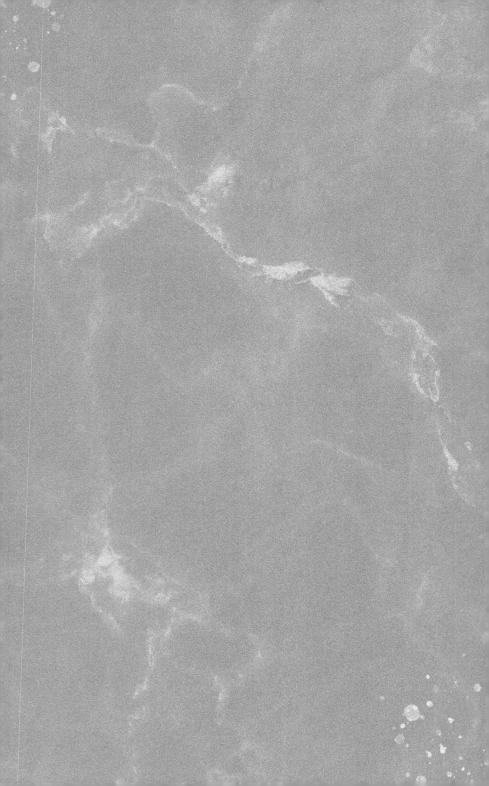

I

"Breathe. You can do this."

I bit my dark pink–painted lips, pushed open the door, and stepped into the chaos that was the Wisconsin state headquarters for Governor Woodhouse's presidential bid. It was everything I'd expected. Staff seated at cubicles, half-finished signs littered a table, an array of volunteers lined up in front of a row of computers, and the permeating smell of coffee.

I couldn't stop the excited smile from creeping onto my face. I was really here. I'd made it to Madison, and I was officially working for Governor Woodhouse—at a state office, no less. It was as if all of my dreams were finally coming true.

"You look lost," a guy said, stepping up with the biggest, most heart-stopping brown eyes I'd ever seen.

"A little," I admitted. "I'm Lark. I'm supposed to start working here today, I think."

His eyes brightened even further. "The new girl. Right. Toby said you'd be coming in today. He said that I'd be mentoring you." He stuck his hand out. "I'm Sam."

"Hi."

I shook his hand, lingering a second at the firm grasp and long musician's fingers. I drew back shyly. Something I was pretty sure

I'd never been in my entire life. But the look on Sam's face was enough to make me forget who I was. That I was actually Larkin St. Vincent, heiress to St. Vincent's Enterprise, a multibillion-dollar company headquartered in New York City. Not that I wanted anyone to know that here.

"Well, welcome to Madison. It's not New York—that's where you're from, right?" he asked, continuing without waiting for my answer, "But I think you'll like it."

I smiled, taking in everything about him in one sweeping glance. One thing was for sure; he was hardly the typical Upper East Side prep guy I was used to. There was something more to him. Something intensely masculine and unpolished in all the right ways.

"Yes, New York," I said. "Are you from here?"

"God, no," he said, gesturing for me to follow him into an office. "I don't even know how I survived the winter. I'm from North Carolina. Tar Heel born and bred."

I laughed and tugged off my scarf. I stuffed it into my purse, which I dropped onto a brown cushioned chair.

"I wouldn't get too comfortable," another voice said from the door.

I turned around and came face-to-face with a gorgeous woman with brown skin and long black hair that she wore in loose, voluminous waves.

"Moira," the woman said, holding out a hand covered in henna. "You're Lark, I presume? Toby gave me your email."

"Yes, that's me," I said, shaking Moira's hand. "Nice to meet you. Is Toby around?"

Toby was the regional campaign director for the Madison area and their boss. I'd interviewed with him twice and found him to be an eccentric, energetic man. The kind of man whose great passion would sustain us through a hard-fought campaign season. Or at least, I hoped so.

"Toby is tied up in meetings with the state team. Sam here is going to take you under his wing. He's been here nearly as long as Toby, so you're in safe hands."

"Great. I'm ready to get started."

"That's what we like to hear. At this point, you, Sam, and I are divvying up most of Madison on the ground for Governor Woodhouse. So, welcome to the team."

"It's great to finally be here."

"Thanks, Moira. I was getting to that part," Sam said with a shake of his head.

"Anytime." She turned back to me. "Are you okay with sharing this office with Sam? We're already short on space, but Josh is working on getting us the building next door."

"Yeah, that's fine by me." I snuck another glance at Sam. I caught him staring at me, and he hastily looked away when our eyes met. "Who is Josh?"

"He's Toby's immediate boss. As the state field manager, he runs the campaign for everyone in the field for the entire state of Wisconsin," Moira said. "Think of this as one big hierarchy. We work for Toby, who works for Josh, who works for the head of the Midwest organization, who works for the field campaign manager, who works for the overall campaign manager, who works for Governor Woodhouse. Our job is to add to the hierarchy and get people to work underneath us. Preferably for free." She turned to the desk, grabbed two clipboards from Sam's stuff, and passed them to each of us. "Now, go bring me back seven voter registrations by five, and then we'll make a hundred phone calls."

Moira smiled cheerily and then jaunted out of the room.

I turned to Sam with wide eyes. "Is she serious?"

Sam laughed. "That's Moira for you. Come on. I'll show you the ropes."

"Just like that? I mean...I don't even get to see the office or drop my stuff at my apartment or anything?"

"Welcome to the campaign," Sam said with a wink.

I looked down at my high heels and shook my head. "At least let me find some sneakers."

His eyes traveled to my shoes, and unbidden, his laughter boomed out of him. I couldn't help it. Suddenly, I was laughing with him.

"Not my smartest move," I admitted.

"Definitely not in the snow."

I tucked the clipboard under my arm, grabbed my bag, and then headed out to the car my parents had insisted on for my time in Madison. I'd managed to keep them from buying a flashy Mercedes. They'd been appalled that I wanted a low-key Subaru but finally relented.

Of course, I hadn't told them it was because for the first time in my life, I wasn't going to be Larkin St. Vincent, but just Lark. Not an heir to an empire. Just a girl.

"Drive all the way here from New York?" Sam asked as I dug through my suitcase in the trunk.

"Oh god, no." I shot him a skeptical look. "I'm not a great driver. I didn't even get a license until I went to college."

"That's insane to me. I grew up driving all the back roads long before I had a license."

I pulled out my sneakers and snapped the trunk shut. I tossed Sam the keys. "By all means, Country Boy."

He laughed. "I'll show you how it's done, City Girl."

II

"You guys getting all of this?" Toby asked, bouncing from foot to foot with excitement.

I sat with Sam and Moira in the rickety plastic chairs. We glanced up at our boss and nodded encouragingly. Sam gave him a thumbs-up.

Moira leaned in and said, "We are one hundred and ten percent focused."

"Excellent. I'm ready to implement all this new knowledge and crush those numbers."

Toby held his hand up, and Moira sighed and then gave him a high five. Toby went down the row, high-fiving Sam and then finally me.

"Okay, back to the material!"

I shook my head as Toby jogged back up to the front of the room to stand with the other field managers as the presentation continued. We'd been at this state-level training at a warehouse outside of Madison all day. It was exhausting and repetitive.

I'd spent the last three weeks with Sam at the office. He'd mentored me through the basics of campaign life. I had my own assignments and tasks to complete for my section of Madison, which primarily included State Street and the University of

Wisconsin–Madison. But Sam was the person I called when I had a question. He was the person who walked me through the voter registration laws, pulling call lists, entering data into the voter system, and a myriad of other things. This statewide training was a lot of the same information recycled back, and I had to admit that I'd liked hearing it from Sam first.

"Are you guys pumped up?" Moira asked with an eye roll. "Or are you snoozing?"

"So pumped up," I said dryly.

"It's not *that* bad," Sam said.

"You've been to at least three of these. Don't you ever get sick of it?" Moira asked.

"Sure. But they really do it for the newbies, like Lark."

I wrinkled my nose at him. "Hey, my teacher already covered this material. I'm pretty sure I aced the exam."

Sam chuckled and leaned back in the uncomfortable plastic chair. "I meant that it pumps up the newbs. Gives you that extra bit of excitement to really make it through the next couple of months."

"Plus, it's the only day we get to sit around and do nothing," Moira added.

"And eat lunch, *sitting down*." Sam wiggled his fingers at me, and I laughed.

"Who knew I'd be so excited to eat lunch like a regular person? Instead of grabbing something on the go and shoving it down my throat as fast as I can."

Sam gawked, and Moira snickered.

"Phrasing," Moira said.

"Oh my god! That's not what I meant!"

"Shh," a girl hissed directly in front of us.

Sam whispered, "Sorry," to the girl and then went right back to chatting. "Anyway, where should we go for lunch?"

"What's even around here?" Moira asked, pulling her dark hair back into a bun on the top of her head with a pencil. "If we were downtown, I'd say Pel'meni."

"You always vote for Pel'meni," Sam said. He turned to face me, and I froze under that gaze. "Do you have a preference?"

I opened my mouth to respond, but then he gently brushed a strand of chestnut-red hair that had fallen loose from my ponytail behind my ear. I lost coherent thought in that second.

"Let me guess. Burgers?" he asked with his award-winning smile. His hand lingered for a second longer. "With no mustard because it's disgusting?"

I swallowed. "Yes, please."

"Burgers it is," Sam said, finally dropping his hand.

I knew that I should look away. That I should ignore the way my heart pitter-pattered in my chest. I didn't have time for these feelings. God, none of us did. I worked from nine in the morning until ten at night every single day of the week. It was hardly sustainable. Let alone adding in anything other than food and the occasional drink. Sleep was more important. I guarded it with my life. And yet, staring into those eyes, I was seriously considering forsaking sleep. Forsaking a lot of sleep.

Then Sam broke the trance, and I bit my lip to keep from sighing. I was ninety-nine percent sure it was one-sided. That was also new for me. Dates had always been easy to get and utterly mindless. But while being around Sam was easy, nothing about him was mindless.

Which was the main reason I was so attracted to him. He was good-looking. By all means, the tall, dark, and handsome thing really worked for him. But it was so much more than that. He was rugged where I was used to preps. He was passionate where I expected apathy. He was driven, motivated, and hard-working where I'd only known privilege and entitlement. His confidence wasn't born out of how much money resided in his bank account, but from the pride he took in his work. I'd never met anyone like Sam Rutherford.

"We only have a few more minutes before lunch," Josh said, drawing my attention back to him. He double-checked his watch. "You'll have an hour to eat, and then I'll need you back in your seats for the afternoon session. Everyone understand?"

The room grumbled a collective, "Yes." We were all ready to get out of there.

My eyes still darted to Sam's. To my surprise, he had just glanced over at me, too.

He smiled that disarming smile and said, "Ready for lunch?"

"Yeah," I said softly. "Lunch sounds great."

"Cool. I'm going to snag a Coke before we head out. Want one?"

"Just a water."

"Got it!"

Sam popped up and disappeared into the ensuing crowd. Lunch was only an hour, and all the campaign workers were in a hurry to make the most of their meal.

"The rest of the campaign is going to be so fun, watching you two," Moira said. Her dark eyes were filled with laughter.

"What do you mean?" I asked cautiously.

"Oh, please. You both have it bad."

"No way, Moira. Sam is a nice guy and he's mentoring me and...he's not interested."

She rolled her eyes. "And I'm a dodo bird."

I couldn't help but ask, "You think he's interested in me?"

"Does he have eyes?" Moira demanded.

"Well, it doesn't matter, does it? I'm not here for a relationship. I'm here to get Woodhouse elected."

"You're right," Moira said, throwing her arm over my shoulders as Sam appeared.

"All set?" Sam asked.

He passed me a water, and I mumbled, "Thank you."

"Oh, we're ready," Moira said. "Right, Lark?"

I tilted my chin up, refusing to back down. I liked Moira and Sam and everyone else on the campaign, but Woodhouse was the real reason that I was here. A boy was not going to get in the way of me following my dream.

"Yep. I am so ready."

III

I held the box of clipboards to my chest. I'd spent all afternoon on campus with a handful of volunteers, doing voter registration at the end-of-semester events at the University of Wisconsin.

With my hands full, I toed the door to the office open and nearly collapsed once I dropped the box onto the counter.

"God, I need to work out more." I stretched my arms and shoulders. "The walk from campus is literally killing me."

Sam strolled out of our joint office and into the main room. "We should get you a rolling cart or something."

"Please do. It'll save my poor, precious arms." I held them out in front of me and shook them like spaghetti.

Sam laughed and reached into the box of clipboards to count the voter registration forms. He whistled. "Forty-seven. What line are you feeding these undergrads?"

"No line," I said with a shrug. "I'm pretty."

Sam guffawed. "Who knew that was all you needed? I'm sure Toby will be happy tonight when we recap numbers."

"I am starving," I murmured. I glanced down at my phone. "We have twenty-three minutes until we have to make calls. Food?" I fluttered my eyelashes at him. "Please."

"Yes, food for sure. Let me drop these off for data entry, and then we can go."

"Oh, thank god."

I sank into my office chair in the space I still shared with Sam. Even though we'd gotten more space and Toby had said I could have my own office, I'd just gotten used to sharing. Plus, I had to admit that I liked being close to Sam.

I picked up my purse and responded to a few texts as I waited for Sam to return. I yawned dramatically and barely managed to cover it with my hand. I'd gone out with Sam and Moira for drinks last night, and I was so fucking tired. I'd been tired all day. I'd really needed that drink last night, but damn, I missed that extra hour of sleep.

"Okay, all set," Sam said.

"Great!" I said and followed him out of the office.

We wandered across the street and into our favorite burger place near the square. The capitol building stood on the hill, overlooking the rest of the city. It was beautiful and a smaller replica of the capitol in DC. I appreciated that I could see it from anywhere on State Street.

We ordered our burgers and took our meals back to our booth in the corner. We came over nearly every afternoon. Sometimes, he just liked to have his mentoring time there instead of being cooped up in the office with everyone else. It was one-on-one time.

"Did I tell you about Kristy?" Sam asked once we sat down.

"Kristy? Like, volunteer-housing Kristy?"

Like most people on the campaign, Sam had been placed in a volunteers' home for the season. He'd been living in Kristy's extra room in the basement for months. But I knew that he'd been looking to get his own place.

"Yeah. I guess her daughter graduated this semester and is moving back home. So, now, I have to find somewhere else to live."

"When do you have to leave?"

"Tomorrow."

My mouth dropped. "Do you have another volunteer's home lined up? Or did you find a place of your own?"

"Toby is calling the other volunteers who offered to house a staff member, but right now, it looks like I'm sleeping on Toby's floor or getting a hotel until we figure it out. I'm going to go through all the listings for houses. I have enough saved for a down payment."

"That's awful. I hate that it happened so fast."

"Yeah. The living situation is my least favorite part of all of this."

I bit my lip. Did I dare say what was on my mind?

"Well...you know, I have a pull-out couch in my apartment," I said, staring down at my food. "You could stay with me for a while. You know...until you find your own place."

"Oh, well, I'm trying to avoid paying rent," he said with a laugh.

"Actually, my parents pay for it." I took a huge bite of my burger to keep from saying anything more.

My parents had flat-out bought the condo on the top floor of one of the buildings in downtown Madison. They were the controlling type, and money was never an issue. So, they'd simply looked for the nicest place they could find and purchased it. The only say I'd even had in the matter was to convince them to get as close to the office as possible. They'd relented.

Not that I planned to tell Sam any of that. He didn't know who I was or what my parents did or that I came from money. And I liked it that way. He treated me just like everyone else. Everyone on campaign did.

"Are you okay with me crashing on your couch? I mean, I don't know if you like your space to decompress after work," he said carefully. His brown eyes said something else though. "It would just be temporary."

And I really hoped I wasn't misreading that look. I hoped that Moira was right and Sam really did like me. Because the last few weeks had been torture.

"I don't mind. And anyway, there's no reason for you to sleep on the floor or get a hotel when I have a perfectly fine substitute. At least until you find your own place."

He grinned, and it made me squirm. Why did he have to be so attractive? And so different than every other guy I'd ever met?

"All right. Well, I'll pile everything into the truck and come over after work."

"I can help if you need it."

"You're already a big help."

I tried to hide my pleased grin.

Sam was moving in with me. I probably shouldn't have offered. It would put us in close quarters, even more than we were at the office. I was tempting fate by having him in my apartment. But I couldn't help but tempt fate with him.

IV

It was after ten when we were finally done packing up Sam's belongings and putting them in his truck. I took one look at that truck and laughed. Every time I saw the beaten-up old Chevy, I couldn't keep it together. I was interested in a man who drove an old truck. My parents would probably disown me on principle.

"You ready?" Sam asked, stowing his last box.

"Yeah."

"Were you laughing at my truck again?"

I couldn't help but laugh again. "I'm not used to it."

"Maybe you should drive her." He offered me the keys.

I quickly backed away. "Oh, dear god, no. I'll wreck it, and then you'll be without a home or a car. And I'll ruin all your things in the accident. We'd better not."

"One day, I'll get you to drive my truck."

"No way." I shook my head. "That's not happening."

He chuckled and then hopped into the driver's seat. I followed him across town in my Subaru, which had most of his clothes in it. Then, we spent the next half hour unloading all of his stuff into a corner of the apartment. I was hyper-cognizant of the quality of the apartment. Like it was a ticking time bomb, and any second, it would explode, and he'd know all of my carefully kept secrets.

"This is really nice, Lark," Sam said.

"Thanks," I said softly, biting down on my lip.

He peeked into the open door of my bedroom. It was a massive master suite with enough space for two beds, a walk-in closet that could have been a second room, and a bathroom that I was glad he couldn't see at first glance with its giant waterfall shower and a freestanding jetted tub.

"Damn! This place is crazy. A little surprised it's only one-bedroom."

My parents had wanted a two-bedroom, had insisted on it actually, until they'd found this floor plan.

I shrugged off his comment. "Two bedrooms would probably be better for you right about now."

He laughed. "Maybe. Well, thank you for letting me stay."

"Anytime."

He grinned, and my heart melted.

"I should probably take a quick shower. Carrying all those boxes was quite a workout."

My heart deflated. Right. A shower. There was only one bathroom. So, I'd have to show him that.

I swallowed. "Sure. The shower is the first door on the right. Help yourself to anything you need. I am going to have some ice cream. Want any?"

"What do you have?"

"Pretty much everything, except strawberry. I'm allergic."

"Good to know. I'll take whatever you're having. I'll just be a minute."

I nodded and watched him retreat into the bathroom, worrying at my lip with my top teeth. It would be fine. Or at least, I tried to convince myself of that.

To distract myself, I pulled out a container of chocolate chip cookie dough and rocky road and then combined them with a chocolate drizzle on top. I never had time to go to the grocery store, but I always had time for ice cream.

True to his word, Sam appeared back in the living room in less than ten minutes, freshly showered and dressed in basketball shorts and a gray T-shirt. My eyes snagged on his biceps and went down, down, down. And then way back up.

Color hit my cheeks, and I pushed a bowl into his hands. "Here you go."

"Your shower is pretty epic," he said, sinking into the couch next to me.

"Uh, yeah. Thanks. I was not expecting that," I lied. "Really nice, huh?"

"Yeah. Looks like the showers I installed in the rich houses I built with my dad back home."

"Oh, yeah?" I had known that Sam worked construction with his father, but I hadn't known what kind of work he'd done.

"Yeah, this place is a really great find. Your parents chose well."

My cheeks heated, and I hastily pulled up Netflix. I'd fallen asleep on the couch the night before in the middle of an episode of *Parks and Recreation*, and it picked up where I'd left off.

"The campaign episodes?" Sam said, shifting the topic away from my apartment. "Those are my favorite."

"Ben and Leslie are perfect for each other."

"Yeah, but Aubrey Plaza."

"I know, right?" I said with a laugh. "April always says everything I think."

"No way are you that dark."

"You have no idea," I said, wiggling my eyebrows.

"Nah, you're like the sweet girl from the city."

I laughed, setting my ice cream on the coffee table. He couldn't be further from the truth. "There are no sweet city girls, Sam. That's something you just invented."

Sam reached out and pushed a strand of my hair behind my ear. Our eyes locked, and I swore I stopped breathing. His hand trailed over the shell of my ear and then to my neck. The softest touch, as if he knew that he should stop but he didn't.

"You don't give yourself enough credit."

I swallowed. "You give me too much."

"Well, whatever we might have been before, we're here now. I think that's all that matters."

"Yeah," I whispered in agreement.

We didn't break eye contact. He was still touching me. My heart hammered in my chest. We were so close and yet so far. And I didn't know if I should cross that line. All the logical reasons floated out of my brain. Logic and reason were secondary to matters of the heart.

We moved as one, as if pulled by a string. Magnets seeking out the other. My hands pushed into his hair. His grasped my waist, tugging me tight against him. Our lips hovered an inch away and then crashed together. As if the weeks we'd spent in that small office and days of working together and hours of mentoring and every minute and second in each other's presence had coalesced into this moment.

Our lips moved together. Hands roamed. Tongues met. Fire and tension and rapture exploded all around us. Every kiss before this was muted and then utterly disappeared. There was no kiss before this. There was nothing before this.

Just me and Sam.

Two bodies.

One heart.

Then, we slowed and stopped and looked on in a state of euphoria and wonder.

"I've wanted to do that since the first time I saw you," Sam said breathlessly.

His hands had somehow become tangled in my hair. I was practically sitting in his lap.

"Me too."

I kissed him again—thoroughly.

"We should probably stop."

"Uh-huh," I said against his lips.

"Or not," he said and then kissed me some more.

And then some more.

Heedless of our different backgrounds or what lay ahead, we didn't stop kissing until long into the night when I fell soundly asleep on the couch, wrapped in Sam's arms.

SPRING

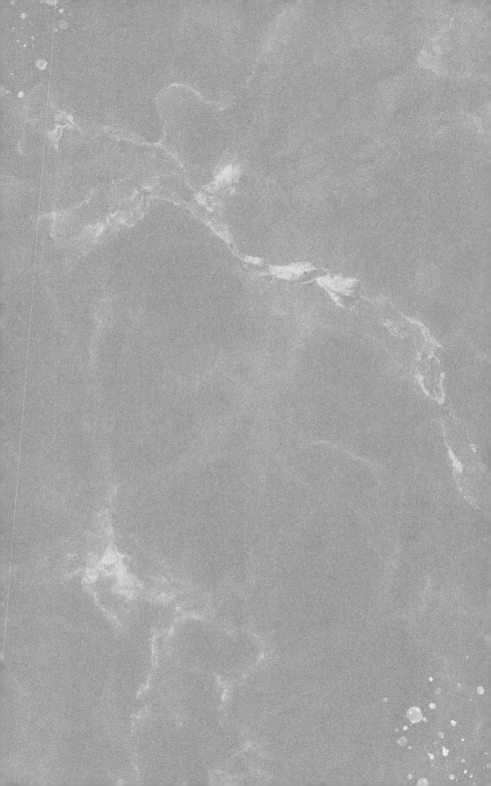

I

If I'd had a two-bedroom apartment, Sam would have moved in with me.

I wanted him to. As irrational as that was. Here I was with a secret identity, and I wanted to bring a stranger into my safe haven. It was close enough that he'd been *to* my apartment, let alone stayed there for the week before he could get his own place.

It was worse when he left.

Because I didn't want him to. And I was pretty sure that I'd never cared this much about anyone. I never wanted anyone to stay.

It wasn't the way I had been raised. The Upper East Side was its own version of fucked up. I'd grown up with controlling parents, four crazy best friends, and too much money. I'd gotten everything I ever wanted and never had any boundaries...except to fall in line with the family.

I'd been raised to follow my family's footsteps. I'd gotten my bachelor's from Brown and a JD from Columbia, and I was supposed to magically take over St. Vincent's Enterprise. Until I'd seen Governor Woodhouse speak in the city, and it had changed everything. He was a man I could get behind. A person I believed in. And I suddenly didn't want to follow the perfect trajectory. I wanted to make a difference.

Which was how I'd ended up here with a one-year term from my parents before I came home and took over my legacy. I intended to make the most of it.

But none of that would make a difference if Woodhouse wasn't nominated for the presidency. He was the front-runner after winning the New Hampshire primary and a spatter of other early states. Wisconsin's primary race was right around the corner, and the campaign was laser-focused on it.

I had planned a vote-athon at the university for the day that early vote opened up. A twenty-four-hour dance party inside the Union ballroom. It would end the next morning with everyone walking from the party to the polling place on campus.

Fifteen hours into it at midnight, I could barely keep my eyes open. The students were really in charge of it all. I'd gotten the student party association to host the event so that we could have it on campus. The campaign hours left me so run-down that pulling an all-nighter sounded like a nightmare, which I hadn't considered when I suggested the event.

"You look like you could use this," Sam said.

I desperately reached out for the coffee. "You are a lifesaver."

He laughed. "I don't want you to pass out. Sleep is our greatest ally. Forgoing it for a night does not seem like your best idea."

I took a long sip of the steaming hot black coffee. "It really isn't. But I'm here now. I can power through until morning."

"That's seven more hours, and you look dead on your feet. Maybe you should get a few hours of shut-eye while your volunteers handle this."

"Don't be reasonable," I said with a grin.

"Just looking out for you."

I waved my hand. "I know. I know. But this is my first big event. I don't feel comfortable walking away, even for a few hours."

"I was afraid you were going to say that," he said, swiping a hand back through his dark hair. My eyes followed the motion with keen interest. "I'm going to have to stay up with you."

"What?" I asked with a laugh. "Don't be silly. You need your sleep."

"You think I'm going to let you early vote before me?"

I rolled my eyes. "They all count the same."

He stepped forward, closer and closer. My heart rate picked up. He was so close and yet so far. We'd kissed a few more times since that first night, but we hadn't decided on anything. We hadn't confirmed anything. This felt like another step. An unknowable step for us.

Slowly, his pinkie slid around my own pinkie. A small, simple motion, and still, electricity zinged through my body. Everything jolted as if he'd zapped me awake for the first time.

We stayed like that for I didn't know how long, watching the night blur on. All the college students moved along to made-up choreography that they planned to dance on their way to the polls. We even joined in with some of them to keep ourselves awake.

We grabbed burgers from our favorite burger joint, which I'd convinced to donate to the event. With only a matter of hours before we could get out of here, Sam and I sank onto the floor of the ballroom and ate our favorite food.

"Lark," Sam said when he finally finished.

I took my last bite of my burger and set the wrapper aside. After I finished chewing, I asked, "Yeah?"

"You don't mind me being here, do you?"

My cheeks flushed. "Mind? No. I...I want you here."

He nodded. "Good. I don't want to step over any boundaries. I know that we're coworkers..."

I put my hand on his. "You're not overstepping."

If anything, he was going slow. So, so *slow*. I wasn't used to guys like Sam. Southern gentlemen who cared whether or not they were going too fast or overstepping. Guys who wanted more than sex from me. We'd been circling each other for weeks and not done more than kiss. To think that he'd thought that was overstepping, I never even would have guessed.

"I just...I really like you," he admitted.

A smile came to my face. "I really like you, too."

I leaned forward then, capturing his lips against mine. It was gentle. None of the hurried rush that I was used to from guys. This was the settling of what had already been brewing between us. The rightness of it sliding into place.

He groaned against my lips and pulled back. "You make it really hard to not just pick you up and steal you."

I chuckled, drawing him in again. "Who said I wouldn't want that?"

He kissed me one more time. "You're too special for that," he said against my lips. "You don't rush perfection, Lark. And I don't want to rush us."

"Us," I breathed the word like a lifeline.

"You are mine, right?" he asked.

I swallowed and nodded, meeting those deep, dark eyes. "I am."

"Good." He tucked a lock of red hair behind my ear. "I feel like I've been waiting forever for you."

"You do?" I whispered in awe. No one had ever talked about me like that.

His smile made his eyes crinkle. It was the most genuine smile I'd ever seen from anyone in my entire life. Sam was one of a kind.

"I'm glad the wait is over."

II

"To Governor Woodhouse! The winner of the Wisconsin primary and presumptive winner of the presidential primary!" Moira cried, holding her beer aloft.

We all lifted our glasses to meet hers and cheered our victory. The primary had been grueling, but now that it was behind us, the future looked even brighter. There had always been the chance that Woodhouse wouldn't be nominated, and then we'd all have to close up shop and hop to another candidate. Or more likely, in my case, head back home.

"God, I love this place," Sam said as a platter of fries were set out before us.

We were currently inside The Station, our favorite bar in town —primarily because it also served after-hours bar grub. Not the best place to eat in town, but they served beer, too. So, win-win.

I reached for the fries, dunking them in ketchup and wrinkling my nose as Moira went for the mustard. "I don't know how you can stand that stuff."

"Well, I don't know how you can be allergic to strawberries. Do you know how good they are?" Moira asked.

I shook my head. "As if I have a choice in what I'm allergic to."

Moira shrugged. "If you say so."

"Says the woman with more allergies than anyone I've met."

"But yeah, I'm just allergic to grass and trees and rabbits and, like, most of nature. Not wonderful, delicious foods, like strawberries."

"You have such an interesting view on this," Sam said.

"Hey now," Moira said, pointing at him. "I don't need the boyfriend to gang up on me."

A flush moved up my neck and into my cheeks. I still wasn't used to that word out of anyone's mouth. Sam *was* my boyfriend. And I was his girlfriend. It felt surreal and like it was absolutely perfect. No wonder I'd never really had a serious boyfriend before this. Just lots and lots of casual dates.

Sam stuffed another fry in his mouth. "Don't get mad at us because you're pining over Toby."

"Whoa!" Moira said, holding up her hands. "I am not *pining* for Toby."

I snort-laughed. "Yes, you are."

"That is outrageous."

"We all know it, Moira," Sam said with a shrug.

Moira looked on indignantly. "I do not pine. I can have whoever I want. And I'll have you know that I left an ex back home, pining after me. Might hook back up with him when this is all over."

Sam laughed. "Whatever you want us to think."

Moira stood from her seat and rolled her eyes. "I'm going to the other table where they appreciate me."

I reached for Moira's hand. "Come on. Don't be like that."

She winked at me with her own giggle and then wandered to the other table of campaign workers from our state office.

"She's so touchy sometimes," Sam said.

"She's Moira. I love her."

He nodded. "She's the best." He finished off the fries and dove into the basket of wings. "What about you?"

"What about me?" I asked as I reached for a barbecue one.

"Do you have someone waiting for you back in New York?"

"Oh," I said, biting my lip. "No. I don't have anyone."

"Really? No exes?"

I shrugged. "I mean, I dated people, but I was never serious."

Sam looked at me like he wanted me to continue. He was eating a wing and patiently waiting for me to say more. Which was...fuck. Okay, I'd have to say more. But what could I say that wouldn't incriminate myself?

"My parents are kind of controlling," I told him evenly. "Weirdly controlling about some things...like my career path. And also, somehow, very flippant about most other things. They don't care who I date or really anything I do as long as I stay on the right trajectory."

"That sounds freeing and also constricting."

"Exactly," I said, relieved that I could get him to understand without revealing everything. I wasn't ready for that yet. "So, I did a lot of, uh...uh, rebellious things in high school and college to try to find the boundaries that were never there."

"Ah," he said, as if catching on. "So, no boyfriends but lots of...dating."

"Yeah. The only people I ever really had in my life were my crew."

He raised an eyebrow in question.

"I grew up with four best friends—Penn, Katherine, Lewis, and Rowe. We have a fraught history, but we've always been there for each other."

"That sounds nice," he said. "I've always been like that with my brother, Jake."

"I'm an only child. So, my family is the crew."

I glanced down at my plate. I didn't exactly want to tell him that I'd fooled around a lot, growing up. That pushing those boundaries meant pushing them with everyone, including my friends. That I'd actually slept with Penn, Lewis, and Rowe at some point. That I wasn't this person. This *good girl* he knew was an illusion. I'd always been something...someone else. I liked the person he saw. The normal girl he was falling for.

"At least you have them," he said.

I nodded. "Otherwise, this might be the first time I've ever been serious about anyone."

When I looked back up at him, he was smiling broad. "Really? I like being your first."

I swallowed as I felt myself sink deeper into Sam. I wasn't lying about my past. Not really. Just not telling all of the truth. I wasn't ready to see his reaction about who I really was. I'd seen it over and over again. The thought of Sam looking at me differently made me want to be sick. No, I couldn't tell him. Not yet.

"What about you?" I asked hastily instead. "Do you have exes?"

"Ex," he clarified. "Just one."

"Oh?" I asked, my interest piqued.

"Melissa Young," he said with a sigh. "We dated through most of college. She still lives in Chapel Hill and goes to church with my family. It's been complicated since we broke up."

"Complicated how?"

He scratched the back of his head. "I don't know. My parents want us to get back together. They like that she's a local girl. But I knew that I was leaving for over a year on campaign. I knew we'd never survive long distance."

"Why?"

"I don't know. She's...needy." He sighed heavily. "I hate saying that. She's a nice girl, and we were together for a long time." He looked deep into my eyes. "But I think if she was that easy to leave, then she wasn't ever going to be my endgame."

I considered his honesty. Hated that I couldn't reciprocate it. And found a twinge of jealousy creep up in me. That he'd had a relationship like that in the past. That his family still wanted that. If they knew who I was, I was certain they wouldn't approve. Or they'd only approve for my money...if they were that sort of people. I hoped not.

I didn't want to feel jealous. It wasn't like Melissa was here. Sam had left her before we ever met. But somehow...that Upper East Side girl inside of me couldn't hold back the petty.

I dispelled the thought. I didn't need to feel that.

After all, I was the one here with Sam.

III

"Thank you so much, Kennedy," I said to my lead volunteer. We were enjoying an ice cream cone from the university Dairy Store on Lake Mendota. Kennedy had agreed to take charge of the event after working with me on the vote-athon.

"You really don't have to thank me, Lark," she said. "I'm so happy that we have a presence for Governor Woodhouse on campus. Four years ago, I wasn't old enough to vote, and I wanted to so badly. But so many of my classmates don't seem to get how important it is. Like they don't think politics affects them. As if taxes and student loans and tuition aren't decided by the government." She rolled her eyes.

"Well, I agree with you. I'm here after all."

"And thank god," she crooned. "We could have had anyone."

I laughed. "Anyone would have done a good job."

"But you're the best," Kennedy said as if it were a fact.

Then, she waved at another girl nearby and nodded her head to say she was going to go talk to her. I let her go. This was why *she* was here after all. Because Kennedy knew everyone. Which was how she had doubled our volunteers in the time we'd been working together. I was going to miss her over the summer when everyone cleared out of the university.

My phone buzzed in my pocket, and I reached for it, expecting to see a cute message from Sam. We'd been texting back and forth like crazy. I kept wanting to invite him over to my place after we'd had another late night at The Station. But I couldn't bring myself to do it. New York Lark would have done it, but this Lark was waiting for him to make the first move. And I knew he wanted to wait. I just didn't know what he was waiting *for*.

When I glanced down at my phone though, it wasn't from Sam at all. The screen was lit up with one word—*Mother*.

I groaned. Great. This was going to be...fantastic.

With a heavy sigh, I answered, "Mother, what a surprise."

"Hello, Larkin, darling. How is my lovely daughter?"

"I'm doing well," I said evenly. I knew she wasn't calling to hear about the campaign. She wouldn't want details. This had to be about something else. Something I was certain I didn't want to hear. "Can I help you?"

"Now, why would you think that I needed help with something?"

I looked skyward. Games. So many games. I'd almost forgotten how exhausting it was to play them. I hadn't heard from my mother since the day I moved away, set on forging my own path on the campaign trail for the next year. And now, here she was, determined to make my life more frustrating. It wasn't enough that I was working ninety-plus-hour weeks and barely sleeping. No, I had to now deal with my mother as well.

"I didn't expect to hear from you, is all," I told her bluntly. My mother hated bluntness.

"Larkin, you know what it's like. Your father is swamped with the resorts. I'm busy designing the latest line of handbags. We're both running billion-dollar companies." Her mother sighed dramatically. "We could use the help."

Oh god, here it was. The real reason for the call.

"You could come home."

I cringed. "We agreed on a year."

"Your candidate has won the primary. He probably doesn't need your help to get elected now. He's a shoo-in."

That was so far from the truth that it physically pained me. Not that my mother would care. "I can't abandon my position. This is where I'm needed until November."

"Are you really though?" my mother asked. "Needed?"

"Yes," I ground out.

"I know that you think you are, dear. But it's not true. Anyone could take your place on that campaign, and the outcome would always be the same. You're a hamster on a wheel in a giant machine there." My mother didn't sound emotional. It was all rehearsed. A robot. "You can make a difference *here*. Can't you see about what's really important, Larkin? You were raised to take over this company. *This* is where you're needed."

Something cracked inside of me at her words. My hands started shaking. My throat closed up. Tears pricked at my eyes. This wasn't supposed to happen. I was supposed to have a year. A full year without more of the same from my parents. A year free from their expectations and shoving the company down my throat. The fucking company. That was the only thing they cared about. Not me. Not their only daughter.

I couldn't breathe. I couldn't think. Everything felt far away and deathly quiet. As if I'd entered a wind tunnel.

Whatever else my mother said was lost to me. Not that it mattered. I wasn't coming home. We'd agreed on a year. I was going to get my year.

But I couldn't push back the rising panic. I knew it was irrational. This was my mother. This was how she was. She ruled with a heavy hand and didn't so much guide as force people into the shape she wanted. This was nothing new.

None of that mattered. Not as the panic attack took over my body. I didn't know if it was the lack of sleep, the long hours, the constant pressure to perform. Or having to hide a piece of who I was at all times. Or if it was a combination of it all, but it hit me like a two-by-four to the chest.

I hung up on my mother. I didn't even remember doing it. But I couldn't get air in. I was sitting in the grass on the quad, overlooking the lake, hyperventilating. Air all around me...and none of it was in my lungs.

I squeezed my eyes shut and willed myself to stop. But it was a waste. It wasn't stopping. It wasn't going away.

I needed...I needed Sam.

Without another thought, I sent one quick text to him.

Panic attack. Help.

I couldn't see his response through my tears, but suddenly, he was there. His strong arms around my shoulders. His fingers brushing the tears off of my cheeks. His soothing words echoing in my ears. Then without a backward glance, he lifted me into his arms and carried me to his pickup truck.

I had no memory of the drive to my apartment. Just him pulling up in front of the building and rushing around to my side of the truck.

"Wait"—I hiccupped—"I have...to go back to work."

He shook his head, easing me out of the truck. "I don't think so. I think you're going to go upstairs and sleep. You need more sleep, Lark."

"But Toby..."

"Let me worry about Toby," he said more forcefully than I'd ever heard him.

I'd been wrong about Sam. I'd thought that he was quiet and soft and principled. But when I needed him, I realized that he was so much more. Commanding and authoritative. Protective and capable and caring. He could take charge with ease, and I felt... safe in his arms. I knew that he wouldn't let me down.

We made it up to my apartment, and he found clothes for me to change into. Then, he carefully eased me into bed. My tears had stopped sometime earlier, but I still felt a growing sense of panic. A panic that I couldn't erase.

"Sam," I said, reaching my hand out for him. He took it in his and kissed it. "Can you stay for a minute?"

He nodded, kicking off his boots and crawling into bed after me. He wrapped his arms around my waist and held me to him. He was silent for a minute before asking, "What happened?"

I shook my head. I didn't know how to explain. I couldn't tell him about my mother. Not like this. He knew that she was controlling, but he'd never understand why she wanted me to give this all up to take over the family company. And it was more than that. It was the two decades of pressure to perform weighing on my shoulders. The knowledge that I'd have to go back after this was over and fit back into the perfect role of Larkin St. Vincent again. When I was finally getting comfortable with just being Lark.

And damn it, this campaign was important to me! I wasn't ready to leave. Even with the shit hours and my shit sleep schedule and my shit eating schedule and everything else that I hated about the job, I still *loved* the job.

I swallowed. "It all came to a head at once. I talked to my mother, and it went...poorly. And work." I shook my head, brushing at another tear. "My brain couldn't keep up. I'm broken."

Sam squeezed me tighter to him. "You're not broken. You're just stressed. We all are. You need more sleep."

"I'd sleep better with you here," I whispered baldly into the silence.

He chuckled against my shoulder and then placed a kiss there. "Well, maybe we can arrange that here soon."

I shivered at the implication and heat in his voice. "I'd like that."

He kissed my neck. "But right now, sleep," he whispered against my skin. "You can relax. I'll be here for you. Right here for you always."

SUMMER

I

"Do you have everything?" Sam asked from where he was sprawled on my bed.

"You haven't told me where we're going. How do I know if I have everything?"

"We have our first day off since Christmas, Lark. Who cares where we're going?"

When Toby had confirmed that we'd finally get a much-needed day off, Sam had immediately stepped into action, telling me that he was going to steal me and to not make any plans. True to my word, no plans. I'd let him do everything.

"How much more stuff do you need for one day?" he grumbled.

"A lot," I said.

I grinned at him and then threw in the only little lacy bit I'd brought with me from home. My hopes were up that we were going to finally seal the deal now that we were going away. We'd been fooling around for a while. Done everything but sex, and I was *ready*. More than ready. He'd said he didn't want to rush us, but we were past the point of being rushed. It was *time*.

I closed my suitcase and then wheeled it out to him. "Okay, now, I'm ready."

"Excellent."

He hopped off of the bed and wrapped his arms around me, pinning me back against the closet door. His lips were hot on mine. I wanted this and so much more. So fucking much more.

My fingers drifted to the button of his jeans. I flicked it open, and he laughed gruffly against me.

"Now, now..."

I groaned. "Sam..."

"We have a drive ahead of us. We should get going if we want to get there at a decent hour."

"What if I want to keep you and stay here?" I suggested.

He kissed me again thoroughly. "Humor me."

I nodded my head with a small sigh. "All right. Will you tell me where we're going then?"

He grabbed my suitcase and then headed for the door.

"Sam?" I begged, following behind.

He winked at me. "Chicago."

I grinned like a fool. "Really?"

"Yeah, really. Now, get your ass in the car, so we can go."

I did as he'd said, sliding into the passenger seat of my Subaru. The drive was about two and a half hours, and by the time we made it to our hotel, it was late. I was already tired from the exhausting couple of weeks, but the drive had made me sleepy, too. I shook it off as we parked in the garage. He grabbed his duffel and then wheeled my suitcase inside the Palmer House.

I nearly sighed with relief. I hadn't known how much I'd missed a real city until I was back in one. Chicago wasn't New York, but it was better than nothing.

Plus, even I could admit that the Palmer House was a gorgeous hotel. An enormous, high-painted ceiling with columns bracketing the lobby and large red-carpeted staircases. If we weren't staying at a Percy hotel, this was a good option.

Sam quickly checked in and then came back to me. I bit my lip, debating on what I was about to do and then decided it was do or die. Might as well make the most of it.

"I got you an extra key," he said, passing it to me.

"Thanks. You know, let me talk to them. I bet I can get an upgrade."

He laughed. "You think?"

"I'm really good at it."

He handed me the rest of the information and his ID. "If you want to try."

"Be right back."

I walked up to the counter and smiled at the man behind the desk.

"Can I help you?" he asked.

"Hi, I'm Larkin St. Vincent," I said, sliding him my black card. "Upgrade us to the penthouse."

His eyes widened at that name. Even here, my family made waves. "Of...of course, Miss St. Vincent."

Another minute later, and I had the keys to the top floor. I dragged Sam to the private elevator that took us up, up, up, and then we burst into our suite. His eyes rounded in shock.

"You talked your way into *this*?" he asked incredulously. "What the hell did you tell them?"

I carefully shut the door behind me and headed into our living quarters. I didn't know what room Sam had reserved, but this had three bedrooms, a living room, dining room, pool table, Jacuzzi, and the best view of the city imaginable. It was exactly the sort of room that Larkin St. Vincent would get. Just not the Lark that Sam had gotten to know. I didn't know which me was me. But I knew that if I wanted to be with him, I couldn't keep hiding who I was any longer.

"I have something to tell you," I said, turning to face him.

He'd stripped out of his winter jacket and looked at me with confusion. "That sounds serious."

"It is...a bit," I admitted.

"Okay. Should I sit down?"

I shook my head. "I've been hiding part of who I am. I told you that I'm Lark Vincent, but that's not exactly true." I waved my hand. "Well, it is, and it isn't."

"I don't understand."

"Larkin St. Vincent," I blurted out. "Of St. Vincent's Resorts and St. Vincent's handbags and cosmetics." I swallowed. "I'm the sole heir to St. Vincent's Enterprise."

Sam sank into the chair with a plop. "Oh."

I bit my lip and looked away. I hated that *oh*. I knew what it meant. I'd seen it in people all my life. Heat colored my cheeks. Shit. I'd thought that it would be different with Sam. I'd thought that telling him wouldn't change anything. Or at least, I'd hoped it wouldn't. That it would be different than everyone else in my life. For so long, people had seen me as dollar signs or a name. It was exhausting.

"Yeah," I said softly, crossing my arms over my chest. "I guess… this is why I don't tell anyone."

"Why is that?" he asked.

"Because they look at me like that." I pointed at him.

"How am I looking at you?"

I shrugged.

He came to stand before me and tipped my chin up. "How am I looking at you?"

But when I stared deep into his dark depths, it wasn't there. I wasn't just my parents' money in his eyes.

"Usually, people get weird about it," I admitted. "They start to see me for something else."

"Lark, I only see you for you. Who your parents are, how much money you have, whether or not you're an heiress," he said with a soft laugh, "none of that matters to me."

I swallowed. "Really?"

He nodded. "In fact, I hate that you ever had to lie about your identity. Though I think it all makes sense now."

"What does?"

"I've been taking things slow with you because I felt like that was what you wanted. Like…you were hiding yourself from me. You weren't fully into this."

"I was. I *am*," I gasped.

He stroked my cheek with his thumb. "I know. I see that now. I think I thought that you pulling back from me had something to do with our relationship. But I was seeing your fear about revealing who you really are."

"I'm sorry," I told him. "I hated hiding. I just wanted to be...normal."

He chuckled and kissed me hard once. "Normal is overrated."

II

"Sam, please," I whispered against his lips.

I pushed my fingers up into his hair, trying to get more of him. More, more, more. I couldn't get enough.

He didn't try to stop me or slow us down. He leaned into my kiss, sliding his tongue along the seam of my lips and opening me to him. Our kiss deepened, intensified, until I felt like I could barely breathe. I wanted him to devour me whole.

He seemed to sense that in my mood. The next thing I knew, he reached down and hoisted my legs up and around his hips. I gasped, wrapping my arms around his neck and securing myself to him. But he was already walking us toward the open bedroom door.

My back hit one of the posters, and he ground against me. I whimpered in desperation. Fuck, I wanted him. I wanted him so bad. Waiting had been so hard. But he'd known something was off even though I'd never told him. Sam *knew* me. Better than my parents. Better than anyone maybe. He'd seen the truth. He just hadn't known what it was.

And I loved him for it.

The thought shook me to my core. I'd fallen in love with him.

This was what it was supposed to feel like.

Not the sham of relationships I'd had growing up. Not the thing they said it was, but what it *really* was. The highest high. Like I was soaring above the clouds. Everything in the world disappeared. And together, we transcended time, space, and reality. Until there was just this moment. I was perfectly okay with that. I was perfectly okay with falling in love with Sam Rutherford.

But I was done waiting. We were stronger, happier for it, but it didn't mean that I wanted to wait a second longer now that we were on the same page.

"God, Lark, I've wanted this for so long," he said, breaking from me and lowering me to my feet.

"Me too. So much."

He stripped me from my jeans with practiced ease. My sweater came next along with the tank top I wore under it in lieu of a bra. I stood before him in nothing but a thong, and soon, that was gone, too.

We'd gotten here before. Done everything but sex. And I trembled with need at the knowledge that there would be no stopping, no complaints about getting sleep or having to work the next day. Just us together. Like I wanted.

Sam dropped to his knees before me, lifting one leg over his shoulder. He slid his hand up my inner thigh until he brushed against my core. I jerked slightly at his touch, but soon, his mouth replaced his fingers.

"Oh fuck," I groaned at the first flick of his tongue against my clit.

I reached up and grasped the poster on the bed to hold myself in place. I felt like any second I was going to collapse as he pleasured me with his skilled tongue. A second later, he inserted a finger inside of me, and my moans were audible. A second finger followed, and I half-wanted to ride him I was so turned on. My orgasm hit me in a rocking spasm all at once. It was like the two-and-a-half-hour ride up to Chicago had been all the foreplay I needed.

"Fuck, Lark," he said.

His eyes were glazed with need as he rose to his feet and removed his own clothing.

"I want you," I told him.

He grinned a cocky smile that I claimed as my own. I'd only ever seen him use that particular smile with me. And I was perfectly okay with that.

My eyes rounded at the sight of him as he stripped out of his boxers. He jutted upward, hard as a rock. As if my own climax had made him as hot as it had made me. I reached out and took the length of him in my hand. I experimentally pumped up and down, up and down. He twitched in my hand, clearly enjoying my ministrations.

"Lark," he groaned.

"Should I taste you?"

He clutched my arms and pushed me back a step closer to the bed. "I've waited for you this long. I'm not waiting any longer."

My smile was teasing. "How do you want me?"

He withdrew a condom and placed it in my hand.

I tore the foil and removed the condom. "Tell me."

He chuckled softly. "You're issuing commands now?"

I stroked his dick one more time and then pressed the condom to the head of him, ever so slowly dragging it down his length. "I like to know."

"I want to get inside of you, Lark," he told me. "I want to make love to you."

Make love.

My heart stuttered in my chest.

Not fuck.

Not have sex.

He wanted to *make love* to me.

"You do?" I whispered, losing my bravado.

His eyes were bright with need when he looked down at me. "Yes. I love you, Lark."

I inhaled sharply at the words. The words I'd thought but hadn't been able to say aloud. It was as if he'd read my mind. Seen deep inside of me and known my soul. It amazed me that we were on the same page. Thinking the same thing in nearly the same moment.

"I love you, too," I whispered back.

Something I'd never told another person. Not once. And I was glad because they never would have been true before this.

I crawled backward on the bed, and Sam followed me, laying his weight across me. Our eyes caught and held. I loved him. It was a surreal moment. And it felt utterly, perfectly, unanimously right. That we had always been leading up to this moment. From that first day on the campaign when I'd walked into the office.

He brushed a lock of my red hair out of my face and then eased forward into me. I was already so primed that there was no resistance. He slid in like he was always meant to be there. My missing puzzle piece.

Our bodies moved together. A fluid motion so smooth and familiar, it was as if we'd done this before. And I didn't want to stop. Not as he brought his lips onto mine. Not as I snaked my legs around his waist to draw him closer against me. Not as his hands dug into my hips so that he could drive into me faster. Not when we hit the peak and fell off together.

Stars exploded in my vision as I cried out into the night. He was right there with me.

My body turned to mush. Sweat coated my pale, freckled skin. My chest heaved up and down from the exertion.

And I felt the best I'd ever felt.

"Please tell me that you brought more condoms," I said in between deep breaths.

Sam laughed and kissed my shoulder before sliding out of me and heading for the bathroom. "You're in luck, City Girl."

I chuckled and threw my hands above my head in delight. Exhaustion took me just as hard, and by the time he returned, I was nearly asleep. I never slept enough on campaign. It was hard to calm down after such crazy days and harder to wake up. To feel this relaxed was almost unheard of.

"Going to fall asleep on me already?" Sam asked, running a hand down my back.

"So comfortable."

"I have a present for you."

I rolled over and groggily opened my eyes. "A present?"

He nodded. Then he held out a carefully wrapped gift.

I grabbed my sweater off the end of the bed and pulled it on over my head before reaching for the package, which was about the size of my palm. I slowly unwrapped it. My hand went to my mouth as I realized what I was looking at. Nestled in the center of the paper was a small wooden lark.

"Is this...me?" I asked. My eyes lifted to his. "Did you make this?"

He sank onto the bed next to me. "Yeah. My dad taught me to carve when I was young. It's a hobby that soothes me when I can't get my brain to shut off. So, I've been working on it for a couple months right before bed."

I pulled the bird to my chest. "Sam, thank you. This means so much."

"I know it's not what you're used to," he said after a minute.

I shook my head. "No, don't condition it. It's perfect."

"I'm glad you like it," he said and softly kissed me again. "And I'm glad that you told me who you are. That must have been difficult."

"No, I never should have hidden from you in the first place."

"I understand why you did. You didn't want to be judged for who you are. A lot of people look at me and see dumb Southern hick," he said with a shrug. "But I hope that I show others that I'm more than that."

I laughed at his description. "I think we're both a lot more than we seem. Even though, under normal circumstances, we'd be complete opposites."

"Then thank god for the campaign," Sam said, pulling me into him. "Otherwise, I would never have met you."

"Yes," I said, sinking into him. "Thank god for the campaign."

III

From that moment on, our summer was dedicated to the national convention. Unfortunately—or fortunately, depending on how you looked at it—the convention was in Milwaukee in the middle of July. Which meant that our entire office and as many volunteers as we could muster were supposed to drive into Milwaukee to be part of the process and fill seats.

I loved campaigns. From the outside, it might look frustrating. But from the inside, it was packaging a candidate into a believable platform and selling them to people like any other household product. It was taking something I believed in and making it consumable for others. People were twice as likely to vote every time they talked to someone about who they were going to vote for. They were even more likely to vote if someone knocked on their door or if they gave money to a candidate or if they volunteered for a campaign. Getting out there and organizing the campaign meant that I was having a literal impact on not just the campaign, but also the country. And it was worth it to me. The long hours and the high stress were all worth it.

But I hated the convention.

Yes, I wanted to see Woodhouse get nominated officially. The rest of the fanfare gave me a headache. A lot of pomp and posturing that did little to change anyone's mind. That money would be better off on the ground as far as I was concerned.

Not that I could say that to anyone but Sam and Moira as we got our volunteers off of the bus and directed them to their designated seats.

I was already tired by the time we snuck away with our staff badges to find a good place to grab a beer.

"I'm thinking beer and then a nap," I said with a yawn.

Moira nodded. "I'm down for that."

"Don't y'all want to see the nomination process?"

"No," Moira and I said in unison. Then we burst into laughter.

"Your loss," Sam said with a shrug.

"Oh, look, delegates," Moira said as we passed a group of men and women in expensive business suits, wearing floor credentials.

I scanned the crowd with excitement. These were the people who actually got to cast the ballots for the primary nomination. It was purely a formality at this point, but still, it felt like an important job. And they got the best seats, too.

"I recognize a few of them," Sam said. "That guy is a state senator from North Carolina. That woman is a governor of, I think, Nevada. The redheaded man is the mayor of San Francisco."

Sam continued on, pointing out people that I'd had no idea how he knew. He must have had a knack for names and faces, or he studied this information extensively. It was damn impressive.

"Beer," Moira said, trying to pull him away. "You can fangirl later."

Sam laughed. "I'm not fangirling."

"Yes, you are," I said with a grin.

Then a voice called out from the crowd, "Lark!"

I glanced up, immediately on guard. Who the hell would know me here?

But then I saw a woman melt out of the crowd and stride toward me. She was a tall, imposing figure in a white power suit.

I heard Sam say next to me, "That's Leslie Kensington. She's a state senator in New York. She was barely defeated in her governor race a few years ago."

"I know," I said as I stepped up and embraced my best friend's mother. "Leslie, it's so good to see you."

"You too, dear. What are you doing here?" Leslie asked. "I thought you were in New York."

I held up my staff credentials. "I'm working as a campaign organizer for Woodhouse in Madison."

"That's incredible," she said with a genuine smile. "I had no idea you had an interest in politics."

"I didn't either. I saw Woodhouse speak in the city last year and decided I had to join up. I'm loving the work though. It's very rewarding."

Leslie smiled at me. And my heart swelled. I hadn't realized that I'd missed my home so much. I hadn't had pangs of homesickness, but here, with Leslie, I felt different.

"I'm so glad you're doing it. We need hardworking people like you. What do your parents think?"

I waved away the question I had no intention of answering. "How's Penn? And Court?" I added hastily.

"You know my boys." Leslie rolled her eyes, avoiding the question as deftly as I'd avoided hers.

I laughed. "I sure do."

"Anyway, I have to return to my delegate duties. But when you come back to the city, come find me. I need some new, young talent. I'm thinking of running in the next mayoral race."

"Leslie," I gasped. "That's incredible. You'd be so great in that job."

Leslie patted my hand twice. "You're sweet. Seriously, come find me. If Woodhouse wants you, then so do I."

I grinned as she headed confidently back into the fray. When I turned back around, Moira and Sam were staring at me, slack-jawed. My smile faltered. I'd entirely forgotten they were standing there.

"Sorry about that. Beer?" I suggested.

"You know Leslie Kensington," Moira said, bouncing up and

down. "And she offered you a job, working for her when she runs for the mayor of New York City. Lark, that's amazing!"

"Oh, thanks," I said with a half-smile.

"What an offer," Sam said, wrapping an arm around my shoulders as Moira directed the rest of the conversation and us to a bar.

When Moira went to get the first round, Sam and I settled into the last available table.

Silence stretched, and I finally got too anxious and broke it. "I'm not going to work for Leslie after this."

Sam furrowed his brows. "Why not? It sounds like a great opportunity."

"Well, maybe you could take it," I suggested.

He laughed. "I don't think it's transferable, Lark. And anyway, I'm going to apply to law schools."

I already had a JD. I'd gotten it so that I wouldn't have to start working for the company yet. My parents had indulged me. Just like they had with this. One day, I was going to have to stop running.

I looked down at my hands. "Well, actually, I made a deal with my parents."

"About what?"

"That I'd work here for a year on campaign, and then after that, I'd come home and takeover the company."

"Really? Is that what you want to do?"

"Yeah," I said unconvincingly, and then with more gusto, I continued, "Yes. Yes, of course. I've spent my entire life preparing for this. I wanted to grab ahold of more of my youth, you know? Once I start there, it's not like I can stop."

He put his hand on mine. "You know it's just me and you, right? You can tell me what you really feel."

I deflated. "I don't know, Sam. I thought for a long time that was what I wanted. And right now, that's the path I'm on. It's the family business. It's what I was born for. My parents aren't getting any younger. I don't want the board to have to take over when they decide to retire. It feels important."

He nodded. "Okay. If you say so."

"Maybe you could apply to NYU or Columbia Law," I suggested with excitement. "Then we could both be in the city."

"Yeah, maybe," he said softly.

Moira plunked three beers down in front of us at that moment. "Here we are! Drink up."

And we did. Letting the conversation slip away as easily as it had come.

FALL

I

The general election was a struck match.

One minute, nothing happened. The next, the entire world was on fire.

With only weeks to go before Election Day, we ran around as if we were all about to be burned. Like this was life or death. Our hours were extended. Our stress levels at max capacity. There was hardly enough time for me to see Sam outside of work. And when we did, we were zombies.

We'd all taken on assistants to ease the burden, but still, it wasn't enough. My first assistant had been a bit of a psychopath. She'd stolen someone's cat from their yard while canvassing and then lied about being sick to go out to eat with her friends for brunch. It obviously hadn't worked out. So, I was pretty desperate to get a new assistant.

I hadn't expected the one that I got—Melissa Young.

"Melissa," I said slowly. My eyes lifted to Sam's. "My assistant is Melissa Young. Why does that name sound familiar."

He cringed. "Uh...that's my ex-girlfriend."

"What?" I asked through gritted teeth.

"She messaged me and asked to join the campaign. She's out of school and wanted to help make a difference."

"So, you suggested she come here?" I asked with mild hysteria.

"No," he said at once. "I mean...yes, kind of."

"Sam!"

"Look, I can't turn down volunteers. I told her how to sign up. I had no idea that she was actually going to be assigned to work in our office."

I blew out a harsh breath. Great. Just great. This was going to be a disaster. But I could tell that Sam hadn't intended this to happen. Not that intentions meant anything when I was the one who was going to be saddled with his ex-girlfriend for the next two weeks.

Melissa showed up the next day.

"Oh my god," she cried. "You must be Lark."

She dragged me into a hug. She was a good five or six inches taller than me, and I didn't like how she hovered over me. I tried to fight back the urge to snap at her. I didn't know her. But as much as I wanted her gone, I also wanted to do the right thing and give her the benefit of the doubt. We had to survive each other for the next three weeks. I didn't want it to start off on the wrong foot.

"Hi," I said, withdrawing. "Yes, I'm Lark. And you're Melissa, I'm guessing."

"Yes! Of course. I'm Melissa. And I'm so glad to be here." She swiped her brown hair out of her heart-shaped face. She had the kind of smile that seemed to be plastered on.

"We're glad to have you," I lied. Then, I went for the truth. "I really need the help."

"That's what I heard!" she said, her Southern accent coming out on the edges of her words as she got animated. "Sam said this whole thing is exhausting, but I just had to be a part of it all. Too important not to be, right?"

I nodded once and bit my tongue. I'd been here for almost a year. I knew how important it was.

"So, you won't have your own office. But you can flit in and out of mine and use the open space as you will. We're a bit cramped," I told her.

"No worries. Where should I put my stuff?"

"Uh...over here." I gestured to my office that I still shared with Sam despite Toby fighting to give us each our own space.

Luckily, Sam was out canvassing with a group of volunteers and wouldn't be back for a while.

Melissa deposited her suitcases into the office and dumped her giant purse on top of them. "All right," she said eagerly, her smile reaching her big brown eyes, "what do you need me to do? Put me to work!"

I assessed her and tried to be objective. Melissa seemed...nice. Even genuine. It surprised me. But I didn't know why.

Maybe because I had everything to lose. What I had with Sam, I'd never felt this way about anyone else, and the last thing I wanted was for Sam's ex to show up and take over. We had three more weeks to permanently be in each other's lives. I wanted to make it count. I didn't want to think about what would happen after.

I was pushing my own insecurities on Melissa. Maybe this wouldn't be so bad after all. Maybe I'd been stressed about all of this for no reason.

"All right, let's get started," I said with a smile.

"Well, what do you think?" Sam asked me later when we were seated at The Station with the rest of the office.

"Of Melissa?"

He nodded.

My gaze shifted to where she was animatedly talking to Moira as if they were long-lost friends. I sighed. "She seems really nice, Sam."

He laughed. "I knew you two would get along."

"I still think it's kind of weird," I admitted. "But she was a huge help today. She fit seamlessly into my established organization and took so much stress off of my shoulders."

"Good." He leaned forward and kissed me once on the lips. "I'm so glad, Lark. You really need the help."

"God, I really do," I agreed. "Especially after dealing with Virginia."

Sam groaned. "Virginia. What a nightmare."

"I still cannot believe that she tried to steal that person's cat."

He chuckled under his breath. "Like, what was she even thinking?"

"I have no idea. It's hilarious now, but when Maria called me in a panic because Virginia, my own paid assistant, had stolen someone's cat, it was awful. Calling Virginia and figuring out why the fuck she had stolen a cat and demanding she return it with an apology?" My head sank into my hands. "The worst."

Sam couldn't stop laughing. "It's probably the best-slash-worst thing that has happened on campaign."

"I'm glad that she's gone. She hated working but fooled everyone into thinking that she liked to work."

"Melissa will be better for you. She worked on campaigns back in North Carolina. She'll do a great job."

I looked at her one more time and nodded. "Yeah, I think you're right."

He patted my hand once and then stood. "I'm going to the restroom. If they come back with my fries, try not to eat them all before I get back."

I grinned devilishly. "No promises."

He shook his head at me as he walked away.

As soon as he was gone, Melissa plopped down in front of me. "Hey there, boss."

"Hey. How was your first day?"

"Great, great," she said cheerfully. Then, she conspiratorially leaned forward. "So, between us girls, are you and Sam serious?"

"Uh, yeah," I said, warning signs blaring. This was not a good conversation. I needed to back away slowly.

"And you think...what? You'll stay together after the campaign?"

There was something else in Melissa's brown eyes now. Deceit.

"That's the plan," I ground out.

Melissa laughed softly. "That's cute."

"What is?" I asked despite myself.

"Sam doesn't do long distance." She shrugged her shoulders as if she were sympathetic. "So, if you go back to New York, that's that." She wiped her hands together twice.

"I think I'm done with this conversation," I said, rising to my feet.

Melissa smiled dangerously as she stood to meet me. "We might work together, Lark, but I'm here for Sam. He's going to be mine. By the end of this, I'm going to win him back."

Something snapped inside of me. The Upper East Side bitch inside who didn't take shit, who could eat someone like Melissa Young for breakfast. I channeled that girl who owned Manhattan and knew that Melissa stood no chance against Larkin St. Vincent.

I leaned in real close and gave her my best eat-shit-and-die look. "If you try, Melissa," I crooned, "I'll ruin your life."

Then I pushed back from the table and went to sit with Moira instead. My blood was boiling. I wanted to tell Sam, to get it all out in the open, but Melissa would deny it. I was sure of it. And it would make me look bad.

No, we'd handle this between us girls.

If she made a move on my boyfriend, she'd find out that hers wouldn't be the first life I'd ruined. And I followed through on *all* of my promises.

II

F all in Wisconsin was way too cold for my sensibilities. I was used to perfect New York falls, and this did not cut it.

I shivered as I stepped out of my Subaru and entered the office. It was swamped. With so little time until Election Day, our schedules were jam-packed. I wished that I were doing something mindless right then. Instead, I'd sent Melissa out to canvass and not heard from her in hours. She hadn't responded to any of my texts or calls.

I stuck my head into my joint office with Sam. "Hey," I said when I saw him inside.

"Lark, you're back," he said with a smile. "I thought you'd be on campus all day."

"Well, I would be, but I can't find Melissa. She was supposed to be canvassing. I had her down as a team lead this afternoon. But I haven't seen her in hours. Have you seen her?"

"Shit, she didn't call?"

My brows furrowed. "About what?"

Sam ran a hand back through his hair. "Her volunteer housing fell through."

"What?" I asked, confused and also suspicious. "Already? It's only been a few days."

"I know. She came here freaking out because the volunteer had to get her out within the hour. I guess the guy was a real jerk about it."

"That doesn't even make sense. All of the housing is vetted months in advance. How would that happen?"

"I don't know, Lark. But it did. It was awful. She was a crying mess when she talked to me. I helped her get out of there as fast as she could."

My stomach knotted at those words. "Did you talk to Toby? What house is she staying at now?"

He shook his head. "I didn't even think. I kind of...invited her to stay with me."

I straightened. "You did what?"

"She was in such a horrible place. I figured, it's two weeks, and she can crash on my couch like I did at yours."

"We hooked up the entire time you stayed on my couch," I reminded him.

His cheeks turned red. "That's not what I meant, and you know it."

"What I know is that you're letting your ex-girlfriend stay in your apartment, Sam."

He sighed. "Fuck. Lark, I swear it's not a big deal."

He couldn't be that naive to think that Melissa wasn't playing the long game. He really believed her bullshit that something had happened with her housing. It sucked because he didn't see it.

"Sam," I groaned. "What are you doing?"

He stood and pulled me to him. "I'm not doing anything. I'm just being nice. You know I love you."

"I do," I whispered.

"Melissa is staying for two weeks on my couch. We're never home, except to pass out. I swear it isn't going to be a big deal. Why don't you come over tonight and see for yourself?"

I really, really didn't want to do that. But I also *had* to do that. Because I knew that Melissa was after Sam, and this was the start of her game plan. I needed to be there to cockblock her. To show her that he was already mine.

I nodded. "Fine. Okay. But I still don't like it."

"I understand, but I'll show you that it's nothing. Promise."

He kissed me, and I almost believed him.

"Wait, you're telling me that your boyfriend is letting his ex-girlfriend stay in his apartment?" one of my best friends, Katherine asked over the phone.

I paced my bedroom in frustration.

As soon as I'd gotten home, I'd called Katherine. It was late, but she was a socialite and never slept. I had known she'd be up and available to talk. And also, she was maybe the most dangerous, conniving person I knew.

"Yes," I muttered. "It's a disaster."

"Tell the bitch to move the fuck out, Lark."

"As much as I'd love to do that, I think it'd hurt Sam. He's never seen me act that way."

Katherine laughed. "He sounds like a nice guy."

"He is."

"Nice guys bulldozer hearts," Katherine told me. "And they do it with a smile on their face."

"I don't think they're hooking up or anything. But I don't want Melissa to make a move on him."

"You know what I'd do?"

I sighed. I knew where this was going. "What's that, Katherine?"

"Establish dominance. If you don't, she will."

I tipped my head up to the ceiling. "I don't think playing a game of What Would Katherine Do is productive."

"That means, you'd win. Now, buck up, St. Vincent," Katherine said with a tinkling laugh. "Go get your man."

I laughed and then ended the call. Katherine was a bit of a head case, but she was basically family, and I loved her. Her pep talks worked, too. I was already feeling better.

And I did know what I needed to do.

I hastily changed out of work clothes and into a sexy off-the-shoulder sweater and skintight jeans. Then, I drove over to Sam's place. I knocked once and then let myself inside. Melissa's suitcases were pushed into a corner. She was seated on the couch in what I guessed were her pajamas—a teeny-tiny tank top and even smaller shorts. She had to be freezing, considering the lows right now were in the thirties.

"Hey, Lark," Melissa said with her sugary-sweet smile.

Sam came out of the back bedroom in gray sweats and a hoodie. "Hey, you made it."

"Yeah, I had to get out of work clothes."

Sam covered his mouth as he yawned. "I get that. You look good."

"Thanks," I said, walking toward him.

He put his hands on my hips as I stood on my toes to press a kiss to his mouth. I definitely shouldn't have listened to Katherine's advice. But I could practically feel Melissa squirming behind me. So, it felt worth it.

I gently pushed him back into the bedroom. He laughed softly as I toed the door closed behind us. The connotation was clear. *Mine, mine, mine.*

My hands slid under his hoodie, and I grazed his toned abs with my nails.

"What are you doing?" he asked with that perfect Sam smile.

"Touching you."

"Right now? I thought you were here to see that everything was fine. We've been home for, like, twenty minutes, and I'm ready to crash."

"Uh-huh," I said, running a finger along the waistband of his sweats.

He shuddered under my touch. "I think you have something else on your mind."

I bit my lip. "That obvious, huh?"

I stood on my toes again and firmly pressed my lips against his. He pulled me close at the heat in the kiss, and I could tell that I had him.

"Okay," he whispered against me. "As long as we're quiet."

"Oh, I can be quiet," I murmured as quiet as a mouse.

"You generally are not."

I sank my hand into his pants and ran down the length of him. "Neither are you."

He gasped at the first touch. "Fair."

"I know what I want," I told him as I angled his body toward the wall and pushed him up against it.

His eyes were wide with surprise and hunger. He was not stopping me, even as his back thumped against the wall. Loud enough for anyone on the other side to hear.

"What's that?" he got out. His Adam's apple bobbed.

Slowly, I sank to my knees before him. His eyes went wide as I dragged his sweats and boxers down his legs, letting his cock jut out in front of my face.

"Lark," he groaned as I stroked him and licked my lips.

I leaned forward and took the tip of him in my mouth. His cock jumped in my mouth as I bobbed forward against him. My tongue laved the shaft before coming back and concentrating on the head.

"Fuck," he said. "Fuck, fuck, fuck."

Not a single word was quiet.

I braced myself against his hips as I sucked him off. And despite whatever reason this had all started, I was getting turned on just from doing this. His body was responding so perfectly. Getting bigger and thicker inside my mouth. His hands were buried in my hair. Not quite guiding me, but not exactly leaving me fully to my own capacities either.

I could tell as he tightened his grip on my head that he was getting close. His cock jerked in my mouth. He thrust forward slightly once, twice as he came so close to climax.

My jaw ached, and I nearly gagged as he got deeper and deeper into my mouth. But I wasn't going to stop.

"Close," was the only word he got out before he came into my mouth.

I squeezed my eyes shut before swallowing it down.

"Fuck, Lark," he said. He was practically shaking from his orgasm. His eyes were heavy-lidded and sex-driven.

"I like when you say my name like that."

He bent down and lifted me to my feet. Then he stepped out of his clothes and pushed me back to the bed. It squeaked noisily with every movement. I smiled as it squealed beneath me.

"Your turn."

I bit my lip. "I'm not sure I can be quiet for that."

He was already moving to my jeans and grinned. "As quiet as you can," he said before burying his face between my legs.

I was not quiet. At all.

III

I stayed over at Sam's every night that week. I trusted him. But I didn't trust Melissa one bit. Not even a little. Not after she'd told me that she was going after him. I didn't want to give her the opportunity for an in.

My phone started buzzing as I groggily made it to campus. I checked the number and saw that it was Katherine. I yawned and sent it to voicemail. I had a meeting with my volunteer Kennedy about final poll schedules. She'd been having some trouble with a group of core volunteers who had started to get flaky. End-of-the-semester blues or something. And I wanted to get it worked out ASAP.

My meeting with Kennedy lasted about a half hour. I pulled my phone back out to call Katherine and stared down at it in shock.

"What?" Kennedy asked in surprise.

"I have, like, a dozen missed calls," I told her.

"Did someone die?"

I shook my head. "I have no idea."

My parents had called. Twice. *All* of my friends had called—Katherine, Penn, Lewis, and Rowe. Even people I wasn't as friendly with were listed in my missed calls.

"What the fuck?" I whispered. "I'm going to call my friend back."

"No problem. Let me know if something's wrong or you need my help," she said, packing up her bag and heading out.

Just as I went to call Katherine, my closest friend from law school, Anna English, called. We spoke every week, but this wasn't when she normally called.

"English," I said uncertainly. "What's up?"

"Lark, how are you?"

"I don't know. What happened?"

English was silent a second. "You haven't seen?"

"Seen?"

"All right, I hate to be the one to break it to you. But I check TMZ on the regular now for my new job."

"Oh, right...you're a publicist now. But...TMZ?"

"Yeah." English cleared her throat. "So, you're in a rather, um... unflattering picture, which just showed up in the tabloids. The headline reads, *Upper East Side Princess in the Dirt*."

My hands shook. "What?"

"Yeah, I guess someone found out that you were campaigning. And instead of talking about it like it was a good thing, they posted a shit picture of you an article about how you're slumming it. It's really disgusting."

"Oh my god," I whispered in horror. "Does it say who gave them the information or the picture?"

"No, I've been digging, but it looks like it was an anonymous tip."

"Fuck," I muttered.

"I'm so sorry. I'm going to see if the PR firm can do anything about it, but...it's already circulating."

"And the internet is forever."

"Pretty much."

I swallowed back bile. "Thanks, English. Thanks for letting me know."

"Of course. I'm so sorry. If there's anything else I can do, let me know."

"I will. You're the best."

We said our good-byes. This could not be happening. I'd done everything right. I hadn't wanted anyone to know what I was doing. When you were the heir to a Fortune 500 company, you took precautions to hide your identity. I didn't care if Sam knew, but I hadn't wanted the *world* to know.

I clicked over to my texts and found a link to the article in one of them. My stomach dropped as I read the rest of the text. It was short, no more than two paragraphs, but it was disgusting. I'd been in the media a fair amount, especially in high school when I ran wild. But this was a new level of low. I was here, doing a good thing, and they made it look like I was doing something wrong. Ugh!

Then my eyes scanned the picture, which really could not have been less flattering. I tilted my head and narrowed my eyes. Wait. I remembered what I'd been doing when I wore that outfit a few days ago. To have gotten that shot, it had to have been someone who was volunteering for the campaign.

My body froze as my sickness turned to anger. Melissa. It had to be Melissa. This was how she was fighting. I had no idea how she knew who I really was, but there was no other explanation. I'd been working with most of these volunteers for months. There'd be no reason for them to turn me in...if they even knew who I was. But Melissa had motive.

I shook my head. I couldn't believe this.

I sent the article to Sam and then dialed his number. I knew that he was busy, but this couldn't wait.

"Hey, Lark. Can I call you back in five?" he asked as soon as he answered.

"Melissa sold a picture of me to the tabloids."

"What?" he asked in shock. He cleared his throat and then said something to his volunteers. "I'm free. Now, tell me what's going on."

"I sent you the article in a text. She sold me out to the tabloids."

Sam was silent for a minute. "I just read the article, and it's fucking trash, Lark. Everything posted there is utter bullshit."

"I know," I whispered. Not that it made me feel any better.

"But why do you think Melissa did this? It could have been anyone."

"I've been on campaign for almost a year, Sam. The only thing that's changed is her. And she was *there* that day when I was wearing that outfit."

Sam sighed. "Lark, I love you, but breathe for a minute. You don't really know Melissa. She is a sweet, kind Southern girl. This is not her style *at all*."

"Then I think that you don't really know her, Sam. Because this has her name all over it."

"Look," he said with another sigh, "we are a week away from Election Day. You haven't slept in months, and you're not feeling that great."

Which was true. I'd woken up yesterday with some horrible cold that wouldn't leave.

"Maybe let your volunteers take over and try to relax."

"Sam," I groaned.

"Please, Lark. The election will be over soon, and after a few days of sleep, we'll all be able to see more clearly. Okay?"

"Okay," I lied.

"I have to get back, but call me if you need me. I love you."

"I love you, too."

I hung up the phone and dropped my head back. He wouldn't even listen to me. He thought it was the cold and sleep deprivation talking. But I hadn't told him that Melissa claimed to be here to win him back. Not that he'd likely believe *that* either.

But I *knew* she had done this. I fucking knew it.

If she wanted to play dirty, I could show her what the Upper East Side was really like. Show Sam exactly what Melissa was capable of.

IV

"Hey, Lark," Melissa said with a cheeky smile as she showed up on campus later that day.

I could see in her keen eyes that she was anticipating my reaction.

"Melissa," I said with a head nod. "I'm waiting for a few more volunteers, and then I'll have you take them out to canvass."

"Oh, yeah? You don't want me for training today?" She dropped her backpack down with a clunk.

"No, I think you'll be needed in the field."

Melissa opened her mouth like she was going to argue, but I turned away from her and handed out a clipboard to one of the volunteers. She wasn't going to get a reaction from me. I wasn't going to let her think that she'd gotten to me. But I also wasn't going to reward her behavior by letting her stay here and train volunteers, which half the time meant she sat around on her laptop. I had other people I trusted to do trainings. I wanted her out of my sight.

When everyone was finally here, I paired people off and then sent them out into the field. Melissa hovered by me.

"Do you need something?"

"I saw that horrible article about you this morning."

I blinked. "Okay?"

"You must be feeling awful."

I laughed softly, glad that Melissa hadn't been on campus earlier when I had my breakdown. "I'm from the Upper East Side. Much worse has been said about me. Those tabloids are trash anyway."

"Right. Do you know who did that?" she asked, wide-eyed with innocence.

I just smiled. "We both know who did it."

Melissa arched her eyebrows. "I don't know what you're insinuating."

"Why don't you go work?" I suggested. "You're not really needed here."

Melissa pursed her lips. Then she leaned in close. "You didn't think I'd let you get away with saying you were going to ruin my life, did you?"

I said nothing. Just kept my steady gaze on her. It didn't matter that she'd confirmed that she'd done it. I'd already known that. And Sam wouldn't believe me either way. Not now. Not yet.

"Have a nice day," I said, turning my back on her.

She hovered behind me a second before huffing off after another volunteer. Good riddance.

I dropped into my chair, thankful that everyone had disappeared for the next couple hours. I downed some more cold medicine and blew my nose, and then I went to work. But no matter how much I tried to focus, my mind kept spinning back to Melissa. I needed something to get back at her. To prove that she wasn't what she seemed.

My gaze wandered to her backpack. I bit my lip and then drew it toward me. I fished out her laptop and then opened it in front of me.

Password.

Crap.

I had no clue what it could be. Luckily, one of my crew was a tech genius. Rowe had invented the social media platform Crew, which was sweeping the country right now. I'd seen him hack people in minutes in high school. He'd know how to do it.

I dialed his number.

"Lark," he said in greeting. "I've been trying to get rid of that picture all morning."

Leave it to Rowe to cut straight to the issue. "Thanks, Rowe. But I need to get into someone's computer, but it's password-protected. How do I get around that?"

"Is it a company computer?"

"No. Just a personal laptop."

"Mac?"

"Yeah."

"Okay. Here is what you do," he began.

He didn't care one bit *why* I needed to break into a computer. He'd always had ambiguous morals about tech security. Classic Rowe.

I carefully followed his instructions and was shocked that within a few keystrokes, I'd bypassed the password, and I was into Melissa's laptop. Damn, that had been almost too easy.

"Thanks, Rowe."

"Anytime. I'll keep working on the picture."

I laughed. "Thanks."

I didn't know what I was looking for as I dug through her computer files. Something, anything incriminating. I found a ton of pictures, including dozens with some guy named Joey. They were recent, too. None of them were dirty, but it was a start. I pulled up the browser and opened her Crew account, which she stayed logged in to. I searched for Joey in her Friends list and found the same guy. He lived in Chapel Hill, but his profile was basically empty. No pictures of him with Melissa. No relationship status. I frowned and decided to try her email.

When I typed *Joey* into the search bar, dozens of emails popped up. Bingo.

From some digging through her emails, I gathered that they'd met on Tinder and been hooking up for weeks. It looked like neither of them had put a label on it, and she'd put him on hold while she was out of town. On hold but not finished.

I quickly forwarded their conversations to my email so I could read them later and then deleted it from her sent file. I checked the time with excitement coursing through me. Most people got sick at the thought of doing something dangerous, but a part of me relished it. A part of me wanted to destroy things. I'd spent the last year with Sam, pushing down the darker sides of my personality. Just trying to be Lark. But Larkin St. Vincent got shit *done*.

Then I drafted an email to Joey, copying Melissa's writing style.

Hey,

How are you? Hope you're doing well. I know that the campaign ends in a week, but I've really been missing you. I wish that you could come up to Wisconsin and visit. A girl can dream, right?

Mel

My heart pattered in my chest as I hit the Send button and waited for a response. From previous email exchanges, it looked like he was always on his email, waiting for her to send something. I'd thought it was weird that they weren't texting, but apparently, at his job, he couldn't use his phone. Hence the hundreds of emails.

The screen blinked, and a new message appeared.

Mel,

It's good to hear from you. It's so boring here without you. I've really missed you, too. Are you serious about me coming to visit?

Joey

I responded next, sticking to how they normally talked back and forth.

Dead serious. Do you think you could make it work? —Mel

Gah, I can get the time off work, but I checked the flights, and they're crazy. I don't think that I could afford to do it. —Joey

I tapped my lip. I had a solution to that, but it was mad.

I could pay for your flight. I have more money coming in right now. I wouldn't mind. —Mel

Nah. I could never accept that. Though it would be so worth it. —Joey

I smiled devilishly. *Here we go.*

But I want to. Just send me your info, and I'll book it for Saturday morning. —Mel

You're sure? —Joey

You said it yourself. It'd be so worth it. —Mel

I tapped my finger on the keyboard, waiting. Melissa wouldn't be back for at least another hour, but still, the nerves were making me jittery.

All right. I'll come. —Joey

My smile grew at the response.

Hook, line, and sinker.

I knew how I was going to take down Melissa Young. She would regret ever releasing that picture of me or thinking she could take Sam from me.

V

I couldn't shake my cold. My head felt like it was a thousand pounds, my throat was scratchy, and my entire face was stuffy. And that was *with* medicine.

"You should really go to the doctor," Sam said as I blew my nose for the hundredth time.

"I'll be fine," I said, my voice nasally.

"You are not fine. You're not sleeping. Your body is shutting down."

I pressed my hand to my head. "When am I going to have time to go to the doctor, Sam? It's three days until the election. I have to be here."

"Even this isn't worth killing yourself over," he reminded me.

I sank into a seat at the front of the office. I didn't even have it in me to argue. My eyes were hot and heavy. Though I was pretty sure that I didn't have a fever. Just this stupid cold.

"Ready to go to campus?" Melissa asked, trotting into the office with a bounce in her step.

"Lark isn't going to campus today," Sam said. "She's too sick."

"Oh nooo," Melissa crooned. "That is too bad, Lark."

I glared up at her. "I'm going to campus."

"You're going to a doctor."

"No," I told him flatly.

"Lark," he groaned.

The door to the office opened again, and a bell jingled over-head, cutting Sam off. In walked a tall, burly guy with glasses. My mouth went dry.

Joey.

"Melissa!" he said cheerfully. Then he strode across the room and scooped her up in a hug.

I saw panic skitter across her face before disappearing. She pushed him away as soon as he put her down.

"Who the hell are you?" she gasped.

Joey looked at her in confusion. "Mel, it's me, Joey."

Melissa just blinked. "You must be mistaken. I have no idea who you are. I've never seen you a day in my life."

If I'd been feeling better, I would have gaped. Melissa was a damn good actress. How was she faking this so well?

Sam glanced between them and then put his hand out, ever the Southern gentleman. "Hey, man, I'm Sam."

Joey shook his hand. "Uh...Joey."

"I'm not sure what's going on here," Sam said. "Are you a volunteer for the campaign?"

Joey looked between them, confusion written across his features. "Well, see, Melissa here is my girlfriend. She invited me to come see her at the end of the campaign."

"I did no such thing," Melissa said automatically.

Joey furrowed his brows. "Don't know why you're pretending not to know me, Mel. You're the one who bought the ticket."

Melissa's eyes rounded. "Uh, no, I didn't."

"Hey, man, maybe there was some kind of misunderstanding," Sam said, trying to play peacekeeper.

"No misunderstanding," Joey drawled. "I have the emails here." He found the emails we'd sent back and forth and handed them to Melissa.

She scanned the emails, and Sam glanced over her shoulder.

"That's your email," Sam reasoned.

"I must have been hacked!" Melissa cried. "I wouldn't do this. Does this even sound like me, Sam?"

He shrugged like he didn't want to get involved even though he was already involved. "Y'all can figure that out."

Melissa whipped around on Joey. "You said I paid for the flight? Do you have the receipt?"

My stomach twisted. Oh god. I'd deleted everything else. I'd even blocked Joey after our final interaction so that Melissa wouldn't get more emails from him. But the receipt...shit, could that be incriminating? I'd run everything by Rowe. We'd both thought that I'd covered my tracks.

Joey handed her his phone again.

"Ha!" she cried. "The last four digits of my credit card are 3711, not 5512." She pulled out her wallet and showed everyone. "I didn't do this."

Sam looked even more confused. "So...what happened?"

"Obviously, someone hacked my email." Melissa took a step away from Joey. "They invented this boyfriend, which I never had, and paid for him to come and humiliate me."

"That sounds...outrageous, Mel. Who would ever do that?"

Melissa froze, and then her eyes found mine. I had been carefully blank through the entire interaction. Just holding a tissue to my nose and trying not to fall over from exhaustion.

"Oh my god, *you* did this," Melissa accused me.

"Mel, come on," he said.

I cringed at the way he'd used her nickname. I didn't like the sound of it in his mouth.

Then the little actress burst into tears. She began to cry into her hands. I had to fight back rolling my eyes.

"It's Lark. Sam, she's...she's out to *get* me," she cried dramatically. "She told me the first day that I met her that if I got near you, she'd ruin my life. Now, look what she did!"

Sam put his arm around her and patted her shoulder. I glared at the exchange.

"I did no such thing," I managed to get out.

My head was pounding even harder. Everything felt fuzzy.

Melissa ripped herself out of Sam's embrace and lunged for my purse. If I'd been feeling better, I might have been able to stop her. But as it was, I was too slow. I couldn't get it quick enough. Then she snatched out my wallet. Sam was telling her to stop, but she didn't listen. She reached in and wrenched out my credit cards until she gasped.

"Look." She threw the card at Sam.

His eyes widened as he looked down at the credit card in his hand.

"5512," Melissa spat. Then she started crying again. "I *told* you she was out to get me! I told you! All of this is a farce. She made it all up."

"Sam, I..." I got out as I tried to stand. But I quickly sank back down. Standing was too much effort. Fuck.

Sam's look of disbelief broke my heart. "Lark, did you...did you do this?"

"Sam..."

"Did you?"

"Of course she did," Melissa said, sobbing.

Joey looked uncomfortable, like he wanted to back out of the room.

"Melissa...Melissa started it," I forced out. My stomach twisted. Fear spiked through my veins.

Oh god, that look in his eyes. That look that said he had no idea who I was. It was too much. I needed to get up. I needed to say more.

He glanced between us. "I don't know what is going on here, but I don't want any part of it."

"Melissa wrote that article in the tabloids. She sent them the picture. She told me herself!" I told him. "She told me when she first showed up that she was here to win you back. This all started because of what she did."

Sam shook his head. He looked disgusted. "I really don't know what's true. But this is your credit card. This proof is in front of my face."

"Sam..." I pleaded.

"We have an election to win," he said gruffly. He stuffed the card back in my wallet and tossed it on top of my purse. "We all need to get to work."

With one more glance at me and then Melissa, he strode out of the office. If I'd felt an ounce better, I would have rushed after him. I'd have explained what happened and why I'd done what I'd done. But I could barely scramble to my feet. By the time I got to the door, his truck was already peeling out of the parking lot.

Melissa came to step up next to me. A cruel smile painted her lips. She didn't say a word. Just threw her shoulder into mine, making me stumble and nearly fall with the weight of my sickness. Then she strode out after him.

Leaving me all alone with Joey and how everything had just completely blown up in my face. The realization of what I'd done...what I'd lost.

I felt cold.

Like I was drowning in a frozen lake.

I'd ruined everything.

Everything.

VI

A beer sat untouched in front of me. I'd arrived at The Station a half hour ago when Toby told me there was nothing more that could be done. Election results were on every screen in the bar. Wisconsin hadn't been called yet, but most of the East Coast had. Woodhouse was ahead by *a lot*. We were just waiting for the final outcome.

Moira slid into the seat across from me. "You look like you're feeling better."

I glanced up at her and shrugged. My cold was mostly gone, which I found shocking, considering my mental health had completely deteriorated after Sam walked out of the office. I hadn't seen him since.

"So, what happened with you and Sam?" Moira asked gently. "People said there was a screaming match and lots of crying."

I shook my head. "I don't know, Moira. I blew it."

"I can't imagine whatever happened being serious enough to wreck you two. You've been inseparable for the last *year*."

"I know." I sighed. "I don't know what to do."

She tipped her head behind me. "Fix it."

I turned around to find Sam walking into The Station. He looked around the room until he found me and then beelined in my direction. Just as he reached me, the entire room went up in chaos. We both turned to the TVs. Wisconsin had been called for Woodhouse. *And with Wisconsin, so goes the country.*

"We won," Sam said to me.

"So it appears," I said.

Everyone else around us was hugging and cheering and congratulating. Toasts were made. Drinks were chugged. Celebration ensued. And Sam and I stared at each other in silence. This was not celebratory. I could see it on his face. This was not fixable in his eyes. I knew it before he said a word.

"Was it real?" he asked.

I swallowed and nodded. "Of course. Yes."

"Which Lark is the real one?" he continued. "Were you acting with me the last year?"

"No, Sam. I'm sorry about what happened. But what we had was real."

He sighed and glanced away. "You didn't trust me."

"I didn't trust Melissa."

"Semantics," he said. "You went behind my back to hurt Melissa because you thought that we were going to get back together. You didn't trust me."

"I don't know what to say, Sam. You invited her to *live* with you. You knew I was uncomfortable. And you didn't hear me when I tried to warn you."

"So, you decided to try to ruin her life?" he demanded. "Lark, that's..." He shook his head again and crossed his arms. Closed off. "I'm going back to North Carolina."

My stomach dropped. We'd never said what would happen next after the campaign. I'd said that I had to hold to my promise to my parents and he was applying to law schools. He could have stayed with me in New York while he applied. He could have chosen NYU or Columbia or even Fordham. Anywhere nearby. But now...he was going home.

"When?"

"In two days. Melissa is driving back with me in the truck."

I thought I was going to be sick. "So, with Melissa then?"

Just as I'd always suspected.

"She lives there, too."

"Sam, please," I gasped.

He looked away as if he couldn't witness my pain.

"What about us?"

His gaze fell to his feet. "I don't think there is an us. Not when neither of us can trust the other."

I choked back a sob. "What am I going to do without you?"

"You're going to go back to New York," he told me with a sad smile. "You're going to join your parents and run your empire. Wasn't that always the plan anyway?"

I nodded but felt utterly hollow inside. It *was* the plan. But I couldn't imagine going home without him. Sam would never come to my city. It'd be empty, just like my life.

He looked like he wanted to reach out and hug me one last time. I stepped forward, hoping for it, hoping to find the words to change his mind. Except he didn't want to change his mind. The last year had been an adventure, but the adventure was over. I would go back to being Larkin St. Vincent, heiress to a fortune, an Upper East Side princess. And he'd return to Chapel Hill. He'd go to law school and build houses with his dad. He'd get back together with Melissa.

Our lives diverged like a river. Maybe we had never been meant to cross in the first place.

"Good-bye, Lark," he said, not able to hide the hitch in his voice before he turned and walked back out of The Station.

Movers came the next day to pack up my apartment. I just had to fill a suitcase, say good-bye to the rest of my colleagues, and then get on a plane back to New York. I lingered anyway, hoping to see Sam one last time. Moira pulled me into a hug and promised to stay close. I agreed. Though I wanted to leave everything about this campaign behind me. Without Sam, how could I even think about it?

So, I left the office and headed to the Madison airport. I boarded in first class and tried to sleep as I flew back home alone. Everything ached, and even a drink didn't silence the demons.

This wasn't what I'd wanted. This wasn't supposed to happen.

Sam was my first love.

My first everything.

We were supposed to drive off into the sunset together. Not end up torn down the middle. I wasn't supposed to feel sick to my stomach every time I thought about him.

And worse, this was my fault. Not completely. Not all of it. He'd still invited Melissa. He'd still let her stay at his place. He'd still believed Melissa over me...every time. But I'd done horrible, horrible things to try to keep him. When I should have realized he was mine and he had no intention of letting me go. Until I'd shown him who I truly was.

My whole life, I'd gotten by with my name and my money. This was the first time ever that someone had loved me for who I was, with no pretense. And then my old self had reared its ugly head and destroyed the best thing in my life.

Bad Lark.

That was what had happened. I'd become Bad Lark.

She felt like a separate entity to who I really was. And I wanted to be rid of her. I didn't want to fall into that trap. I never, *ever* wanted to be Bad Lark again.

I felt stronger when I got off the plane than when I'd boarded. Still hollow and empty where Sam's light had previously shone through me. But free of the person I'd been, the one who had sent those emails to Joey and destroyed her own life.

Instead, I was just *me*.

And that was who I was going to be for everyone from now on.

When I wheeled my suitcase out to baggage claim, I broke into a smile. There, standing inside LaGuardia Airport, was my crew. Katherine in a skimpy red dress. Penn dressed in a suit, his eyes lost and contemplative. Rowe fiddling with his iPad. Lewis perfectly put together, as normal. He noticed me first and burst into a giant smile as he waved.

I walked toward them, and they all drew me into a hug at once. Even Rowe, who hated touching. I laughed.

"You're all here," I said in surprise.

"Of course," Penn said with command. "You were gone for a year. We missed you."

"We did," Lewis agreed.

"Yeah, I'm tired of being *completely* outnumbered," Katherine said with an eye roll.

I looked around at my friends—my family. At least I wasn't alone. They'd always loved me for exactly who I was. They'd seen me at my best and my worst. And they wouldn't care which Lark appeared before them that day.

But as I walked out of the airport with my friends, my heart still panged for Sam. And I knew it would be a long, *long* time until I got over him.

If I *ever* did.

CRUEL TRUTH

K.A. LINDE

PART I

THE ONE THAT GOT AWAY

1

LARK

"Larkin, darling, I don't understand why you're mad," my mother said. She turned crisply in her sharp Chanel suit that hugged her figure perfectly.

"You don't understand anything apparently," I snapped back.

I nudged a pile of boxes as high as my head that had manifested in my living room out of thin air. It was six thirty in the morning. I hadn't had my coffee. And I was ready to combust.

"I am just trying to keep you up-to-date on the latest fashions. If you're a part of this family, then you must look the part of a St. Vincent, dear."

"Get them out of here, Mother. I don't need seventeen pairs of high heels," I growled, estimating the boxes in front of me, "or thirty evening gowns or twenty new handbags. Mother, I work on the mayor's campaign. This isn't my *life* anymore."

"Nonsense," she said. "Who doesn't want more clothes? I did find you a dozen new power suits to replace that number you're wearing right now." She pointed up and down at me. "It'll do you wonders."

I ground my teeth and debated whether or not this was worth the fight. My mother, Hope St. Vincent, cared about next to nothing in this world other than appearances. She still probably wondered how she had gotten so unlucky to have a daughter who didn't want to take over the family business and live the same life she presently lived on the Upper East Side—filthy rich, married, and miserable. I swore, my parents hadn't shared a bed in twenty years. The St. Vincents took *fucked up* to a whole new level.

"I honestly cannot handle you right now," I said. "Please have this all cleared out. I have to get to work."

"All this work causes you so much stress." My mother strutted over to me on her six-inch Louboutins and pressed her fingers to my forehead. "There's this new plastic surgeon everyone is talking about. I could get you a Botox appointment. It's preventative!"

I counted slowly to ten, reminding myself this was my mother and that somewhere deep, *deep* down she meant well.

"I'm leaving." I reached for my bag. "Also, I'm having the locks changed. I don't even know how you got *in* here."

"Oh, Larkin, you're overreacting, as always."

Any minute now, she would be inviting me to early morning martinis. It was never too early to drink.

"As you know, Mayor Kensington's reelection campaign is gearing up," I reminded her as patiently as I could. "I have even less time than normal to do anything. Today, I have a huge meeting about the mayoral fundraising banquet next week. So, I have to go."

"Oh, of course," my mother said. "Leslie told me about that. We purchased a table, obviously." She opened a box and pulled out a lavender St. Vincent's handbag. My mother's signature bag—the Larkin. I cringed. God, it had been a nightmare, growing up with my name on a bag. She shoved the bag into my hand. "Too bad that Nina isn't going anymore."

"It is too bad," I agreed.

Then I tossed the Larkin bag back into the box. I was not looking forward to my parents being at the banquet. It made my job so much harder.

My mother continued to fish through the new clothes and pick things out. Sometimes, I dreamed that I was adopted. It was just a fantasy though. My mother and I had the same signature chestnut-red hair. Though she kept it long and straight as a board while mine curled every which way if I let it. And under her layers of makeup, she had the same heart-shaped face, the same pouty lips, and the same bright green eyes as me. I had once thought that we had the same smile, but my mother didn't really smile anymore.

It pained me to think that I'd once been so vapid. The Upper East Side took everyone as its victim. I'd been trying so hard to stay out of that life. Except for my closest friends—my crew, the four people in my life who were more like family than my own parents—I stayed out of the madness. But somehow, it always sucked me back in. Just like my mother tried to do right this very minute.

"Okay. You figure out what to do with all these clothes," I said on a sigh. I knew it was stupid to give in to her. For every inch, she took a mile. But I had to leave. I had too much work to do to deal with this right now. "I'm going to go to work."

"Oh, take the limo!"

I shook my head. "I'll grab a cab."

"Don't be absurd. Your father's Mercedes is only two blocks over. He can pick me up, and you'll be free with the limo."

"That's okay. I'll take a cab. It'll be fine," I said, grabbing my own purse and striding toward the door.

"Will we see you for brunch?"

I rolled my eyes. "Depends on how busy I am after the banquet this weekend! I'll talk to you later."

With a sigh, I pushed out of my door and hurried to the elevator. Dear god, I thought somewhere in my brain that it would get easier to deal with my parents. That someday, they would come to accept that I actually enjoyed working on campaigns. That I liked being a campaign manager for the mayor of New York City. It didn't help that my parents ran St. Vincent's Resorts, a multibillion-dollar company that had been in my family for generations. Or that my mother had created St. Vincent handbags and cosmetics. Not only did they want me to take over the family business, they also had a long list of suitors they found acceptable for me to marry. They didn't even seem to care which one I picked as long as I kept the wealth among other old-money families.

Not that I had any intention of dating any of them or taking over the business for that matter. One day, they would get that through their skulls. I hoped.

I just shook my head and hopped into the first cab I saw. I grinned a little as I passed my mother's limousine.

It took me under thirty minutes to get into the office, even without my parents' goddamn limo. Which was fortunate because I was there a good hour before everyone else arrived. It was the only way I would get through all the work piling up on my desk. The fundraising banquet was our biggest event thus far, and it would set the tone for the campaign season. And that was on top of everything else that was on my plate.

I'd been under a pile of paperwork for who even knew how long when a text hit my phone.

Are we still on for coffee later?

"Fuck," I grumbled.

I had completely forgotten that my friend Anna English was coming into town today, and I had promised her coffee. That was before I'd known how swamped I'd be with the banquet. But English lived in Los Angeles, and I never saw her anymore. I couldn't just bail.

"Ugh," I groaned again. I'd have to figure it out.

Yes! I might be a few minutes late.

When aren't you, babe?

I laughed. At least she understood.

"Ready for the fundraising department meeting, boss?" my assistant, Aspen, asked, popping her head into my office. Her long platinum-blonde hair fell like a waterfall over one shoulder, framing her pale skin and sky-blue eyes.

I checked the time. Somehow, two hours had already passed.

"All set," I lied.

"Okay! Let me know if you need anything else from me."

Aspen was a godsend. I'd gone through so many assistants before finding her. She was always eager to learn, which I'd found out was not a common trait among campaign assistants.

"Will do," I told her.

I grabbed everything I would need for the meeting off of my desk and stumbled into the conference room, scattering papers on the giant table. I arranged them into a neat pile, perfectly ready for this meeting. Even if I would have felt more comfortable after another twenty hours of prep.

Not that I had twenty extra hours. Not as the deputy campaign manager, where I had to oversee all six major departments—fundraising, communications, field, legal, tech, and political. I could spend every day on just one of these areas and not get enough done. But since the mayor's banquet was the most important thing on the agenda, this meeting was at the top of the list. And I was going to be sure that it went off without a hitch.

"Hey, girlfriend," Demi said as she entered the room.

Demi was the head of the fundraising department and probably my favorite person in the office. She was a short, curvy black woman from Brooklyn, who always seemed perfectly put together. In fact, she carried her own papers in a notebook with each person's name labeled on the front and a presentation board with every banquet guest's name on a sticky note.

"Morning, Demi."

"Aspen said you came in early again. Are you always going to show us up?" she asked with a grin. She set the board down on the table and then turned to face me, twirling a short corkscrew curl around her finger.

"Too much to do, so little time," I told her with a shrug. "I'm just going to grab my laptop. We can get started once everyone else is ready."

"Sounds good."

I hastened back to my office and grabbed my MacBook, pulling up the figures I had been looking at yesterday.

"Oh, hey, Lark. Do you have a minute?"

I glanced up to see Kelly from HR, peeking into the office. "Um, I have, like, three minutes before my meeting."

"Perfect! I'm trying to introduce the new attorney we just hired to everyone."

"You finally filled the position?" I asked in surprise.

We'd been searching for a while for someone with the proper qualifications in campaign finance. I hadn't thought it would be hard to find someone like that in New York City. Didn't everyone have a JD here?

"Yep! Come meet him real quick. I sent him to get coffee."

I shut my laptop and passed Kelly as she sank her hip against Aspen's desk and started chatting. Clearly, this *meet the new guy* thing was an excuse to chitchat, but I really *did* like to know everyone who worked here.

I stepped into the break room just as the new guy turned from the crappy coffeemaker. Our eyes met. Time slowed. Then froze. For the first time, I understood the meaning of my heart skipping a beat. Because it did.

I took in the deep dark brown orbs. Let my eyes crash over the swish of brown hair, the lethal cut of his jawline, the Cupid's bow of his perfect lips. That body. Holy fuck, the way that body filled out that black suit. And those hands. Builder's hands.

A part of me ached to step forward.

A part of me remembered what had happened.

How we had fallen apart all those years ago.

"Lark?" he asked in disbelief.

My traitorous heart fluttered.

"Hi, Sam."

2

LARK

Sam's eyes swept down my own black suit as he took me in from head to toe. I felt exposed in that look. As if he saw so much more than the rumpled suit to the vulnerable girl I'd been once upon a time.

He reached a hand forward as if he was trying to make sure that I was actually there. Then he quickly withdrew like if he got too close, I'd burn him.

"What are you doing here?" Sam finally managed to get out.

"What am *I* doing here?" I said in disbelief. "What are *you* doing here? I'm from New York. I thought you were still in North Carolina."

"Oh, right." He rubbed the back of his head. "You're from New York. I just...I thought you were working for your parents."

"Oh."

Because of course he did. That had been the plan after all. One year on the presidential campaign in Madison, Wisconsin. One perfect year with Sam. And then I would come home to New York and take over St. Vincent's Enterprise. Except everything had changed when I got home. I'd never been the same after that fateful November five years earlier.

"I decided to join Leslie's campaign instead," I told him. "I mean, Mayor Kensington's campaign."

"Really?" he asked, shock registering on his face. "But...I thought it was just a year."

"Yeah...it was."

We were.

I swallowed back the bile at the thought of what had happened with us five years ago. A year of bliss that had gone down in a fiery pit of destruction.

We stood together then like ghosts of our former selves. An echo of what we'd once been. Hurt, betrayal, and still that aching want burning at the edges. That had always been there with Sam. An inevitable force that blew us together, only to slam us into a wall, screeching tires, locked brakes, and cracked windshield, leaving us both a mess.

And still, despite all the walls I'd built up around myself since Sam, seeing him made it feel like my still-bleeding heart was exposed all over again.

"Hey, Lark!" Kelly interrupted, popping into the break room at that exact moment. "Glad you met Sam. He's going to be a big part of the team from now on."

I swallowed back bile. Oh no. Oh god. I'd known when Kelly sent me in here that Sam was the new attorney she had just hired. But I hadn't put two and two together that I was going to be seeing him every single day from now until November.

"That's great," I said. "Welcome...to the team."

"Thanks," he said softly.

Brown eyes met green in the space between us. There was so much more that needed to be said. So much that had been left unsaid when I returned home all those years ago. I'd never thought that I'd see him again. And now that I was, I had no fucking clue what to do.

"Well, come on, Sam. Lark is late to her banquet meeting, and the mayor just got in," Kelly said in her default chipper tone. She strode out of the break room and called over her shoulder, "You'll get your first intro on day one!"

"Ugh, my meeting," I groaned, turning in place to follow Kelly.

"Wait," Sam said.

He reached out and this time gripped my elbow. I turned back to face him with wide, shocked eyes. He towered over me. I'd forgotten until that moment how huge he was. All tall, wide-shouldered Southern boy who actually knew manual labor with calluses on his fingers and biceps for days. A man who liked to use his hands...in all the best ways.

"What?" I whispered. I was conscious of Kelly mere feet away and the meeting I was currently supposed to be in.

"We need to talk. Later."

A dormant, broken butterfly wing beat for the first time in ages. I hated my heart for responding that way. But fuck, despite all the shit we'd gone through and how we'd both fucked up so royally, it was *Sam*.

"Okay."

He released me slowly, almost reluctantly. Something uncurled further in my chest...or perhaps lower, much lower, at the way his fingers withdrew from my skin. Oh fuck, I was screwed.

I scurried away from him. My heart raced, and my hands were clammy. I couldn't seem to get my head on straight.

Sam Rutherford was in New York City. Something I'd never thought he would do. He certainly hadn't considered it for *me*. And now, what the hell was I going to do? After what had happened, could I disentangle the anger and pain from the love and lust? Could I find a way to move on from what had happened and work next to him?

It felt impossible.

Honestly impossible.

And by the time my meeting was over, I hadn't come to any better conclusion. In fact, I'd sat through the whole thing with my head in the clouds. Which was something I absolutely could not afford. I had too much to do to sacrifice even one meeting.

Somehow, just seeing Sam for a few minutes had left me feeling like the inexperienced twenty-four-year-old girl who had never been on a campaign before. Rather than the deputy campaign manager to the mayor of New York City.

I needed to shake it off. Get him out of my head. I'd worked hard to help Leslie get elected as the first female mayor. I absolutely deserved to be one of the highest-ranking people on this team. Many people had come and gone since we started, but I'd stuck with her, forgoing other campaigns to work with a candidate that I believed in. Which was the whole reason I'd moved to Madison six years ago for the presidential campaign in the first place.

Before the campaign, my parents had controlled every aspect of my life. I was their perfect little Upper East Side princess. Read: monster. I had all the right friends and boyfriends and high school accolades. I attended Brown, of course, because I was a legacy and got a business degree with the goal of taking over the company. Even when I decided to get a law degree, it didn't ever feel like a choice. I went to Columbia Law so that I could work with my parents and be close to home.

But then something happened. Something changed. Governor Woodhouse held a rally at Columbia. English had heard he was an awesome speaker and dragged me and Whitley to the event. Then I heard him speak. Heard the eloquent speech he delivered to the packed, entranced audience, and something shifted in me. This was a man I could get behind. A race I could believe in.

I applied for a position the next day in every swing state.

Two weeks later, I'd gotten the job in Madison.

It was the only real choice I'd ever made in my entire life. And it was the start of everything. The start of getting out from under my parents' thumb and finding my own life.

And then there was Sam.

I shook my head. He was all jumbled with that choice. Inherently connected to it in a way that I had never been able to pull apart. How the fuck was I going to do it now?

My phone buzzed just as I stepped back into my office, prepared to lock myself away all afternoon and obsess endlessly about this issue. As one did.

Just got to Coffee Grounds and managed to snag a table. I'll grab our drinks. See you soon!

"Oh, right. Fuck." I'd forgotten about my coffee meeting with English. I jumped out of my seat and grabbed my purse on the way. "I'm out for a meeting. I'll be back in thirty."

"Roger that," Aspen said. She gave me a little salute as I passed.

I was out the door and jogging the few blocks to my favorite coffee shop in the East Village. Somehow, I managed to only be ten minutes late. It might be a record.

"Sorry I'm late," I said, plopping into the seat across from my friend.

English removed her enormous sunglasses and brushed her long Hollywood blonde hair off of her shoulders. "You're always late."

"Well, yeah, but this time, I have a reason."

"You were in a meeting for the campaign and forgot?" She laughed as my eyes rounded and pushed my drink toward me. "I know you too well. Now, drink up before it gets cold."

I took a fortifying drink of my coffee. This was going to suck.

"Sam is back," I blurted out.

Her bright blue eyes rounded. "Sam? Like, *the* Sam?"

"Yeah. Yep. He's here. In New York City. And I don't know what to do," I told her in a rush.

"Wait, what?" she spat. "Sam Rutherford, the guy who did you dirty on the last campaign, the guy who ran your heart over with his truck and then blamed *you*? That Sam? Please tell me you didn't actually talk to him."

"He just got a job in my fucking office,"

"No way. What a douche!" she gasped out. "He had the nerve to get a job where you *already* work? What, did he use you as a reference to get an in?"

I shook my head. "No. As far as I know, he didn't even know that I worked there. He thought I was still working for my parents."

"Ew."

"Tell me about it. But it was what he'd thought was the plan before our fallout. So, I think he probably didn't know I worked for the mayor. It's not like my picture is on the website."

"Girl, we are going to need to get something stronger than coffee to deal with this conversation," English said.

"You're not wrong," I said, gulping down the coffee. "What am I going to do? He's in legal. It's probably the department I deal with the least, but it's not a big office. I'm going to have to see him every day from now until November."

English reached into her bag and pulled out a planner that was stuffed to the brim with notes and tabs and stickers. She flipped until she found a blank page, immediately going into fixer mode. She might look like a movie star, but she chose to handle their publicity and generally clean up everyone's messes instead of acting herself. Her work as a celebrity publicist was top notch. She was one of the best in the business back in LA. And she worked nearly as hard and as many hours as I did to prove it, and that was saying something.

"Let's make a list of what we can do," she said. "First things first. I'm not saying that I know someone who could plant blow on him so that he could get fired, but...I do work with rockstars."

I burst into laughter. "I love you, but no. I can't do that. Bad Lark might have considered that option, but that's not who I want to be anymore."

"You act like Bad Lark is a physically different entity than you," English said, jotting the word *blow* down on the Maybe list.

"I hope she is," I said with a shrug. "I don't want to get him fired. I don't want to jeopardize his career or anything. I just...don't know what to do."

English put her pen down. She sighed. "Because you still care about him."

I bit my lip. "And I hate him."

"And you're wondering if this is your second chance."

I immediately shook my head and then frowned and nodded slowly. "I don't know. Can we get past what we did to each other?

Five years is a long time. I'm a different person than I was. Maybe he's different too."

"I'm going to go on record and say this is a bad idea," English said, adding *second chance* to the No list. "You just had to deal with all the Thomas shit. That asshole still works as a senior executive for St. Vincent's Enterprise. I mean, your parents actually sided with your ex-boyfriend over you in the fallout. I don't think you're ready to head straight into Sam-level territory. Can't you just find a nice, normal guy?"

"Says the girl married to a movie star."

English laughed. "I mean, we're not all lucky enough to find a Josh Hutch. But I know there's a guy out there for you. I just don't know if it's Sam Rutherford."

"Jesus, I need to get it together. He's just an ex, right?" I glanced up to find her nodding approvingly. "He's just this guy I dated for a year, like, five years ago."

"Exactly. I mean, you still hang out with your crew, and haven't you slept with Penn, Lewis, and Rowe?"

I glared at her. "We do not bring up Bad Lark when we're trying to get me to do the right thing here."

English snorted. "Fair point."

"I can put the past behind us. I'm a professional. I can deal with Sam being in the office for the next six months. It'll be fine...right?"

"Well, if it's not, we can always drink," English offered. She scribbled *wasted* into the Yes column. "I was thinking we could go out tomorrow night with Whitley before I leave for LA. You could even invite Katherine."

"Oh god, Katherine and Whitley in the same room. That sounds like a perfect way for me to forget that Sam is in town."

"Exactly. You game?"

I nodded. Even though I knew that I'd pay for it the next day at work, I really needed a night out with my girls. Maybe I could get drunk enough to forget this disaster had even happened.

3

LARK

I headed back to the office with more confidence than I'd left it.
Thank god for Anna English. I didn't know how I would have
gotten through the rest of the afternoon without her. Just being
able to talk to her had made it all seem better. Even if she didn't
actually use her fixer capabilities on me. Or maybe...she had.

I knew that I'd have to face Sam later. But I was hoping to get
through all of my work first before it came to that. I still needed to
go through the field report from Robert on what the campaign was
doing on the ground to reach voters before the primary. Plus,
Aspen had told me this morning that new messaging was coming
in from Matthew, head of the political department, and she'd
scheduled a joint consult with him and Beth, who ran the tech-
nology department and disseminated policy information on the
website and social media. I was already anticipating then having
to take it to Christine in communications for the speech Mayor
Kensington would give at the fundraising banquet next week.

Just putting together the flow of the departments that I coordinated with helped to calm me down. But the look on Aspen's face
when I got back to my desk ruined it all.

"What happened?"

Aspen rolled her eyes. "Nothing. The mayor's son is here."

I frowned. "I'm guessing it's not Penn based on that face."

"Out of luck. Court's here."

"And causing problems?"

"Doesn't he always?" she grumbled.

I sighed, letting all the work I'd planned to do spiral out of my head. "I'll deal with him."

"You're a godsend."

"Could you just go through the field report from Robert and mark it up for me? I'll look at it when I get back."

Aspen frowned. "Um, I haven't gotten that yet."

"Jesus. Okay, email Robert and ask him to send over the field report ASAP. You know what? Email Matthew about the messaging, too. I want to go over it before it gets to Beth and Christine."

"On it," she said with another salute.

Then I turned and went in search of the number one problem on the mayor's campaign—Court Kensington.

I'd been friends with the Kensingtons my entire life. Penn Kensington was still one of the closest friends I had. The only other person in our five-member crew who had gotten *out* of the Upper East Side cycle. He was a philosophy professor at Columbia, bucking all tradition, and trying to live the good life with his girlfriend, Natalie.

Court was another story. He was a straight trainwreck. As far as I could tell, he had a very loose, open relationship with his girlfriend, Jane. That led him down all the wrong rabbit holes. His mother had had to get him out of more than one scandalous situation. Plus, he ruined every campaign event at which he was in attendance. As if he had been prepped to self-destruct.

I rounded the corner, ready to find out what mayhem Court Kensington was causing, and my stomach dropped. There he was. With the inimitable Gavin King...and Sam.

Sam seemed animated, clearly in the middle of a story. He hadn't seen me yet. And for a second, I just watched his expression. The easy grin that came to his face. The laugh that came from all three of them when he hit the end of the story. It was so effortless.

He was handling Court and Gavin like a pro. They didn't even seem to know they were being handled. Sam had that way with people.

My heart thumped before I could remind it to stay professional. That I couldn't deal with this right now. And it was going to be *fine* having Sam in the office for the next six months.

"All right," Sam said with another laugh, "I have a meeting with Gibbs soon. I have to get back into the office. Good to meet you both."

He shook hands with Court and Gavin. They all joked around for another minute, and then he disappeared into the legal department. I stepped out from where I'd surreptitiously been watching their interaction.

"Ah, looks like we've been caught," Court said as he turned to face me. "Larkin St. Vincent, always a pleasure."

"Hello, Court," I said dryly. I nodded at his partner in crime. "Gavin."

"Lark, my love," Gavin said with a wink.

"I heard that you're causing trouble again."

Court shrugged and leaned back against the wall. He was the classic too-hot-for-his-own-good type. Everything about him exuded confidence and charisma until it turned on a dime.

"Does that sound like us?" Gavin asked. He was also devilishly handsome with dark hair shot through with red and keen, cunning eyes.

"Yes," I said automatically.

Gavin came from old Texas oil money. He wasn't Upper East Side rich, but considering his ancestors had found the oil in the Permian Basin, he had just as much power. He'd gone to Harvard with Court and his best friend, Camden Percy. I'd met him a few times since he'd taken over the New York branch of his family company, Dorset & King.

"What exactly *are* you two doing here?"

"We heard that you needed a new speaker for the banquet after Nina Warren had to drop out because of that Warren business scandal," Court said easily.

He looked to me for a reaction, but I refused to give him one. I could play Upper East Side politics as well as he could.

"And?"

"Well, Gavin's family is longtime friends with Jay Neville."

"Oh, wow. You're friends with Jay Neville?" I asked, momentarily lost in my political nerdom.

Jay Neville was the former deputy chief of staff in the White House and now a successful political consultant. He was a legend.

Gavin laughed. "Here I thought, I'd have to woo you with sweet platitudes. And it turns out, my connections win out. Yes, Jay lived next door to my cousin. I grew up with his daughters."

"That's incredible," I said honestly. "You think he'll speak?"

"Sure," Gavin said with a wink. "Anything for you, love."

Court shook his head and pushed Gavin backward a step. "Sorry to disappoint. You might be my friend, but you have no chance with Larkin St. Vincent. The St. Vincents wouldn't sully their good name for you."

My cheeks flushed as Court laid out my family as if it explained why someone like Gavin King had no chance with me. My family name ruining everything all over again.

"Thanks, dick," Gavin said, punching Court in the shoulder.

I forced a laugh. I wasn't actually interested in Gavin anyway. He might be good-looking and charming, but if Thomas was any indication, guys either wanted me for my money or thought they couldn't get me because of my money. And the only guy who hadn't known who I was had shattered my heart and was now working for me. Great.

"Okay, back to the point," I said.

"We need to get in line?" Court guessed.

"Yes, please." I pointed between them. "I'm not sure who is keeping whom in line, but figure it out."

"That'd be me," Gavin said with a grin.

"We're doomed," I muttered.

Both guys laughed, and as they headed toward the exit, I considered my job accomplished. I'd managed to get out of that situation with laughter instead of frayed nerves. It didn't guarantee that either boy would actually behave, but it was looking up.

My eyes strayed to the direction of the legal department. I wanted to go back there and confront Sam right now. Get everything out in the open. But I wouldn't do it. For one, I had too much work to do. I'd already lost enough time today, and I couldn't afford any more.

So with a sigh, I backtracked to my office, thanked Aspen for getting me the documents I needed, and barricaded myself inside. The work was slow and tiresome even if I did enjoy it. While I was the deputy campaign manager, my direct boss was the actual campaign manager, Shawn. He was the big-picture guy who controlled access to the mayor and was the last say on basically everything. And we went back and forth all day about the new messaging research that had come in.

Sometime later, a knock sounded on my open door. I couldn't even remember leaving it open. My head snapped up. I was prepared to tell them I was busy, but then I faltered.

Sam was standing in my doorway.

"Hey," I said.

"Hey," he said with that easy smile. He leaned against the door-frame, taking up nearly the whole damn thing. "How are you doing?"

"Um...I'm kind of busy actually. Did you talk to Aspen?"

"I think she left already."

"She did?" I asked in surprise.

He laughed. "I think everyone's left, Lark. It's late."

I checked the time and groaned. "How is it almost nine? Christ."

"Burning the candle at both ends already, I see."

Sam stepped in the room, uninvited, as if he belonged in the damn place. His steps were even and measured. No rush or hurry to him. As if nothing affected him. Not even me.

"I just have a lot to do," I told him.

He grabbed a chair, unbuttoned his suit jacket, and sank into it before my desk. He crossed one leg over the other at the ankle and stared back at me. "Don't you always?"

"What are you doing here?" I asked instead of answering his question.

"I said that we needed to talk." He shrugged. "It's later."

"Right. I guess we should talk."

I closed my laptop and shut down my desktop as well. Then I stacked the paperwork in front of me into an easy pile for me to work from tomorrow, keeping out the few things I needed Aspen to do. I'd add them to her desk on the way out.

All the while, I avoided Sam's steady gaze. I didn't know what he was thinking. Or what he felt about this situation. Technically, I was his boss. Or his boss's boss. We had history. And as much as I didn't want to think of him, he *was* my ex-boyfriend, and we were now working together full-time. I was a professional. I'd told English that I could handle this. But now, sitting in my office with the charged chemistry blistering between us, I was having all sorts of doubts again.

Finally, when the silence was too much to bear, I looked up into those big brown eyes. "When did you move to the city?"

"About a year ago."

My stomach dropped. A fucking year ago. He'd been here that long...and I'd never known. God, what did I even expect? That he'd rush here to see me? I was delusional. I didn't even know if I would have wanted that anyway.

"Wow," I muttered.

"The firm I was working for back in North Carolina transferred me up here," he continued as if that news wasn't a gut punch to me. "And then the company folded."

"That sucks."

"Yeah. When I saw the mayor had a legal spot open, I jumped. Which is how I'm here now. But what about you?"

"What about me?" I asked.

"One campaign. One year. And then you were going to go back

to the Upper East Side," he said almost as an accusation. "How the hell did you end up working for the mayor?"

"Well, I got home after..." I swallowed hard. "After us. And my parents were ready to bring me on board, and so...I did. I worked there for about five or six months. I was miserable. So, I decided I would just work part-time for Leslie. Get my campaign fix." I held my hands out in front of me. "But I loved it too much. I wanted to make a difference and do what I loved. So, I quit with my parents and came on full-time."

"Bet your parents loved that."

"Yeah, they still hate it," I said, finding myself relaxing with the lull of the conversation. It had always been easy to talk to Sam after all. "They try to force their way into my life. God, just this morning, my mother showed up with, like, half of Barneys in my apartment." I shook my head. "I still have no idea what to do with all that shit."

He laughed and leaned back in the chair, watching me with warm, attentive eyes. "That sounds right."

I sighed. "Look Sam, I know that we have history, but..."

He held up his hand. "I get it, Lark. You don't even have to say anything. This is your life. And I jumped into the middle of it. I don't want to get in the way."

"Oh. Okay," I muttered. "We can just keep it professional."

"Yes," he agreed. His eyes slipped from mine to travel down my neck and to the opening of my white blouse and then snapped right back up. "Strictly work relationship."

I flushed at the attention. At the way he could make me feel both sexy as hell and like the room was burning up in one look.

"Good," I forced out. "I'm glad we're...on the same page."

Sam stood then. He slipped the button through the hole on his suit jacket, shrugging it back into place around his broad shoulders. My eyes memorized those lines. The shape of him. The brake I'd just put in the middle of our relationship. We were just friends. I couldn't keep staring at him like this. Fuck.

He shot me a half-smile as if he could read my mind. "I'll see you tomorrow."

"Yeah, tomorrow," I said as he strode to the door. And every other fucking day after that.

He reached the door and glanced back at me just once. "It's really good to see you, Lark."

"You too," I whispered just as he slipped out the door.

Wanting to be professional felt like the biggest lie I'd ever told.

4

LARK

Katherine Van Pelt was bathed in a puddle of light that seemed to have been made just for her. That was how it always was with my oldest friend. The universe revolved around her. She had that something that everyone else would kill for.

"How do you do that?" I asked.

Katherine turned to face me. Her brown hair was down past her shoulders in supermodel waves that looked effortless. Her big brown eyes were lined with kohl, making them appear to be twice their normal size. Her lips were painted a deep, dark red. The kind of lipstick that had a name like—Uncensored, Siren, or Don't Stop.

She arched one perfectly groomed eyebrow. "Do what?"

"Make the light bend your way. We're in a club, for Christ's sake," I said, gesturing to the gyrating masses before us. "How do you have a fucking spotlight?"

She shrugged. A keen look coming into her eyes. "I have no idea what you're talking about."

I rolled my eyes and turned back to face the crowd. English and Whitley should have been here already. I hadn't heard from either of them yet either, except a text after work from English, saying that they'd meet us.

"Where are they?" I muttered. "I'm usually the one who is

late."

"Stop worrying." Katherine took another glass of champagne from our waitress.

She'd procured a booth for us by dropping the Van Pelt last name—old Upper East Side money. Unlike me, Katherine had no qualms about using all the advantages she had to get what she wanted.

Katherine gestured for the waitress to hand me a drink as well.

I gratefully took it. Two days with Sam in my office, and I *needed* this drink.

"I'm surprised we're at Sparks," I told her to get my mind off of him. "I thought you liked Club 360."

A cloud passed over her face. "I did. But...Natalie happened," Katherine said dryly. "The audacity of that girl."

"What'd she do?" I asked, surprised I hadn't already heard about it.

Katherine waved a hand. "What hasn't she done? I'm over her. I don't even want to go to her party, but I won't let her try to dethrone me."

I would have laughed if Katherine wasn't deathly serious. For as long as I could remember, I'd had my crew. Penn was the ringleader. Katherine was the instigator. Lewis egged them both on. And Rowe was...well, Rowe—a tech genius and the quiet type. And then there was me. I was the glue that kept them all together. And lately, that had been a lot harder than it used to be.

Katherine and Penn had been hot and cold, on-again/off-again since, well, ever. Until Natalie. It didn't matter that Katherine had entered an arranged marriage with none other than the devil himself, Camden Percy. Only that Natalie had thrown down the gauntlet with Penn, and so she was a problem to be disposed of.

I was saved from trying to navigate that mess when I saw English's blonde head bobbing toward us. She waved once and nodded her head back as if to say Whitley was the problem.

But what else was new?

I loved Whitley Bowen with a fiery passion, but she was a handful. She'd been in medical school while English and I were in law school. Now, she was on her way to becoming one of the best plastic surgeons in the city. For someone who was borderline genius, she was total a head case.

English finally pushed through to our box. Her pale skin was flushed, and she glanced back once to look for Whitley. She shook her head and then pulled me in for a hug. "Hey, babe. How are you holding up?"

"I'm doing...okay."

"She's anxiety-ridden," Katherine said, tipping her champagne at English. "We need to get her drunk."

"Great idea," English said, brightening. "If only Whit could get her ass over here, I'd say we should do shots."

"Why wait?" Katherine said. "Tequila?"

"God, yes."

English stepped toward Katherine to greet her when Whitley appeared at the entrance to our box. She was five foot nothing with olive-toned skin that glowed with gold highlighter and the best pink ombré to her natural waves. For all her lack of height, she had a giant personality.

"Larkin!" Whitley tipped back the rest of her drink and then threw her drunk ass toward me. "I've missed you so fucking much."

I laughed as she hip-checked me. "I missed you too, Whit."

"Sorry we're late. Ran into a guy I used to date." She made a face that said it was not a good run-in. "You know how, like, no one *ever* gets over me? Well, he hasn't either. *Awkward.*"

English snorted. "Your tits were in his face, and then you got a free drink out of him before ditching him, Whit. I wouldn't exactly say that he hasn't gotten over you, honey."

Whitley just rolled her eyes. "Oh my god, is that tequila? Pour me some of the good stuff." She winked at Katherine. "Ren, baby. Bring it in."

Katherine shook her head.

My friends—the pinnacle of self-restraint and letting loose. Watching them together was like waiting for the clock to run down on a ticking time bomb. As much as Katherine complained about Whitley's behavior and Whitley complained that Katherine had a giant stick up her ass, they actually loved each other. At least...in small doses.

"All right, shots all around," English said, passing out the tequila, lime, and salt. She raised her glass. "To my last night in the city and not having to deal with hookers and blow for once."

We all laughed and then threw the shots back. I coughed over the burn of the tequila.

Whitley patted my back. "Let's get you another. How hungover can you be tomorrow at work?"

"Um...probably about as hungover as you?"

"Oh, I can do my job drunk with a blindfold on," Whitley said. "So, you should be good."

I snorted as she grabbed the bottle of Patrón out of the waitress's hand and poured the liquor into my empty shot glass.

Then she winked at the waitress. "Thanks. What's your name?"

"Keri," she said automatically, taking the bottle back. She gave Whitley a small, secretive smile.

"Keri. I like that." Whitley grinned big at the waitress. "You're hot."

Keri laughed. "Thanks. So are you."

Whitley leaned back toward me. "I think I'm going to take her home. Girls are so much less complicated than stupid boys."

"Are they?" Katherine asked. "I wouldn't think that."

Whitley looked her up and down. "Girls like you maybe."

English just shook her head. "Can't we just have drinks and dance and leave worrying about going home with someone to Lark? Because she needs it."

"I do not need a one-night stand."

Whitley nudged my glass. "Yes, you do. Drink up."

I narrowed my eyes at her but tipped the second shot into my mouth. It went down better than the first. And I felt the effects almost immediately. I went from steady to shaky as soon as it hit my stomach. If I didn't slow down, I was going to be throwing up in the bar restroom.

"You know...maybe you do," Katherine finally said.

"Traitor," I said, sidling up to her.

Katherine arched an eyebrow. "It's not like it's your first time."

"Well, I haven't since...right after Thomas," I admitted.

"Are you telling me that you haven't gotten laid in over a year?"

I blushed. "No. That's not what I'm saying. I just...well, I had an arrangement."

"With whom?"

English's eyes rounded. "Oh my god, yes, tell us who."

"Um...Kurt Mitchell."

"No!" Katherine gasped.

English and Whitley focused intently on me now.

"Who is Kurt Mitchell?" Whitley asked.

"A guy who got kicked out of our prep school freshman year and bounced around European boarding schools. He's like the Upper East Side fuckup. I didn't even know he was in the city," Katherine said. "How did that happen? And how the hell did you keep it from me?"

"My mother," I admitted, ashamed. "She set us up when he came back."

"You didn't!" English gasped.

"It was never serious."

"And when did it end?" Katherine asked.

I shrugged. "A few months ago."

"So, you *do* need to get laid," Whitley chimed in. "A few months is a lifetime."

English turned back to face the crowd in front of us. Even on a Wednesday night, the place was packed. "Well," she mused, "we should look at our options."

Whitley laughed and shook her head. "I'll go scope them out from the floor."

Then she vanished into the crowd as quickly as she had come.

"Are we ever going to see her again?" I asked.

English shook her head. "It's probably fifty-fifty with Whit."

Katherine asked Keri to make us a round of drinks. "You know, I think she's toned down some."

Our eyes met, and we both burst into laughter. Because this

was toned-down Whitley, and that was pretty terrifying.

I took a dirty martini from Keri and knew this was a bad idea. But what the hell? I was with my girls.

"I swear, in my next life, I just want half of her confidence," English said.

"Whatever. You're insanely confident," I said.

She pointed at a guy standing at a high-top table nearby. "Him?" she asked.

I shook my head, taking a long sip of my drink. "I'm definitely tipsy, but I'm still firmly in the *I don't need dick to feel better about Sam* category."

"The fact that you just said that proves otherwise," Katherine said.

"Both of you are married," I said, gesturing between my two closest girlfriends. "You seem to be doing just fine. But neither of you found your significant other because of a one-night stand."

Katherine's eyebrows rose, saying everything that I'd left out of the conversation. She and Camden had an arrangement. She got access to the considerable Percy hotel fortune, and he got...her. I was still unclear if that just meant sex or what. She'd been totally weird about it all since the honeymoon. It used to be clear that she hated Camden with a fiery vengeance and was only doing this by the contract, but now, I didn't know.

"So, okay," English said, "I didn't meet Josh in a club, it was a film party at the Beverly Hills Hotel." I rolled my eyes. "*But* we slept together on the first date. Does that count?"

"Nope."

"God, Josh Hutch. He's so...Hollywood," Katherine said with mild disdain. "But damn, does he have a rocking body, and he's a great actor."

"Yeah, I locked that down quick," English said. She pointed out another guy, dancing in the middle of the room.

He was in a business suit, and his hips swayed to the beat.

I shook my head again.

"Are you going to disagree with all of them?" English asked.

"I think we should just stick her out in the middle of the room and let the guys flock to her," Katherine said. She twirled my red hair around her finger. "Guys go crazy for redheads."

"That's a big no," I said. I polished off my drink and reached for another one from Keri.

English grinned. "This is way more enjoyable than work. If I have to deal with another movie star throwing up in a limo or a rockstar getting caught with a groupie or have to try to calm down another irate wife, I might quit."

"Is it that bad?" I asked, leaning forward and nearly falling over. "I thought you loved it."

"I do," she said, blowing out a breath. "I really love the PR part. Working for Poise PR is like the best thing that could have happened. And I don't even mind fixing things. It's just, sometimes, I wonder if I'm fixing the right things, you know?"

I blinked back the alcohol. "I think I'm too drunk to know."

"Well, I get it. Everyone thinks it's easy to be me, to work as a socialite. But it's a literal job to keep my place in this world. And sometimes, I just want to fucking stop." She shrugged one petite shoulder and downed her martini. "Poor little rich girl."

Wow. Katherine had to be drunk to be opening up to English. She didn't open up to anyone. Hardly even to *me*.

I opened my mouth to reach for something profound, but nothing was there.

Then Whitley appeared with a super-hot guy from the dance floor, and I didn't have to respond.

"Y'all," she cried, "look what I found."

"What *did* you find, Whit?" English asked with a shake of her head.

"A guy for Lark." Whitley not-so-subtly winked.

"Oh," I muttered.

He *was* incredibly good-looking. Platinum-blond hair, bright blue eyes, and a dimpled chin. He wore fitted dark jeans and a short-sleeved button-up. He wasn't exactly *my* style. But then again, I was used to Upper East Side guys. And while they all dressed nice, they were also douche bags.

"Hi," he said, stepping forward. "I'm Chad. You must be Lark."

"I am."

English nudged me toward him. I stumbled forward a few feet, suddenly losing control of my legs with all the alcohol. It was like it all hit me at once. I'd thought I had control over it. I wasn't a lightweight. My parents had started me drinking wine at a *very* young age because they said that you were never too young to develop tolerance and taste. They'd hardly approve of the option before me. But maybe that was perfect.

"Yes, I am," I said more forcefully. I stepped away from my friends, and Whitley hustled over to the other girls. "So, do you live in the city?"

"Yeah. Queens."

"Nice," I said.

"You?"

"I'm on the Upper East."

His eyebrows rose. "Oh wow. So, I guess your place is closer than mine."

I opened my mouth and then closed it. "Uh, yeah. I mean, physically speaking, yes?"

He chuckled. "Cool. Well, you ready to get out of here?"

"Already?" I asked in surprise. I was drunk, but I couldn't be *that* drunk.

"I mean...you do want to hook up, right?"

I whirled around. "Whitley, what did you say to him?"

Whitley just grinned back at me. "I told him that you wanted a one-night stand."

I shook my head at her in frustration. "Jesus Christ, Whit! I do not want a one-night stand! Let alone with a guy I just met!"

"Uh...guys," English muttered.

Katherine had skipped over to the front of the box, and for the first time, I realized through my drunken haze that we had an audience. Camden had just shown up. Katherine must have let him know where we were.

Next to him stood Court and Gavin.

And then, to my shock and utter horror, I locked eyes with Sam Rutherford.

5

SAM

Larkin St. Vincent stood in front of me.

And she had just screamed something about a one-night stand.

Fuck. Me.

Well, this night had just spiraled completely out of control. I should have known better than to agree to hang out with these guys. I liked Court and Gavin a lot. When I'd met them at the campaign office, we'd hit it off immediately. Camden...I was still getting to know. But Court had assured me that Camden's frosty behavior wasn't personal. He just didn't like new people, and it took him a long time to warm up to anyone.

But still, I should have put two and two together. They were Upper East Side. Just like Lark. Why wouldn't they frequent the same nightclubs and know the same people?

This was a mistake.

I'd just felt like we were on the right foot in the office. Agreeing to be professional. Well, that was fucked now.

"Sam," Lark said gutturally. Her big green eyes were wide. Her mouth slightly parted. She swayed a bit forward.

She was drunk. And fucking beautiful.

"Oh, *you're* Sam?" the girl with the pink hair next to her said twice as loud. She whipped around to the guy on Lark's other side. She waved her hands away from her. "Shoo, shoo, you. No one-night stand for you."

Lark looked like she might kill the girl. "Whitley," she groaned.

Ah. So *this* was the infamous Whitley.

The guy glanced around in confusion. "This is fucked." Then he stormed off as if he was personally affronted.

Gavin seemed to take the pulse of the room. "Well, if we're talking about one-night stands..."

Court just shook his head at him.

English muttered, "Typical," under her breath.

Katherine was already diverting Camden's attention.

And just like that, the tension in the room was defused. Gavin called for a round of drinks, and Court seemed to purposely move into place so that I was all alone with Lark.

"What are you doing here?" she asked.

I raised an eyebrow. "I feel like we keep asking each other the same questions on repeat."

She laughed and leaned toward me. Her green eyes gleamed in the shifting light. "I meant, with these guys...not New York."

"We met at the office, and Court invited me out," I said stiffly.

The Lark I knew was particular about this sort of thing. She also got drunk and did stupid shit. We were two for two so far.

"I thought this wasn't your scene."

"And it's yours?" I asked a bit harsher than I'd intended.

She heard my tone even through the drunkness. She cringed away from it, but she answered anyway, "English is in town, all the way from LA. Normally, I don't have time, what with living the campaign life—you know how it is."

I didn't know why I was provoking her. Maybe it was just the way she seemed right at this very moment that brought back a slew of bad memories. And I couldn't disentangle the Lark from when we'd fallen apart from the one standing in front of me. They were one and the same. And it didn't matter how gorgeous she was after what had happened.

"Well, I guess this isn't professional," she said with a small laugh.

"I guess it isn't," I agreed.

Her eyes skimmed my face as if she were looking for something but couldn't find it.

"Don't let *me* keep you from a good time," she said and then turned to head back to her friends.

I reached out and grabbed her arm. She glanced back at me in drunken confusion.

"What?" she asked when I didn't say anything.

But I didn't know what to say. My feelings toward Lark were dark and tangled. I shouldn't even be touching her right now.

So, I hastily released her. "Nothing."

She stiffened at the harsh way I'd said it. She swallowed hard. For a moment, I thought she might actually be fighting back tears. But no...had I ever seen Larkin St. Vincent cry, except out of campaign-induced exhaustion and anxiety?

"Come dance with me, Lark," Whitley called from where she was twirling her body in place.

Lark looked me over once more, waiting. And then when I didn't say anything, she stepped away toward her friend. Whitley grabbed Lark's hand and spun her in place, putting Lark in front of her. English giggled and then jumped in behind Whitley. The three girls danced and twirled, grinding up against one another in a way that made me adjust my pants.

Court appeared then with two drinks. "Hope you like your whiskey strong."

"That I do," I agreed easily. I took a long, fortifying drink. I'd already had a few, but the encounter with Lark had left me uncomfortably sober.

We both watched as Whitley touched her toes and shook her ass in a way that I'd thought only professional dancers were capable of. English reached forward and smacked her ass and then Lark's.

"That is quite a sight," Court said.

"It's something," I said.

The girls all gasped out loud as Gavin unceremoniously jumped into the middle of their trio. Whitley ran her hand up her legs and then shook herself against Gavin's crotch. English and Lark jumped into the action, dancing around Gavin like he was some god.

"So," Court said, turning his attention back to me, "you and Lark, huh?"

"Oh, uh...no."

Court arched his eyebrow. "Really?"

"Uh...well, we dated in the past. But it's been five years since I've even seen her. We just work together now."

"Just?"

I shrugged. "Nothing is going on."

Court shot me an exasperated look. "Let me tell you something, Sam. You seem like a nice guy. I've known Larkin St. Vincent for a long time, and I have never seen her look at anyone the way she looks at you."

Fuck.

"I don't...know what to say to that."

"Be less obvious when you lie," Court said with a wink. Then he downed his drink and headed to the group dancing. "Hey, don't let Gavin have all the fun."

I glanced around the room in frustration. I didn't want to leave. I wasn't ready to go back to my small, sad apartment in Brooklyn. I'd been in New York for a year, and I still hadn't made any lasting friendships. The guys I'd worked with at the law firm always felt more like colleagues than friends. This was the most fun I'd had in the city, period.

But at the same time, I wasn't sure I should or even could continue to watch Lark move her body in ways that my brain and my cock remembered vividly.

"Sam!" Whitley cried from where they were dancing.

She crooked her finger at me, but I shook my head. She rolled her eyes, clearly not taking no for an answer. Then she left the group and dashed toward me.

She grabbed my arm with more force than a tiny pixie of a girl should be able to. "Dance with us!"

And I should say no.

Not a single part of this was smart.

But I let Whitley drag me over anyway.

A minute later, even Camden and Katherine were dancing with us. Which, if I had to guess by the others' expressions, was out of character for them both.

I let the concern wash away from me. We were all dancing and having a good time. I finished my drink and had a pleasant numbness come back over me. Maybe it would be fine to do this. To pretend to be the kind of guy who drank top-shelf liquor in a box at the hottest nightclub in New York City. To spend time with Lark outside of work. Even if she seemed both exactly the same and completely different and I couldn't decide which I preferred.

Then the song changed from whatever techno beat had been playing to a remix of Ellie Goulding's "Lights." Without even meaning to, I drifted into Lark's personal space. Her eyes widened with alarm and something else. Something I remembered all too clearly. Heat. We moved closer. Our bodies almost but just not quite touching.

"This song," she whispered.

I nodded. This song had played over and over and over again when we had worked on the presidential campaign together. At some point, it had just *become* our song.

"What are the chances?" I asked her.

"With us?" She bit her plump bottom lip. "Always."

And then the hairbreadth space vanished. Her arms wound around my neck. Mine found her hips, my hands digging into the material of her slinky green dress. Our bodies moved in time, remembering the hours and hours we'd spent together. The easy way she moved. The pace I set. The time we had done all this with no clothes at all.

"This feels...familiar," she breathed into my ear.

I closed my eyes. "We used to do this."

She leaned her forehead into my shoulder before whispering boldly, "We used to do *a lot* of things."

Jesus Christ.

My grip tightened on her. "Yes...yes, we did."

She was just drunk enough to pull back and look up at me with those big green eyes so full of want. Her tongue flicked out and wet her bottom lip, drawing my attention to them. She was so close. So familiar. So...Lark.

I could kiss her. I could kiss her right now.

Except I couldn't.

"I have to go," I said, dropping my arms and taking a step back.

Her mouth popped open in shock. Her hands fell to her sides. "Go? Go where?"

"Home," I said automatically.

Her eyes hardened into something lethal.

There she was. That was the Lark I knew.

"I'll see you tomorrow at work." Then I took another step back.

"Yeah," she said in confusion, "work."

I forced myself to turn around and walk out of the nightclub. Because if I stayed another moment, against all reason, I'd kiss her. And I didn't trust myself not to.

6

LARK

S am made *no* sense.
      None.
   At all.

   I was still fuming about his abrupt departure and then the subsequent cold shoulder at work. One minute, he had been a dick to me. And the next, I had been in his arms, about to kiss him. Then he'd freaked the fuck out and ditched the entire party. Hello, mixed signals.

   English just thought this was proof that I needed to leave Sam in the past where he belonged. I wished that she was still in New York instead of back in LA. Katherine and Whitley had polar-opposite advice about the whole thing, and I felt battered back and forth like a tennis ball.

   Luckily, I had work to keep me company. The fundraising banquet for the mayor was tomorrow, which meant the office was in full panic mode. I barely had time to think, let alone eat lunch or take a break. We had to finalize all plans today, and then I'd head over with the advance team in the morning to make sure everything was set up.

   I was reviewing the paperwork that Demi had just sent out to the team. It included the full script for tomorrow and everyone's specific jobs for the event. My eyes narrowed when I saw Sam's name next to legal staff.

I sighed.

Of course they'd send Sam to the banquet. He was the new guy. It made perfect sense. But that meant that I wouldn't even be able to escape him tomorrow. I bristled and wondered if I could convince Gibbs to send someone else. He was in charge of the legal department. But I wouldn't be able to tell him why I wanted someone else without lying. Saying that I wanted someone with more experience. But it was bullshit. It would just draw more questions.

I flipped to the next page when a notification for an incoming email appeared on my screen. I almost closed out of it, but then I saw the name attached.

Why was Sam emailing me?

I narrowed my eyes as I clicked on the email and watched it pop up on my screen.

Lark,

Do you need a break? Want to go get coffee?

Best,
   Sam

A thrill ran through me before I could prevent it. I wanted to get coffee with Sam. I wanted him to think of me when he went on break. But at the same time, this was just another one of those fucking mixed signals. Why would he want to go get coffee after what happened when we went out?

Unless he wanted to apologize.

I closed my eyes and slowly counted to ten. I didn't have time for this. For whatever Sam was going through. I'd turned over a new leaf. I wasn't the same Lark I'd been when we first met. And I didn't want to play games. I didn't want to deal with any of this.

No matter how familiar things seemed.

I remembered how it had ended. And I just needed to keep reminding myself of that.

Sam,

The banquet is tomorrow. No time for breaks. There's coffee in the break room.

—Lark

I gulped before I hit Send. It was abrupt. And said everything I hadn't.

Translation: *I don't want to see you. Even if I had a few minutes, I would rather drink the shit break room coffee than step out of the office with you.*

I pulled up the banquet itinerary again and then nearly groaned as another email came in. Had he not understood the first one?

Lark,

I understand that there is coffee in the break room. But I think a ten minute break might be good for the both of us. Don't you think?

Sam

No. No, I did not think a ten minute break would be a good idea.

Why was he pushing this? I'd already wasted more than ten minutes on these stupid emails. I couldn't afford to walk out of this office today. Not even to find out what other mixed signals he wanted to send me in person.

Sam,

I don't need a break. Thanks though. Feel free to run out and get coffee. I recommend Coffee Grounds. You're perfectly capable of leaving without me. Right?

—Lark

Translation: *You ran out the fucking door at the club earlier this week. Get your own coffee!*

Lark,

I suppose I am. I will take your recommendation. I have something I'd like to discuss with you. Since you're so busy, perhaps we could meet after work? I heard there's a good burger place not far away. No mustard, right?

Think about it.
    Sam

Why, oh why did he have to remember how I liked my burger?

I closed my eyes, and my finger hovered over the Reply button. This had gone on long enough. I didn't need to respond. I could just say no. That would be easier. But now, I was curious.

Damn it!

Why had he made me curious?

Sam,

I don't know what you need to discuss with me. But can't you do it in an email?

—Lark

Translation: *Get this over with. You are killing me slowly.*

Lark,

I could. I'd rather do it in person. I owe you that much.

Please.
    Sam

He *owed* me that much? What the hell did that mean? Was this about the club? Was he finally going to explain why he'd run out?

I chewed on my bottom lip. It could just be a line to get me to agree to see him again. I didn't know why he needed it, but I didn't really understand Sam at all anymore.

Sam,

Fine. I'm signing off now.

—Lark

I exited out of the email and returned to my work, but my heart wasn't in it anymore. Now, I was wondering what he wanted to talk about. And despite it all, I felt nerves take over. Wondering if this was good or bad or somewhere in between.

All I knew was that I wanted answers.

I probably should have just gone for that damn coffee. Then I'd have them now. I wouldn't have to wait until after this very, very long day. But I'd dug my grave. Time to lie in it.

It was another late night by the time I was finally able to leave. Aspen had left ten minutes earlier with the promise of seeing me bright and early to manage setup. I shut down my computer, stuffed everything I would need for tomorrow in my bag, and then stepped out into the hallway. I half-expected Sam not to be there and that I'd imagined the bizarre emails we'd sent back and forth that morning.

But no. He was there, waiting for me.

I forced my eyes to remain on his face and not examine the gorgeous body wrapped in a suit that fit him like a glove. The Sam I'd known never even owned a suit. He'd come straight off three years of construction work with his father and joined Woodhouse's campaign to try to find purpose before applying for law schools. He wore blue jeans and flannel button-ups. His hair was always a little too long, falling into his eyes. He drove this ancient pickup truck that I swore was going to fall apart at any moment. I'd insisted we drive the Subaru I'd convinced my parents was a low-key alternative for Wisconsin winters.

Somewhere underneath the new facade was the same old country boy who had tried and failed to hide his Southern drawl. Who had carved me a lark with his own two hands and given it to me as a present when he found out my birthday was coming up. I still didn't know where he'd found the time.

I wished that I could reconcile that thoughtful and endearing man with the one who had left me...and the one standing in front of me.

"You look like you've seen a ghost," he said with a half-smile.

I have.

I shook it off. "Burgers?"

He nodded, rubbing the back of his neck. "Yeah. Have you been to Buns before?"

"Yeah. Once or twice," I said, falling into step beside him as we exited the office. "The best part of the city is that everything is open late. There's always something to eat on the campaign schedule."

"I've noticed that. Not like Madison, where we essentially had three choices."

"Three excellent choices though."

"True enough. I still have dreams about Pel'meni's dumplings."

I groaned. "Me too. You'd think I could find Russian dumplings that compared. But nothing is like Paul's."

"At least it's not just me."

We crossed the street and headed north toward Buns. Sam held the door open for me, and I stepped into the brightly lit burger joint. I ordered my burger. No mustard indeed. I was quick to grab a water and pay for mine before sinking into a booth in the corner.

Sam dropped down across from me with his own water, and our burgers appeared a few minutes later.

I would have thought after all the back and forth between us, this wouldn't be comfortable. That somehow, it would be awkward. He'd ditched me at the club. And then I'd tried to blow him off today in our emails. But this actually felt exactly right. We'd done just this every night for nearly a year in Madison. Some activities were just ingrained with certain people.

I polished off my burger in record speed. "God, I just realized I haven't eaten in, like, twelve hours."

"You? I'm shocked."

"I sometimes just forget food when I'm this intensely focused."

He frowned and nodded. "I remember."

Silence stretched between us for the first time. Sam seemed to be stalling. I didn't know what he needed to tell me. But I wanted him to just say it.

"So...you wanted to talk to me?" I nudged him.

"Yeah, I do," he said.

He glanced up and met my gaze. And it was then that I knew something was wrong. Seriously wrong.

"Just tell me." My stomach churned.

"I have a girlfriend," he said in a rush.

My stomach dropped entirely out of my body. "What?"

"I was trying to keep my professional and personal life separate."

"You failed," I spat.

A flush suffused my features. I knew my freckles were making it all the worse. I was angry and ashamed and humiliated.

No *wonder* he'd run out on me at the club.

We'd almost kissed. We were inches away. He'd expected a guys' night out, and he'd gotten me instead.

And still...he hadn't told me then about the mysterious girl-friend. How convenient.

Sam nodded with a deep frown. He dug through his bag and pulled out the paperwork that Aspen had handed out this morning to everyone who would be working at the fundraising banquet. He flipped to the second page and pointed at a name— New York City Symphony Orchestra.

"She's in this orchestra," Sam said with a pained expression. "She's going to be at the banquet tomorrow. And I didn't want you to be blindsided."

"Like I am now?" I hissed.

"Yes," he muttered.

There was regret in his eyes. I felt no sympathy for him.

"Great."

"Lark..."

"Okay." I stood from the table, pushing the empty burger basket away from me. "Got it, Sam."

Before he could respond, I wrenched my purse out of the booth and walked out of the restaurant. I didn't need to say another word. He didn't need to say anything else either.

I was shaking with anger by the time I made it out onto the New York City streets. I turned northward and just started walking. I knew I'd have to hail a cab before long. I could never walk the entire way to my apartment. But I was so furious right now that there was nothing else I could do but ferociously walk and walk some more.

Then the anger turned to sadness. My body felt weighed down and heavy. Like I might fall apart at any moment.

And I vowed that I was never, ever going to let anyone make me feel like that again. Not *ever* again.

PART II

PLAY BY THE RULES

7

LARK

The fundraising banquet was the biggest event we'd put together on the campaign thus far. It was a test of how smoothly our team could work as a unit. And how much money we could bring in from huge donors in one evening.

I had every intention of breaking every record we'd set for ourselves.

I'd spent all morning helping the advance team prep for the event. Finally, Demi had sent me to eat something and get ready. Apparently, I was a tad bit...intense today.

No surprise there.

Not after what had happened the night before.

Or what I knew I would have to deal with today.

I even dug through the boxes of clothes and shoes that my mother had left for me. I picked out a stylish little black dress, fitted jacket, and muted black snakeskin pumps. A part of me had wanted to rebel against all the purchases, but I needed armor for today. And designer clothing was as close as it got.

With a deep breath, I strode back through the banquet hall and into the back room where I'd left Demi an hour earlier.

"Oh thank god you're finally back," Demi cried.

"I wasn't gone that long."

Demi shrugged. "No, and you needed the break. But damn, I missed you."

I peeled off my jacket and hung it up before turning to face Demi. "I missed you too. What's up?"

Demi waved her hand. "Girl, look at you!"

"What?"

"That dress! Aspen, come look at this dress!"

I rolled my eyes as Aspen came into the back room.

She whistled. "Looking hot, boss."

"This isn't that different than normal," I assured them.

"Yeah, sure," Demi said.

I shook my head at them. "What's the emergency?"

Demi tossed me a headset. "We're an hour from start time. The interns aren't answering. We're down three ushers. I just heard that Mr. and Mrs. Chambliss thought that the two tables they'd ordered were for ten people each and not eight tonight. So now, I have to find space for four extra attendees and figure out how to politely ask for ten thousand more dollars," she said with an eye roll. "Mayor Kensington will be here in fifteen, and everything needs to be done before then."

"You work on the seating chart," I told Demi and then turned to Aspen. "Can you figure out the usher situation?"

"On it!" Aspen said.

She turned to leave just as Robert from the field team, Beth from tech with her social media girl and the photographer, and finally, Sam stepped through the door and into the back room. My eyes snagged on Sam for a second before wrenching away.

I continued speaking as if he weren't there, "We'll send Leslie over to the tables at the end to warm up the Chamblisses, and then I'll have Shawn do the big sell before they leave. He's the best at it."

"Perfect," Demi said.

I slid on the headset and grabbed a clipboard. "I've got the interns. Let me know if there's anything else."

"Oh!" Demi cried. "Also, the musicians aren't in position and haven't practiced in the space at all."

I froze, grinding my teeth together. Right. The orchestra.

"I can take care of the musicians," Sam said from where he'd just set up his computer.

My gaze slid to his, my eyes narrowing. He looked guileless. As if he were just trying to help me out. But I didn't *need* his help. I was the deputy campaign manager for the mayor of New York. I could handle anything thrown at me.

"You do your job," I told him. "And I'll do mine."

Then I left the room to do just that.

I strode into the banquet hall decorated with dozens of large, round tables. Red-white-and-blue Mayor Kensington banners hung from the ceiling around the perimeter of the room. A painstaking adventure I'd witnessed earlier this morning.

Sticking to the perimeter, I angled toward the stage and saw the answer to the first problem. All the field interns were congregated in one corner, chatting rather than working.

I rolled my eyes. This would be fun.

"Bailey, Kolby, Marcel, Sonya." I clapped my hands twice. "Let's get moving. Headsets on and responsive."

Their eyes rounded in shock, and then they immediately dispersed with mumbled apologies. It was like none of them wanted paid jobs at all.

"Interns are a go," I said into the headset.

"Roger that," Demi said.

I shook my head and then took a deep breath, continuing toward the stage. I had to put my feelings about the orchestra behind me for tonight. I needed them to do their job. They *were* getting paid.

I was nearly to the conductor when the short, squat man tapped his baton two or three times, and the orchestra moved seamlessly into their chairs.

"It's a Christmas miracle," I muttered sarcastically.

At least something was going right. One fire I didn't have to fix.

I should have turned around right that minute and headed back to Demi. I was sure she could use some more help with the seating chart. Beth would want access to Leslie for photographs.

Their messaging for the night needed to be on point. In fact, there were a dozen things that I could be doing at this moment.

Instead, I stared up at the orchestra. Their music was perfectly in harmony. It was gorgeous and so full. I knew why we'd hired them.

In the thirty or forty members they had sent for this ensemble, only three of them were young enough females who could potentially be Sam's girlfriend—a tall Hispanic girl on cello, a pale blonde, and a mousy brunette, both on violin in the back.

I wondered which of the three girls was Sam's girlfriend. None of them looked like me. None of them looked like his ex, Melissa, whom I'd unfortunately met. I had no way to judge from here. And even if I could, I shouldn't. I didn't really want to be the girl judging others on or off stage.

My stomach turned as I gazed a second longer. I was purposely torturing myself with not knowing. And I'd decided yesterday that I wasn't going to do this. That I was going to be strong and not let myself think about it. It was why I wore my Upper East Side armor. I needed it. But I didn't need the subsequent devilish personality that came with it. That was dangerous on so many levels for me.

With a sigh, I turned away from the orchestra and said into the headset, "Orchestra is rehearsing. Heading your way now."

"Actually, Lark, the mayor just arrived. Shawn asked for you," Demi responded.

I sighed with relief. That would be better than going to the back room to deal with last-minute fires while Sam was there. I didn't want to be in the same room with him...even though I knew it wouldn't be that easy forever.

"Got it," I told Demi and then left the ballroom behind.

I set out to find the mayor. Even though I'd been working for Leslie since the beginning, my nerves still thrummed with excitement when I was in the thick of it all.

I slid on my game face as I entered the mayor's inner sanctum. And found only madness.

Hair and makeup frantically applied finishing touches. Hairspray and setting spray clogged the small room. Christine ran

Leslie through the final stages of her speech. She kept correcting emphasis on key words, marking them up, and then handing them back. My boss and Leslie's campaign manager, Shawn, was listening with half an ear to the speech as he texted relentlessly.

"No, no, no. We've said five times not to use that word," he said, glancing up from his phone. He was a trim six-foot-four black guy who always ran a hand over his short, cropped hair when he was nervous. Which was always. "The word *feminism* has negative connotation. Our audience might be fine with it, but if your opponent gets ahold of it, it's going to be in every ad from now until November."

Christine whipped her blue hair—which was shaved on the sides with long, edgy bangs—out of her eyes. "We're keeping it."

"Tonight, we need money," Shawn added. He pocketed his phone. "If our audience doesn't like it, then we're doomed."

"Come up with something better for me then."

Shawn opened his mouth to respond, but the mayor held her hand up. "Enough. I put the word back in, Shawn. It stays."

"With all due respect..."

Leslie shook her head. Then she looked right at me, hovering in the periphery of the room, waiting to see if there was about to be a showdown. "Lark, come in. Remind everyone why we're keeping the word in."

"Mayor Kensington is most known for being tough on crime, but her other main platform and personal project is promoting female equality. She *could* talk about how she's increased the number of female-appointed officials, worked hand in hand with women who want to run for office, and lowered the wage disparity in the city without saying she's a feminist." I nodded at Shawn. "But it's a word that stands in for all of her great accomplishments."

"I know," Shawn said with a sigh. "I'm not saying remove that from the speech, just that we replace *feminism* with *advocate for women's rights*."

Mayor Kensington closed the speech and nodded at Christine, who promptly exited. Hair and makeup did the same. "It's fine,

Shawn. The fundraiser is our base. If it bombs here, we'll tone it down."

He spread his hands before him. "What if Quinn gets ahold of it?" he asked, referring to our major opposition. "Can you stomach a feminism sound bite for the next six months?"

"I've had to stomach worse," the mayor said evenly.

"All right," Shawn said, knowing when he'd lost.

"Are we ready?" the mayor asked.

"Yes, we're all set," I said.

"Mr. Neville is being introduced first," Shawn said, checking his watch. "We should hustle you down to the stage and get you in position. Go over that line one more time."

The mayor smiled at him. "I don't hustle for anything, except votes."

I laughed. "Hardly."

"You know me too well, Lark. I hustle for everyone in my city. Just not from one place to another."

"Everyone should wait for a lady."

She winked. "If they know what's good for them."

We all laughed and walked purposefully down the hallway toward the stage door.

Leslie touched my arm. "Oh, I meant to thank you for dealing with Court the other day when he came into the office. I've been so busy preparing for this that I didn't get to mention it. I know that's not exactly in your job description."

"I've known him my whole life. Handled with ease."

"What would I do without you, Lark?"

"I hope we'll never find out," I responded.

"Me too, dear."

My smile was wide, and all the drama with Sam evaporated in that moment. When Leslie said things like that, it made my heart soar. I wasn't just needed; I was necessary.

This was why I was on campaign. This was why I did it. I wished that I could explain to everyone else what I loved about campaigning. Maybe then I could get my parents off my back about being behind the scenes rather than a politician myself.

But it was working for someone that I believed in, who valued me. It was the joy of packaging and marketing and selling a candidate. To reaching out to thousands of people through phone calls, knocking on doors, volunteering, banquets, rallies, and more. At the end of the day, when all the votes were tallied, there was nothing more satisfying than my candidate winning. I worked hundred-hour weeks for that high. And I'd keep working at it for as long as I could.

"Now, wish me luck," Leslie said with a smile.

"You don't need it," I told her honestly.

Leslie patted my shoulder. "How right you are."

8

LARK

For all the nerves I'd had all week, the banquet was a hit. Jay Neville had given an amazing speech. Leslie had wowed the audience, as she always did. Donation numbers had gone through the roof. For a whole ten seconds, I could breathe again before worrying about the next step on the campaign trail.

"Awesome job, Demi," I said as I stepped into the back room to grab my jacket. "This success is all on you."

She laughed and shook her head. Her curls bounced around her face. "No way. My success is everyone's success. I couldn't have done this without any of you."

"Well, you killed it. It was great," I told her.

"Thanks." She beamed. "Hey, a bunch of us are going to go to this pub around the corner to grab a celebratory drink. You interested?"

I winced. "I would, but I am so beat. I still have to see my parents, which is always super fun." I rolled my eyes. "I think I'll have to pass on this one. But have fun."

"We will. But we'll miss you," Demi said, nudging me.

"Next time," I assured her before stepping back out to go deal with the inevitable.

My parents.

They donated considerable money to Leslie through the company and tried to come to her bigger events. They'd been doing that before I joined the campaign, back when Leslie had been a state senator and a close friend. It would look bad if I didn't say something. Even though I would rather send Shawn over.

I brushed my hands down the sides of my little black dress and then headed out into the mostly empty ballroom. My mother, Hope St. Vincent, was easy to spot in her floor-length red dress that formed to her curves and the black fur coat draped across her shoulders. My father stood next to her in a sharp, custom-designed, handmade black suit. He worked with a handful of designers each year and had his collection redone to perfection. It made him look effortlessly powerful. They said Alexander St. Vincent was not to be underestimated.

My mother noticed me first. "Larkin, darling!"

"Hello, Mother," I said, seeing how she very carefully didn't hug me. She wasn't affectionate like that. Never had been.

She held me at arm's length. "That's one of my dresses!"

Shit! I'd forgotten that I was wearing the clothes she'd picked out. "Uh...yeah," I stammered. "I like it."

My mother beamed as if I'd finally done something right in my life. "I knew you would if you just gave it a chance."

I veered toward my father to avoid responding to my mother's enthusiasm. "Hi, Daddy."

"Sweetheart," my father said. He put his hand on my back and then kissed my cheek. "What a good event this was."

"Yes," my mother agreed. "If you did *this* all the time, I might actually understand why you work here."

I bit back the cringe. Showing no emotion was better than letting them know how much it got to me that they hated my job. I knew it wasn't glamorous. I could be doing something much, much flashier than this. I didn't have a bachelor's from Brown and a JD from Columbia for nothing. But it just didn't interest me. And I was done trying to be someone else for my parents. Or anyone for that matter.

"You know, if you enjoy the event-planning side, we could have you work with the STV Foundation," my father mused. "Our charity always needs a boost. You'd be perfect for the job."

"What a great idea, Alexander," my mother said.

I stared between them blankly. So much for just thanking them. Perhaps they'd coordinated this attack. They knew that wasn't what I wanted.

"Well, thank you. But I'm not the event planner. Our fundraising chair, Demi, did most of the planning work. She's brilliant. Maybe after the campaign, I could give her your information," I suggested blithely.

My parents shared a look. *The* look. Like they were going to move into plan B.

I spoke before they could. "I just wanted to thank you both for coming and for your generous donation to the mayor's campaign. It's donations like yours that keep this campaign running and put the mayor in a position to help the people of New York City. We can't thank you enough," I said as if reading from a script. "If you have anything to discuss with the mayor, feel free to reach out."

"Larkin," my mother said with a tired sigh.

I kept my smile painted on. "Again, thank you. The campaign will be in touch!"

And even though I knew I was supposed to be sucking up to them, I just couldn't do it tonight. Not after the week I'd had. So, I turned around and headed out of the ballroom. I'd probably hear about it later, but right now, it just felt really damn good.

A smile returned to my features by the time I made it to the nearly empty back room to grab my purse. Shawn stepped in just then.

"What are you grinning about?" he asked with his own smile plastered on his face. He got like this after events. Like he was on top of the world even though, a few minutes ago, he'd been a stress and anxiety-ridden mess.

"Just happy about how well the event went."

"Yes!" he said, holding his fist out. I awkwardly bumped his fist. "We're all going out for drinks. Come on. You can walk with me."

"Oh no, I'm beat. I just need to sleep before work tomorrow."

He threw his hands out. "I gave everyone the day off. I wanted to celebrate our accomplishment while we have the time. Once we get to the primary, we'll have few days off. Helps to keep morale up."

I opened and then closed my mouth. "Oh."

"So, no excuses!" he cheered. "Be a team player and come have a beer."

I didn't even like beer.

But what the hell was I going to say?

"All right. Sure," I said with a nod, trying to search for that smile again. "One drink won't hurt anything."

"That's the spirit!"

We headed out of the building and down the street to a dingy-looking Irish pub with Guinness signs all over the windows. The room was dimly lit with a long bar on one side, a row of booths on the other, and billiards set up in one corner. We easily spotted the campaign group, considering we were the only ones in evening dress attire in this dive bar.

It was about night and day from Sparks earlier this week. But it had its own charm. Something I never would have been able to acknowledge before working that year in Madison. You couldn't walk a foot without hitting a bar in Wisconsin. It was the only state in that country that I was certain had more bars than people. You could even drink in the union on campus at the University of Wisconsin-Madison. I'd grown up drinking, but Wisconsin was something else entirely.

"What do you drink?" Shawn asked. "I'll grab the first round."

"Um...I'll just have whatever you're having."

I was certain there wasn't a good wine in the entire establishment. And I didn't want liquor. It'd be easier to just pretend to drink the beer. I could probably pass it off to Aspen without Shawn even noticing.

I headed to the row of tables the campaign had commandeered. There were two empty seats next to Aspen and Demi, and I took the first one.

"You decided to come out!" Demi said.

"Shawn," I said by means of explanation.

"Oh yeah, he gave us the day off."

Aspen laughed. "What are you going to do with yourself, Lark? I didn't think you took days off."

I shrugged. "I was thinking of sleeping all day and eating a lot of junk food."

"No way. You'll come into the office anyway. Even if no one is there," Aspen said, nudging my shoulder. "It's who you are."

She wasn't wrong. I'd done it before. But with everything that had gone on with Sam, I felt like I needed a mental break. Work had always been my escape. The thing I loved so much. But now, he was there. At work. And when I went there, I thought of him. I needed a day off from that.

"Maybe," I said with a shrug.

A shadow fell behind me. "Oh, I guess I'll pull up an extra chair."

I turned around in confusion. I hadn't thought for a second why there were two open chairs at the end of the table. I figured that they'd held one for Shawn or maybe just that they had more than they needed. I hadn't realized I'd taken someone else's seat.

"Hey, sorry," I said, standing. "Did I take your seat?"

I turned to face the girl who had spoken. She was dragging an extra chair over. And when I caught sight of her, my breath hitched. She was the blonde from the orchestra. The violinist who had been seated at the very back of the group. Her hair had been pulled back into a bun at the time, but now, it hung in loose waves to her shoulders. I couldn't even get that look with a curling iron. And she'd managed it by pulling it out of a bun. She still wore the nondescript black dress pants and a fitted, long-sleeved black blouse. Somehow, it didn't look stupid.

"Oh, no worries!" the girl gushed. "I can just grab another." She stuffed a chair at the end of the table between me and Aspen. "See, this works for me." She held out her hand. "I don't believe we've met. I'm Claire, Sam's girlfriend."

I took her callous hand in mine and shook. "Lark."

"Ohh!" Her eyes widened.

For a moment, I worried that she knew. That Sam had confessed it all to Claire and that things were about to get *really* awkward.

But then she just grinned bigger. "Sam has told me so much about you. You run the campaign, right?"

I stared at her blankly for a few seconds too long before responding, "I'm the deputy campaign manager. Shawn"—I pointed toward him at the bar—"is the head campaign manager."

"Well, still, I hear you're the one who keeps everything running."

"She does," Aspen interjected. "Lark is, like, literally the best."

"See," Claire said, gesturing to Aspen.

"Don't try to deny it, Lark," Demi said. "Shawn is great, but he's no Larkin St. Vincent."

"You all are too much," I said, uncomfortable with the praise... and Claire.

"Here's your drink," Shawn said, setting the beer down in front of Demi and pushing it across the table. "I'm going to go catch up with Christine. See if we can talk about the feminism topic again."

I gave him a thumbs-up. "Have fun with that."

Aspen snorted, and Demi tried to hide her own amusement.

Claire glanced around with wide blue eyes. "Y'all are so cool. I wish I had more people my own age in the orchestra."

"How did you get into that?" Demi asked her.

I shifted, looking around the room as I took a sip of the beer in front of me. I choked on the dark liquid. God, it was gross. What had I been thinking?

I was looking for Sam.

Of course.

Where the hell was he? And how had I been left alone with his girlfriend?

That was the minute he appeared out of the restroom. Our eyes locked across the room. I could see his thoughts clear across his face. I was there. Claire was there. What the fuck had he gotten himself into?

It was the same question that I was wondering.

But to his credit, he still strode across the room toward us.

I missed everything Claire had said to Demi and Aspen in the brief exchange with Sam. Claire didn't even notice him until he was standing right in front of her.

"Oh hey! Look, Lark is here," Claire said with a big smile.

"Should I...scoot down?" I asked with my poker face firmly in place.

"No!" Claire gasped. She waved her hand at Sam. "We don't have to always be together. Take the other seat."

Sam wavered for a second. But what could he say? *Sorry, I don't want to sit next to Lark because she's my ex-girlfriend and this is insanely uncomfortable?*

Nope. He took the seat.

And now, I was fucking sitting between Sam and his girlfriend.

Kill me. Just kill me.

"So, as I was saying..." Claire continued.

But I didn't hear what she said. My ears were ringing. This was such a bad idea. I hadn't thought that Sam would be here. Let alone with Claire. I should have anticipated it, but after the confrontation with my parents, I hadn't even considered that option.

"Are you drinking Guinness?" Sam asked next to me. "Don't you hate beer?"

I glanced down at the drink I'd barely touched. "Shawn got it for me."

Then I pushed it toward him. Sam loved Guinness. I remembered one of the UW-Madison bars had this guy who had studied in Dublin to pour Guinness. That was how serious he was about the authenticity of their staff. Sam had raved about it. I wouldn't touch the stuff. Except that one crazy night that involved an Irish car bomb and lots of fuzzy blackout memories.

Our fingers brushed against each other as he took the drink from me without comment. I jerked away on instinct.

"How did you and Sam end up in New York?" Aspen asked. "I always love these stories. Everyone has their own *how I got to the city* story."

"Except Lark, right?" Claire asked. "You're from New York."

How much *had* Sam told Claire about me? Christ.

"Uh, yeah, I am. Born and raised."

"So cool," she said. "Well, Sam and I met my senior year of college, which was his last year of law school. We had mutual friends and ended up at a party together. We were together, what, about a year when I auditioned for the orchestra?" she asked Sam. He nodded, his head buried in his beer. "Yeah, a year. And when I got the position, he took the New York bar and transferred up here to be with me. It's been about a year since we've been here too."

I kept my gaze from wandering to Sam. He'd lied. He'd lied to me. He'd said that the firm had transferred him. But he'd only been transferred after Claire had gotten a job here. He must have requested it. He'd moved her for *her*. When he'd *never* done that for me.

My throat tightened painfully.

"I love that," Aspen said. "I wish I had a cute story like that for how I met my girlfriend. We met in a bar." She laughed and shrugged. "So cliché."

"That's not cliché. That's great!" Claire said. But then turned her attention back to me. "So, Sam says that y'all worked on the Woodhouse campaign together. Isn't it just crazy that y'all met up again on a campaign here in New York?"

"Wait," Demi said with an arched eyebrow, "you and Sam knew each other before this?"

"Hey, I didn't know that," Aspen said.

"I didn't know it was a secret!" Claire said.

I forced out a laugh. It was hard to speak around the knife in my chest. "It's not a secret. We both worked in Madison, like, five years ago. I didn't even know he was in the city or anything. Just coincidence that he's here now."

"Yeah, I actually thought she was working with her parents still," Sam said.

Which meant...*if I'd known, I might not have applied for this job.*

"What a small world," Aspen said.

"It's all about connections," Demi said. "I really believe that the world is so much smaller than we think. And that once we make a connection with someone, we're more likely to see that connection everywhere."

I gulped and glanced over at Sam. That was exactly how I felt.

"Like, think about when you test-drive a car. You *immediately* see that car everywhere on the road. But before, you never even noticed it. That's how it works with people too. We're brought together for a reason. It's serendipity."

Yeah, and what happy accident brought me to this incredibly uncomfortable situation?

"I love that idea," Claire agreed. "I lived most of my life in rural North Carolina. I like to think that it's not so big after all. And people come into our lives for a reason."

I swallowed. I needed to extract myself from this conversation.

I coughed hard into my hand. "Ugh, guys. I think I caught something. I'm really not feeling well. I wish I could stay longer, but I think I should just go."

There was a chorus of people trying to get me to stay. But I pushed my chair and coughed a second time, apologizing through coughs. Sam glanced at me once, seeing through my facade. But he didn't try to stop me as I made my excuses and headed toward the exit.

I'd seen enough anyway.

Claire seemed like a perfectly nice, perfectly normal woman. She had heart. She was genuinely curious about people. She seemed interested in being involved in Sam's life. I could see how they worked together.

Even if I didn't like it, there was nothing I could do about it.

Not that I even would if I could.

That was the *old* Lark. Bad Lark.

The separate entity that I didn't want to rear its ugly head ever again.

I already knew how this played out. There was no point in sticking around and enduring it any longer. I didn't want to be made a fool of...again.

9

LARK

I woke up the next morning around noon. It was the most I'd slept in weeks...maybe months. I felt like a new person after a full night's sleep.

I planned to spend the entire day wallowing in front of my television, eating junk food. It seemed like the best way to convince myself not to go into the office or think about Sam. But even a marathon of Jane Austen movies wasn't enough to completely distract me. I spent the time scrolling social media and texting with Katherine.

God, you must have no work to do after your banquet last night. You never text me this much.

I laughed.

No work today. Shawn gave us the day off.

I included a picture of me in sweats and a Brown T-shirt with my hair in a messy bun on top of my head. No makeup. I knew she'd cringe. But I did it for the joy in seeing how much she'd freak out.

Larkin St. Vincent! I must come save you. Put on something presentable. We're going shopping.

I loved her. Her and every inch of her ridiculousness. Others might find her rude, catty, and heartless, but she wasn't with me. She knew exactly what I needed, and she dropped everything to help.

Ugh! I don't want to leave. Can't you just let me wallow?

Over Sam? Still?

Yes. He has a girlfriend. I met her. Am I not allowed to have an ounce of your melodrama?

No. I'll be there in twenty.

I snorted. *Oh, Katherine.*
Then another message came in almost immediately.

And brush your hair. We're not animals.

I couldn't help the laugh that escaped me. At least she was making me laugh instead of letting me be miserable. It would be easy to do after the past week of hell. I grumbled the whole time, but I did eventually get up, change, and fix my hair.

When Katherine texted me to say she was here, I headed downstairs. I rolled my eyes when I saw the vehicle outside of my building. A limousine. Christ, she was as bad as my mother.

"Miss St. Vincent," the driver said, opening the door for me.

"Thank you."

I slid into the backseat next to Katherine, who was dressed in stylish denim with a fitted white cotton tee and nude high heels. Her dark hair was parted down the middle, glossy and straight. She looked every bit like a model who was about to head to a photo shoot—put together and effortlessly stunning.

"The limo, Ren?" I asked, switching to the nickname Penn had given her at prep school.

She shrugged one shoulder as we pulled away. "It's the Percy limo. Why not use all the benefits of this marriage?"

"I suppose."

Though...my own mother had offered me the family limo, and I'd declined. But Katherine and I were far from the same people. She could live her life however she wanted. No matter how many times I tried to save her from herself, she was going to do whatever she wanted.

"It's nice to see you out of business suits," Katherine said.

I'd opted for an athleisure look with Lululemon leggings, a tank, and Nikes. My hair was in a sleek ponytail, as managed as I could get the curls in twenty minutes. It wasn't as fancy as Katherine, but I never was.

"Where are we going anyway?"

"Bergdorf, of course."

I shook my head. "I should have guessed."

"Probably."

"You know my mother bought half of Barneys and left it in my apartment last week. I really don't need anything."

Katherine arched an eyebrow. "Define need."

Which was how we ended up in the dressing room of Bergdorf Goodman with a personal shopper or two bringing us a dozen or more outfits to try on. None of which seemed practical for my job. But it was fun to actually have a day to relax and hang out with my friend.

"So, melodrama," Katherine said. She turned in place in a pink sundress that looked like something she'd wear to a polo match. "What's going on? You met Sam's girlfriend? How?"

I explained the awkward situation that I'd found myself in the night before. Hearing it from my own lips made it sound extra ridiculous. "Anyway, it was really awkward."

"It sounds like you should have taken charge," Katherine said with her hands on her hips. "Why are you letting anyone push you around? Don't you know who you are?"

"Being a St. Vincent doesn't actually matter for everything."

"Doesn't it?" she asked. "I swear, you used to know that."

"I don't want that life."

"God, sometimes, you sound just like Penn," Katherine moaned. "Why don't you want that life? What is so wrong with being the sole heir to a billion-dollar enterprise? How is your life hard when both of your parents are dying for you to take over and make them even more money? Do you know how many people would kill for that? What kind of power that commands?"

"Nothing is wrong with it. But my entire life was spent doing exactly what my parents wanted. There was never a question of what *I* wanted."

"I don't understand you. You *used* to want this."

"No, I didn't," I told her vehemently. "That's the thing. I never wanted it. I just did it because that was what was expected from me. From all of us. And even if I was interested in running a business instead of a campaign, I don't want to become the person I had to be to survive living a hundred percent in the Upper East Side. You know my parents don't sleep in the same room. They haven't since I was a kid. All that matters is money. And I didn't like who I was when that was my life, so I gave it up. I know I'll always be a St. Vincent. I can't escape my name. I just want people to accept both sides of me."

"You're insane," I said as I changed into my next outfit.

"But effective. Now, can we move past Sam?" Katherine asked.

I stepped back out of the dressing room in cigarette pants and a skintight blue bodysuit. I put my hands on my hips.

"I'll admit, he's good-looking. But he's not worth your time. He's just so out of your league."

"Apparently, I'm out of every guy's league."

Katherine shrugged. "Can't deny facts."

I rolled my eyes. "Not helping."

"You just need someone more like us. Someone who will understand you."

"What? Like Thomas?" I ground out.

Katherine wrinkled her nose. "Definitely no. That was a

mistake. I still think that asshole should go down for what he did to you. We can make him suffer."

I adamantly shook my head. "I'm not that person anymore."

"Fine," she grumbled, changing out of her polo outfit. "But not every guy on the Upper East Side is Thomas."

"Have you met the guys on the Upper East Side? They're all kind of pretentious douche bags."

"They're not all that bad."

"Really?" I asked with raised eyebrows when she appeared again in a canary-yellow cocktail dress. "What? Like Camden?"

Katherine froze mid-spin in front of the mirror. "No...Camden Percy is the king of assholes."

"I know that. But are you going to tell me what's really going on with you two?"

"What?" She tried to sound cool. "It's just an arranged marriage. A trade of money and sex. It's not that uncommon with old money, Lark. You know that."

"And nothing more?" I prodded.

Katherine stood perfectly still. And it was a tell on her part. I knew there was something else. I just wanted her to tell me. If I had to sit here and listen to her judge my love life, I was going to make her divulge her own.

"Come on. What happened on your honeymoon?"

Katherine dipped her chin. "Nothing of importance. We were in the Maldives for three weeks. Beach, sun, sand, salt."

"Katherine," I groaned.

She whispered something that I couldn't even hear and then turned away from me.

"Wait...what was that?"

"You heard me."

"No...no, I didn't," I said, stepping close to my friend.

She looked up at me with wide eyes. And for the first time, I realized she was...afraid.

"I think...I like him."

"Camden?" I asked. "Camden Percy?"

She blanched and looked away from me. "I think I'm...I'm falling in love with him."

"Whoa," I breathed. "But...you hate him. We all hate him. We've always hated him."

"I know," she whispered. Then she sighed heavily. "Fuck, do I know it."

"Then what's changed?"

She shrugged, nonchalant. "Nothing. Everything. I don't want to talk about it. God, this is painful. I hate him. And I'm falling in love with him. And I don't even know what is going on."

"Okay," I said, realizing when not to push her.

This was a huge revelation for her.

Katherine had only ever loved one person as far as I knew. And we both knew that she wasn't going to end up with Penn Kensington. For her to have real feelings about anyone else...let alone her husband...had to be the hardest look she'd ever given at her life.

"Let's forget it," she said. Her Upper East Side mask slid back in place. "Let's talk about nabbing you a gorgeous, extremely wealthy businessman at Natalie's atrocious Happily Ever After party on Saturday."

"Ugh," I groaned. "Do I still have to attend?"

"I got you a dress, so you're fucking going."

I chuckled as I stormed into the dressing room to try on another outfit. "This is going to be such a disaster."

"It is not," Katherine said.

I came back out to find her staring darkly into the trifold mirror. She looked like a woman possessed.

"It's going to be fine," she insisted when she caught me looking. "You're going to get a hot, new guy. I'm going to hold on to my throne. And Natalie will be put back into her place. All will be right in the world again."

She sounded like she was convincing herself.

I wanted to believe that it was all going to be fine too.

Not just for me...but also for Katherine and Natalie and my whole crew. But only Saturday would tell.

10

LARK

It was not fine.

Not dealing with Sam the next week at work.

Not at Natalie's party.

Not for Katherine's throne.

Or my crew.

I stood there in the crowded ballroom as everyone I cared about yelled at each other. Tears rimmed Katherine's eyes. Natalie looked like she was ready to spit actual venom. Penn could barely keep it all together. Camden had already raced out of the room, furious with Katherine.

I didn't know how it had all gone so wrong.

One minute, I'd been trying to take Katherine's advice and meet a new guy—unsuccessfully, I might add—and the next, Katherine was almost crying. I hadn't seen her cry since high school.

"Oh god," I whispered as they continued to go at each other's throats.

Then I saw it. The moment that Katherine admitted defeat, turned on her heel, and left. I glanced between her retreating form and Penn. He gave me a sad look. One that said I should help Katherine. That he couldn't do it right now.

Fuck.

I whipped around and raced after her. I didn't care that people were watching. Just that Katherine was hurting. I reached her right before the exit.

"Wait, Katherine. Don't leave," I said, grabbing her elbow and hauling her to a stop.

"No, let me go," she said through her own tears.

"Talk to me. What happened with Camden?"

She sniffled and looked away. "He saw me with Penn."

"Were you *with* Penn?" I asked. It was a valid question. Being in a relationship hadn't stopped either of them before.

"No!" she gasped. "No, I was actually telling him exactly what I'd told you...about Camden. And Camden drew his own conclusions. He said he was going to go see Fiona."

I winced. "He wouldn't!"

But of course, he would. Camden had had an on-again/off-again thing with Fiona Berkshire for as long as Katherine had been interested in Penn. It was half the reason I suspected he'd wanted something arranged. Fiona wasn't quite marriage material, but he didn't want anyone to interfere in his dalliances.

Katherine just shook her head, her tears damming up. "I don't even know what he'll do. We agreed. We agreed not to be with anyone else after the honeymoon." She choked on her words. I could see it cost her to admit that. "And I haven't. I...I didn't think he had either. But now, I don't know. I don't know, Lark. I just want to go home."

"Okay," I muttered. "Okay, we can figure out what to do about Camden in the morning."

"You should stay," she said. "You were talking to that guy. Just because half of our plan is ruined doesn't mean it all has to be."

"Are you sure you want to be alone?"

"I've never wanted to be more alone," she said and then walked off into the night.

I cursed colorfully and then turned back to the party. I had no interest in talking to anyone now. Except maybe Penn and Natalie and Camden and knocking some sense into them. Katherine might appear indestructible, but she wasn't.

And neither was I.

The realization hit me hard. I didn't know if I could last another six months with Sam in the office. I didn't know what I was going to do.

It was impossible not to have feelings for him. Even if it was just anger about what had happened, the choice he had made, and the way it had all ended. But I knew that anger was so mixed up with other emotions. Ones that I couldn't act on. And yet, I had to be around him.

It was like a festering wound. When I was away from him, sometimes, I could forget that I was rotting from the inside. But every time he was near, the wound would throb with a white-hot, pain-filled reminder.

I was done with this party. I couldn't think clearly. And I was done lamenting the gaping hole in my chest.

Just as I turned to follow Katherine out, the lights switched off. I stalled as everyone in the room screamed. I blinked a few times as my eyes adjusted to the light. A few people turned their phone flashlights on, illuminating the space like a horror film. But the floodlights appeared overhead a few seconds later.

The screams died down, and everyone just looked around the room in confusion. But instead of standing around like an idiot, I immediately went into action. This wasn't my event. I shouldn't care less what happened with it. But it wasn't in me.

So, I hustled past the stunned group toward the stage where I could see a crowd forming. I pushed up to the front and then stopped, my jaw dropping when I saw what everyone was staring at.

Court Kensington was in handcuffs.

His girlfriend, Jane, was also handcuffed, standing next to him, staring blankly.

Penn and Natalie were speaking to the arresting officers, but it didn't look like they were getting anywhere. In fact, it seemed to only get worse. Because Court couldn't let anything stand. He had to run his big mouth.

I ran a hand back through my perfectly sculpted hair. Fuck. This was bad. This was really, really bad.

Not just for Court and Jane.

No, it was bad for the campaign.

It was bad for Leslie.

What the fuck was the mayor of New York City going to do when she discovered her son had been arrested? What would the press say when they found out? Leslie was tough on crime. This was going to be a *huge* setback. And I didn't even know how to process this.

But I did know one thing...someone needed to call the mayor.

And with Penn talking to the police and dealing with his brother, I knew that...it was going to have to be me.

I groaned as I pulled out my phone. This was not going to be pleasant.

I swallowed hard and then pressed the number for the mayor. She answered on the third ring.

"Lark, it's one in the morning. This had better be an emergency," Leslie said into the phone.

"It is," I said with a sigh and a trace of fear. "Court was just arrested with Jane at the big Happily Ever After charity function."

"Arrested?" she demanded. "Whatever for?"

"It's unclear. The officers don't seem to be explaining what happened. Jane is remaining silent, but Court is..."

"Not," Leslie guessed. She sighed, but she sounded rattled. "Tell him to keep his mouth shut, and I'll be there soon to deal with this."

"I'll let him know. I think Penn is going to the police station with him. I'll go with him and let you know which one."

"Thank you, Lark. Once again, you're a lifesaver in helping me deal with my son." She was silent for a second. "Well, we will fix it."

"Yes, we will."

"Lark," she said softer than before, "does he seem okay?"

I looked between her two sons. And no...neither of them seemed okay.

"I don't know," I admitted.

She sighed. "That's what I was afraid of. Go help my son. I'll figure this out."

"Yes, ma'am."

I hung up the phone and stepped forward, passing the predetermined demarcation. The police were telling everyone to leave the building, that the party was over, and Trinity was closed. That couldn't be a good sign for whatever was going on with Court and Jane.

Penn stepped away from Natalie and toward Court.

"Penn," I called.

"I thought you'd left already," he said when I approached him. He looked physically shaken. Like his world had just imploded.

"I was going to, but I had a change of heart. What's going on with Court? Do you know why he's being arrested?"

Penn shook his head. "Court is denying anything happened. The officers are being tight-lipped. I guess we'll find out at the police station. It's bullshit. I need to call my mother."

"I already did," I told him. "She's coming to fix it."

"She's coming?" he asked with raised eyebrows. "Herself?"

"Yes. She said that she'd be there. She seemed...shaken."

"It's an act," he said without skipping a beat. "She's only thinking of the campaign."

"I don't think so. She didn't mention the campaign on the phone."

But I could see that Penn was second-guessing his assumption. I was the asshole who had thought of the campaign first.

"My car is out front," he said. "We should probably follow them."

I nodded. "All right. Are you okay?"

"No. No, I'm not." His eyes were sad and distant. "You?"

And I realized...I wasn't. I wasn't okay with any of this. My best friends weren't speaking. Everyone was arguing. Court had just been arrested. Leslie was even upset. Leslie, who was impenetrable.

I wanted to put it all back together. Just like with my now-nonexistent relationship with Sam. If I'd tried to put it back together then...maybe we wouldn't be here. Or maybe we would.

All I knew was that things weren't okay. I fixed things for a living, and I didn't know how to fix this.

11

SAM

Buzz. *Buzz. Buzz.*

"Sam," Claire hissed. "Your phone is ringing. Silence it or answer it or something."

I blearily opened my eyes and reached for my phone on the nightstand. The screen lit up again. I squinted at the name that appeared on the device. What the hell? Why was Lark calling me at one o'clock in the morning? Was she drunk?

I silenced the phone and set it back facedown with a yawn. "Sorry about that."

"It's fine," she muttered, already half-asleep.

But then the phone started to ring again.

I snatched it off the nightstand with a curse. I threw the covers off of me and stumbled out of the one bedroom and into the tiny living space.

With a deep breath, I answered the phone, "Hello?"

"Sam," Lark said in relief, "you answered."

She didn't sound drunk. Not even a little. She sounded...uncertain, almost soft...vulnerable.

"It's one in the morning, Lark. What's going on?"

"I know. I'm sorry. I wouldn't have called if it wasn't an emergency. Court has been arrested," she got out in a rush.

"Arrested?" I gasped. "What for?"

"It's complicated. Apparently, his girlfriend, Jane, is being booked for fraud, theft, possibly...I don't know...grand larceny."

"Holy shit!"

"Yeah. It's, fuck—" She broke off, clearly shaken. "It's horrifying. I knew her. I mean, we weren't friends, but I've been to a lot of events with her. She was close with Natalie."

"Who is Natalie?"

"Sorry. Penn's girlfriend. I'm getting off track. We're at the police station. It's a fucking nightmare here."

"Jesus, Lark," I breathed. I could hardly believe this was happening.

"Yeah. Court claims he didn't do anything and that the officer put him in cuffs because he'd mouthed off to him. But Penn said that he might be an accomplice because he was giving Jane money."

Fuck. An accomplice to grand larceny. Yeah, that was going to be a fucking field day for the office.

"We're waiting for the mayor to show up. And I'm totally freaking out. I feel worthless. I have a law degree. I've passed the bar here, but it was years ago. I'm not practicing." She was beginning to ramble. Getting more incoherent as she went.

I knew what she wanted but hadn't asked.

"I'll come down," I told her.

"Really?" she whispered.

"Yeah. It's part of the job, right?"

"Right." Her voice got this far-off quality. "The job. Yes."

"Plus, I like Court. He doesn't seem like the type of person to do this."

"I don't know," she said. "I really don't."

"Look, hang tight. Shoot me the address, and I'll grab a cab."

"Thank you," she told me sincerely. "I really appreciate it."

"No problem."

I hung up the phone and ran a hand over my face. What a night. Court and Jane arrested. This was going to be a nightmare. I couldn't even imagine what the office would look like tomorrow.

And I was in legal. I'd probably have to handle some of this shit. Fuck.

I slipped back into the bedroom and went to the small closet to grab one of my suits.

"What are you doing?" Claire murmured from the bed.

"That was Lark. The mayor's son was just arrested. She asked me to come down to the station."

Claire shot up in bed. "Oh my god! That's horrible."

"Yeah. You don't mind, do you?"

"What? No, of course not. This is your job. You have to go." She rubbed her eyes. "Do you want me to come too?"

I shook my head as I pulled on a suit. "That's okay. You should sleep. You have rehearsal tomorrow. I'll just go. I'll text you when I'm done."

"Okay," she said, lying back down and getting comfortable again. "I hope it's all just a misunderstanding."

"Me too."

Though I didn't think it was.

I watched her already falling back asleep as I grabbed my phone, wallet, and keys. I hurried out of our apartment and out to our barely mediocre Brooklyn neighborhood. Thankfully, this was New York, and cabs were out at all hours. I flagged down the first one that I saw. It had been idling out front of a nearby bar. And I was in Manhattan and at the police station within a half hour.

I strode past a half-dozen people at the entrance, who appeared to either be reporters or paparazzi, and into the building. For one thirty in the morning, the station was pretty busy. I supposed they dealt with a lot of petty crimes on the weekends—underage drinking, turnstile jumpers, public indecency, et cetera. But there was a buzz in the room. As if what had happened with Court and Jane was something else altogether.

I found Lark in a poufy plum ball gown. Her dark red hair had been tamed and fell in soft waves almost to the middle of her back. I'd never have guessed it was that long when it was in those unruly curls. Her gaze shifted my direction, and I saw she had on heavy makeup, but her eyes were wide with alarm.

She stood abruptly at my presence, and I walked over to her.

"A little overdressed for the circumstances, don't you think?" I asked with a smile, hoping to break the tension.

"What? A custom-made designer dress isn't how everyone goes to a police station?" She brought her bottom lip into her mouth, betraying her unease. "Thanks for coming."

"Of course."

The person seated next to her sighed and then rose to his feet. He was nearly as tall as I was but trimmer through the shoulders. And he was in a tuxedo that probably cost more than my monthly salary. Even if I hadn't known who he was, it was obvious right away because he almost looked like an exact replica of his older brother.

I held my hand out. "You must be Penn."

Penn looked me up and down with the attention of someone who knew my history with Lark before he took my hand. "And you're Sam. *The* Sam."

My eyes flicked to Lark's once, and she just shrugged guiltily.

"Yeah, I guess I am."

Penn's eyes darkened. Oh, he didn't like me. He had definitely heard Lark's side of the story.

"I hear that you're working for the campaign now."

"Legal counsel. That's why I'm here."

"And you're just friends," Penn said in a way that made it seem like Lark had told him that.

"Penn," Lark said with a sigh, "it's really not the time. We're dealing with your brother."

"We're just friends," I told Penn even though he didn't believe me. "But I agree with Lark. We're not here to discuss the past. We're here because your brother was arrested. Have you heard what's going on so far?"

"Leslie stormed back there a few minutes ago with another attorney," Lark said. "They wouldn't let Penn or me do anything. We've just been waiting."

Lark had barely finished her statement when the door burst

open, and Mayor Kensington sauntered out of the police station as if she owned the place. Which, as mayor...it wasn't too far off.

Behind her was a diminutive man with almost completely white hair in a boxy suit, who must be their attorney.

And behind him...was Court. His shoulders were back, and he looked like he was on top of the world. But I could see the strain behind his eyes, the forced set of his shoulders, and the way he walked like he was going to collapse at any second. It was there, and it wasn't. As if he were two people overlapped. The real Court and the fake Court.

The mayor stalked right over to where Penn stood with Lark and me. "We're putting this ridiculous mess behind us. Court did nothing wrong, except perhaps act with some stupidity. They're not going to file any charges. We're leaving. Are you coming with us?"

Penn nodded. "Yeah. Of course."

Leslie's eyes shifted to Lark. They softened in a way they hadn't quite for her sons. "Thank you for everything." She reached out and gripped Lark's hand. It was then I realized the mayor was trying to keep herself from trembling. "Could you call Shawn and get him caught up? We'll need everyone in the office bright and early. This is going to be a circus."

"Yes. Yes, of course. I'll call Shawn," Lark told her. "I'll take care of it. Go be with your boys."

Leslie nodded once and then released her. Like a hurricane, she left as quickly as she'd arrived, sweeping everyone else out with her.

Slightly delirious, Lark and I hustled out in the wake of the crowd, avoiding the reporters who were camped out front. Without a word, we started together down the sidewalk. Away from the media circus that Leslie had already predicted.

This whole thing wasn't really in my job description. I primarily did campaign finance law. I didn't even know if I would have been able to get Court released. The mayor had so much clout. I should have considered that. But instead, at the sound of

Lark's shaky voice and the knowledge that my friend had been arrested, I'd bolted.

Even though...it was clear that I hadn't ended up being needed, I didn't feel like this was a waste.

I walked side by side with Lark as she clutched her phone, trying not to lose it. I'd seen her exhausted and sleep-deprived and sobbing from anger at the election. But I'd never seen her like this. She was so strong. This was...unnerving.

"Are you okay?" I finally asked.

She nodded. "Yeah," she lied. "I mean...I have to call Shawn." She stopped and turned to face me. Her hands were visibly trembling now. She looked down at her phone and tried to get it to work. "I have to...tell him what happened."

"Hey. Hey," I said. I put my hand over hers. She flinched, but I didn't let go. I pried the phone from her hand. "How about I call Shawn?"

"No, I need to do it. Leslie told me."

"Yeah. And you're delegating." We passed a bench, and I veered her toward it. "Have a seat. You're shaking."

"Am I?" she whispered.

"Yes."

"It's just that...I've never seen Leslie upset before. Not really," she admitted. "I don't know why I'm so freaked out."

"It's okay. It's normal. Just sit."

So, she sat. She sat the entire time I was on the phone with Shawn, explaining the situation and why I was talking on Lark's phone. It didn't take long, but now, Shawn was in charge. By the time I handed the phone back, she was a little more composed.

"Shawn is on top of it now," I told her.

"Why are you taking care of me?"

I sank into the seat next to her. "Because...we're friends."

Her impossibly green eyes found mine. They were wide and watery and disbelieving.

"Friends," she repeated. "Can we be that?"

No.

I didn't think that we could. But I had to be around her for the next six months, and I didn't know how I'd survive it any other way. The last week of cold shoulders and anger hadn't helped. And we couldn't be more. We just...couldn't. Not with our history. Not with the pain between us. Not with...Claire.

"Yeah. Friends," I lied to her.

It was a simple lie. One that was hardly even there. Meant to comfort someone. It shouldn't have made me feel like an asshole for saying it. But it did. Because I was a total jackass. Lark and I would never just be friends.

She was trying to read my expression. To see the lie I'd told. But I hid it the best that I could. Let her see that this was possible. Because she needed it tonight.

"Okay," she finally said.

And even I wanted to punch myself for the break in her voice on that word. The lie she had just accepted as truth.

12

LARK

The mayor's prediction came true. As I had known it would.

The press latched on to Court's arrest like leeches trying to suck us all dry. They were camped out in front of the campaign office, City Hall, the Kensington residence. Court was under unofficial house arrest. Which I'd gathered meant his mother had threatened him within an inch of his life if he left his penthouse.

It wasn't ideal.

A week ago, we'd joked about the opposition using the word *feminism* against us for a sound bite. Now, we had this mess.

I could already see the television ads screaming how the mayor claimed to be tough on crime while she had a delinquent son. Whether Court had done anything or not was irrelevant. It was the headline, the flashy story, the sensationalized side of it that sold newspapers. And so that was what would be reported.

We'd all had to show our campaign clearance to get into the building, passing the reporters. What a nightmare.

"We just have to make it clear to everyone that if they talk to the press, they're fired," Christine said. She swiped her blue hair out of her eyes. "It's already in their contracts, and we coached everyone, *especially* field workers, on it when we brought them in. But this is different. And we need to be vigilant."

I nodded absentmindedly, writing notes onto my legal pad. We'd been in this meeting for an hour. Leslie had only slipped in a half hour ago, after she got away from City Hall. She'd scheduled a press conference that afternoon to address what had happened.

The party line was, Court had done nothing wrong. The arresting officer had made a mistake. Justice would be had.

Not that the media gave two fucks what she said. I'd seen the press conference and still cringed. How she'd kept her composure before letting her press secretary take over was beyond me. I knew she was furious. I was furious. We'd worked so hard to get to where we were. No scandals in almost four years. And now...this.

Christine continued speaking about what we could and couldn't say while Matthew kept chiming in with messaging information from the political department.

But my eyes drifted out the glass door to the offices beyond this conference room. I still couldn't believe I'd called Sam last night. I didn't know what had possessed me to do it. One minute, Penn and I had been waiting for the mayor to show up, and the next, I'd felt like I just couldn't sit there and do nothing. So...I'd called.

Or at least...that was what I'd told myself and Penn when he asked. Though he hadn't been any more convinced than I was.

I'd confessed to Penn that Sam was in New York. That we were just friends, just working together. But he remembered the mess I'd been after I came back from Madison. He remembered the shell of a person I'd been as I forced myself to work for my parents. Before something had shaken loose and I'd realized it was all a mistake and come back to the campaign.

Penn didn't want to see me become that person again. I didn't either.

And still, when push had come to shove, I'd called Sam.

Sam wasn't needed, but in some way...he was necessary. He didn't look put out when he realized that he'd driven all the way down from Brooklyn for nothing. He'd just silently taken care of me and handled the campaign while I shook like a leaf on a park bench.

It was the first time in my career I hadn't been able to handle my job. It wasn't because of Court's arrest. I'd seen many a friend get arrested and immediately leave the police station because we all had wealthy parents who could make things disappear. It was the worry that Leslie had. The worry that said...this one would stick.

Sam had taken care of me. We'd walked back to my apartment. Me in my ridiculous ballgown. Him in a rumpled suit and messy hair.

Friends.

Or at least, sort of. Closer to that than anything else. Closer to that than we'd ever been.

I'd always thought we were either in love or we weren't. There was no in-between for us. Especially not with him having a girl-friend. But last night, he'd been my friend when I needed one. Just like I had been Penn's because he needed me. It had been a relief.

I hadn't seen him today. I'd been stuck in this meeting since the dawn of time. I wondered if last night would stick for us too.

"That's fine. That's all fine, Christine," Shawn said. "There's another announcement. Leslie has brought on Jay Neville for strategic consulting after this."

My ears perked. "He agreed?"

I knew that Leslie had been courting him for months now. That she'd wanted him last election too. He'd said he wanted to stay in Texas and remain near his family. But this Court situation must have been serious enough for him to finally get on board.

"He did," Leslie said. "Which is wonderful. I think we need him. He's working with his own pollsters to see how this will look. But we won't know until the end of the week. In the meantime, I'm working on finding someone else to...handle Court full-time."

"That's smart," Shawn said. "We should have had that last election."

It wasn't a bad idea. Court tended to cause trouble wherever he went.

"Yes, well, nothing was this serious," Leslie said. "I have a few people in mind. They'll be another paid staff, and we'll need to onboard them in the campaign and in Court's lifestyle." She turned to look at me. "I hate to put more on your plate, Lark, but do you think you can be in charge of that aspect once we find a person? I realize most people who were even trained in PR don't quite get the Upper East Side like they do other celebrities."

"Of course," I agreed immediately. "I'd be happy to."

"Great. Once we can get him a handler, we're going to have to put together messaging for him joining the campaign in some capacity. I think it's the easiest way to deescalate this situation at this point. Jay agrees with me."

"We need him on message," Shawn agreed.

Leslie nodded. "Yes, we'll figure it out."

I leaned forward as something clicked in my brain. "I know someone who is a fixer—Anna English. She's a celebrity publicist in LA with Poise PR. She already knows Court and has some understanding of the Upper East Side. She's the best in the business."

Leslie arched an eyebrow. "Oh, really? Well, bring Anna out. We'll interview her for the position."

My smile broadened. This was perfect. English had just been complaining about her job. This might be the break she needed to get away from the less pleasant aspects.

"I'll do that."

"All right," Leslie said, standing to her considerable height. "You all have your assignments. I can't stay much longer. Still have a city to run. Let's look at this as a small setback and not a death sentence. It will be fine. It's far enough away from the election that we can manage this. We can still win. So, let's go out there and do it."

Everyone sat up a little straighter as she spoke. She had that effect. Like her words were almost a glamour. The force of her charisma pushing into us. It was one of the things that I loved about her.

We all stood up and stretched our aching muscles as Leslie walked out of the room. Back to City Hall to deal with her mayoral duties. Leaving us to try to pick up the mess of her son's debacle.

I headed out of the conference room with my legal pad tucked up under my arm. I needed coffee. I'd barely gotten any sleep last night, and it was already catching up with me. I couldn't pop over to Coffee Grounds with the media camped out front. So, I'd have to make do with the shitty break-room coffee.

The room was already full of everyone else who had decided on the same thing. There was a line ten people deep, and man, I could not deal with that today. I whirled around to head back to my office and die from exhaustion in peace. But when I got there, I found Aspen missing and Sam leaning against her desk instead.

"Hey," I said in surprise. "What's up? And where's my assistant?"

"I told her to go grab her lunch. That I'd watch her desk."

My eyes widened. "Oh god."

He laughed. "It's only been a few minutes." He picked up a Coffee Grounds cup from the desk. "I brought you coffee in. She was going to take it to you in the meeting. But hey, now, you're here."

I looked at the coffee like a lifeline. "I don't even want to know how you got in and out of here to bring this to me. I'd die for that coffee right now."

"I can't give away all my secrets." He passed it over to me with a satisfied smile. "I figured after last night...you might need it."

"You figured correctly."

"So, what's the scoop?" he asked, sitting back and sipping his own coffee.

I shrugged. "Court is under house arrest. We're bringing Jay Neville on for consulting. I'm going to try to hire English to babysit Court. And otherwise, we're kind of fucked right now."

"Wait, Court is under house arrest?" he asked. "That doesn't make sense. He didn't even do anything."

"Well, not official house arrest. But he *was* arrested, and it's a fucking media circus out there. He can't leave without making this all worse. So, we're trying to find someone to deal with him before that happens."

"Huh. That seems unfair to Court."

I gave him a *I've been up for way too long to pity Court* look. "He's fucking the entire campaign right now. If he has to sit in his multi-million-dollar penthouse for a few days, is he really suffering?"

Sam laughed softly. "I suppose not."

"I appreciate this," I said, nodding to the drink. "But I should probably get back to work. The world is ending. Didn't you hear?"

He stood up from Aspen's desk and nodded. "Ah, well, I think it'll blow over. Just hang in there." He headed back toward his own office before saying, "And get some sleep."

I waved him off with a secret smile and then headed into my office. I would not overanalyze that conversation. I would not think obsessively about him bringing me coffee. I would not think about any of it.

Not even a little.

Okay. Maybe just a little.

13

SAM

Ever since the conversation with Lark, I'd been thinking about how Court Kensington had ended up on an unofficial house arrest. And how ridiculous it was that it was happening. That no one seemed to care that he was a grown-ass man and should deal with his own consequences or not.

But no, everyone was so focused on the campaign. No one was thinking about Court at all. It was their job to think about Leslie and how this would impact her. I seemed to be the only one wondering how Court was holding up.

Which was how I ended up inside an actual fucking elevator that took me up to his literal penthouse overlooking Central Park.

I knew in some abstract way how the uber wealthy lived. Lark had been different when in Madison—living in a one-bedroom apartment, driving a Subaru, and wearing regular brands. So, I hadn't seen it close up.

Not until today...right this minute.

The elevator dinged on the top floor and slid open to a foyer. It felt pretty surreal to be in an apartment that was nicer than any house I'd ever been in.

"Court?" I called as I stepped out of the elevator.

But no one responded. I crept forward until I found the living room. It was a kind of perfect mix of interior designer meets bachelor pad. Everything was muted and nearly spotless.

Court rounded the corner. He was dressed in dark-wash jeans and a plain gray T-shirt, holding a bottle of bourbon in his hand. "Oh, hey. You made it past the assholes outside."

"Yeah. I came in the back way, like you suggested."

"Cool. Drink?"

He didn't wait for my reply before striding back into what appeared to be the kitchen with a full wet bar. He poured out way more than a knuckle's worth of bourbon into each glass. Then he held one out for me to take.

"Uh, thanks," I said. I took a sip of the drink. It was smooth as hell. Maybe the best bourbon I'd ever had. "Holy shit. This is...great."

"Yeah. I've been saving it for a special occasion," he said with a shrug. "Guess getting completely fucked over by your girlfriend of two years is a special occasion."

"Have you been drinking since you got back here?"

He didn't look sober. But he wasn't completely gone either. As if he was trying to stay perfectly, comfortably numb.

"Why are you asking?" he demanded, finally meeting my gaze. His eyes were this fierce blue like they might reach out and drown you. "For you or for my mother?"

My own eyes rounded. "What do you mean? I'm not here for the campaign."

"Yeah, well, you were at the police station last night. Did my mother call you for that too? Did she try to make you become my friend to keep an eye on me? I wouldn't put it past her."

"Uh, I have no idea what you're talking about. I came to the police station last night because Lark was freaked out and called me. I thought I might need to help get you out of there. But your mother had that handled."

Court snorted and took another long drink. "Yeah, as always."

"I'm here because I found out you were under house arrest, and I thought it was shitty. Just thought...I'd check in on you. That's what I do for friends."

Court narrowed his eyes. He seemed to be searching for something. Something that I wasn't giving him. "Seriously?"

"Uh...yeah."

"You just came over to see if I was doing all right?" He seemed unable to comprehend it.

"Yes," I assured him anyway.

"Shit," Court groaned. He walked over to the couch and sank into the cushions. "Don't tell anyone that you're this nice."

I laughed and took a seat on the chair adjacent to him. "What do you mean?"

"Especially Camden. He'll eat you alive if he thinks you're a nice guy. Be a total jackass around him, and he'll respect you."

"Why do you like him if he's like that?"

Court took another long drink and then set it down on the coffee table. He threw his arms behind his head and leaned further back. "Camden and I go way back. He's the only person who has always been there for me. My best friend disappeared in college. My dad overdosed. You've seen my mother. Penn and I have always been on rocky ground. And now...Jane." He ground his teeth after saying her name. "Camden is a jackass. I know that. But he doesn't judge me. I don't judge him. We don't have to fucking pretend with each other. We're way past that."

"That makes sense," I admitted.

"Anyway, he's not all bad. He just doesn't show anyone else another side of him." Court cleared his throat. "But that's not what you're here to talk about. You want to know about Jane?"

I shook my head. "Nah. You probably don't want to talk about it. I don't need to know what happened."

Court nodded his head once, but he seemed startled. "You... really aren't here for my mother."

"I'm really not."

"Huh," Court said. "Full of surprises."

"I guess."

"So, since I don't want to talk, tell me about you and Lark."

I should have seen it coming. But for some reason, I hadn't. Instead of loathing the idea of talking about it, I actually felt okay.

Not okay about what had happened in the past, but I hadn't ever had anyone to talk about it with.

"Well, we met on the Woodhouse campaign in Madison. I didn't know who she was. She wasn't going by Larkin St. Vincent at the time. Just Lark Vincent. If I'd known her real name, I think even I might have put two and two together. My ex's parents always vacationed at St. Vincent's Resorts. I'm pretty sure I'd heard of the purses. But she was trying to be someone else. To fit in."

"Ah, classic," Court said as if everyone on the Upper East Side had tried that trick. "But it didn't stick."

"No. We got close and then started dating. I knew she was hiding something, but she wouldn't admit it. It came out, who she was, and I think she thought I'd care."

"You cared," Court said. "Everyone cares."

"I cared that she'd hidden who she was. But I understood why. I don't know if I would have treated her differently. Her fear was likely warranted." I shrugged. "It didn't matter. We dated for about a year. We had a falling-out. She came back to the city, and I went home to North Carolina."

Court sat up and leaned his elbows on his knees. "But what's the whole story? Why'd it end?"

I laughed softly. Not a laugh filled with humor, but old anger laced with regret. I could tell him. He'd probably understand. But I just shook my head. "Dude, I don't think you could get me drunk enough to tell the whole thing."

Court leaned back in defeat. "One day, I will."

"Maybe."

"What about your girlfriend? She's chill with you seeing Lark every day like this?" he asked, downing the remainder of his drink.

"Well..." I winced.

Then he started laughing. "Ah, there it is. Claire doesn't know."

"Not...exactly. She knows that I dated a girl on campaign, and it didn't work out. She knows that I worked with Lark on campaign and that I'm working with her now. She just doesn't know those are the same people."

"Sneaky. Maybe you are one of us after all," Court said as he headed back into the kitchen to pour himself another drink.

It was sneaky. But it felt necessary. I knew I should tell Claire. But...there was nothing going on with Lark and me. We'd decided to be friends. Of sorts. Plus, she was technically my boss. Telling Claire would bring undue complications in my already-complicated relationship.

"So, your ray-of-sunshine girlfriend, it's all good there? She's not potentially hiding a secret identity or stealing millions of dollars from overseas banks and her not-suspicious boyfriend, is she?"

I winced. Fucking Jane.

"She is not," I told him. "Actually, she's going on tour with her ensemble next week."

"Is she? Where?"

"Europe," I said with a sigh. "For twelve weeks."

I hadn't told anyone this. Not even my parents, who I checked in with every week. I didn't know how to tell them that I'd moved to New York City, and now, Claire was leaving to go on tour.

Court's eyebrows rose to the ceiling. "Whoa. She's going to be gone for three months, and you're going to be here with Lark every day?"

"It's not like that."

"Isn't it?"

I shrugged and downed the rest of my own drink in one big gulp. Because...Court wasn't wrong.

"Lark doesn't have to know that Claire is gone."

Court tipped his head back. "That's going to go over well."

"Honestly, I've been trying not to think about it."

"I like your style," Court said. "Ignore, avoid, and if worst comes to worst...deny, deny, deny."

"That is not..."

"Hey, I am not judging. Look at the fucked up situation I'm in. I should have seen what Jane was doing. I should have known that it was wrong to give her all the money I did to help her with her stupid fucking nightclub. But she...she got me, you know?" Court sighed and looked up again. He looked like the kind of person who had just been forced to look directly at the sun after wearing sunglasses for so long. "I thought I loved her."

"And now, it feels like a lie?"

He nodded once. "It was a lie. Everything she did and said and felt was a lie. Because Jane Devney doesn't even exist. Did you see? Her real name is Janine Lehmann. German-French dual citizen. She's nothing and no one. And she fooled me completely."

I had seen. The news made it clear how much Court Kensington had been duped. Though...they all thought he had been in on it. I didn't see what the benefit was to him, but no one was asking the real questions. They were too interested in the scandal.

"We're all fools for love," I told him.

But I wasn't thinking about Jane or Claire when I said it.

My mind conjured a pair of green eyes and dark red hair.

I'd always been a fool for her.

14

LARK

"I cannot even believe you convinced me to fly out here," English said three days later as she dropped her suitcase in my living room and pulled me into a hug. "You're insane."

I laughed and hugged her back. "I know, but I couldn't imagine anyone else in the world taking on Court Kensington."

"This isn't even the kind of work I do."

"Yes, it is," I said, nudging her.

"Okay, it is. But I'm used to Hollywood. The Upper East Side and politics are their own craziness."

"Which you already know about because you have me."

"Knowing and living it is different," English said. "But...yeah, I mean, I think I could do it."

"I don't just think that you could do it. I *know* you can. That you'd be kick-ass at it. Plus, you were just complaining about your job. How tired you were of all the same stuff. This would be different. More."

"I complained in a *bar* while I was kind of drunk. You can't use that against me." But she was smiling when she said it.

She wouldn't be here if she wasn't actually interested in the job. I'd known she would be. She also had a JD from Columbia, and though she might be the best in the business in LA, I'd known her long enough to know that she wouldn't turn down a better option.

"Before you say anything else, I'm starving," English said. "I texted Whitley on the way in. She said she'd be game for dinner. You think Katherine would be in?"

I frowned. I didn't think Katherine would. I'd called and texted her a few times since she'd run out of the party Saturday night. She'd been her normal, abrasive self. Claiming that she was *fine*. But everyone knew fine didn't actually mean fine.

"She had a falling-out with Camden," I confessed. "She hasn't talked to me since it happened."

A crease formed between her eyebrows. "Why would she be upset about that? I didn't think she even liked her husband."

I bit my lip. "I think...she does. Though don't say anything to her about it. She didn't seem to even want to admit it. And then, I don't know...she was seen with Penn, and Camden said he was going to go back to his side piece. I think it's pretty fucked up."

English rolled her eyes. "Jesus, they're a train wreck."

"Yeah. I'll text her, but it seems unlikely."

"All right. Well, I'm changing out of these airport clothes, and then we can go."

I nodded as I jotted out a text to Katherine.

Fifteen minutes later, when English was ready to go, I still hadn't heard from her. I didn't like that at all. She must be even more messed up than I thought.

A bomb had erupted at the center of my crew, and everything felt off-kilter. Katherine was MIA. Penn had jetted off to Paris. I hadn't heard from Lewis or Rowe at all. I was glad that English was here because, otherwise, I'd be pretty alone.

A short while later, we were settled into a small table at the back of my favorite pizza place on the Upper East. Whitley had complained about how we should have met in the middle, but as soon as she took the first bite, she relented.

"Okay, this is phenomenal," Whitley said.

I nodded. "Yep. I know. They brought the brick ovens over from Italy. Been in the family forever."

"The Family," Whitley asked with a conspiratorial grin. "Like capital F? Italian Mafia?"

"You are such a conspiracy theorist," English said.

"I am not! The Mafia is real."

"I don't think they're in the Mafia," I said with an eye roll.

"Are you sure?" Whitley asked. "Because this could all be a front."

"Well, if they are the Mafia, I'll be sure to sell your virginity to save the Family," I told her.

Her eyes twinkled. "A little late for that, but hey, I'd be down."

English just chuckled as she dug into her pizza. "I'm still just amazed that I'm even here."

"Why?" Whitley asked. "This is where you belong! Who would want to live in LA when they could live in New York City?"

English arched a skeptical eyebrow. "Like...millions of people?"

"Oh, right," she said with a shrug.

"Also, you? For the three years you were at UCLA?"

"Yeah...I sometimes forget about that."

English rolled her eyes, but Whitley continued on, "But hey, I like seasons. New York has all four. When I was growing up in Dallas, they only had two—*fucking kill me* summer and *fucking kill me* winter. LA only has one. No, thanks."

"You're a strange, strange human being, Whitley Bowen."

"Why, thank you," she said, tipping her head at her.

"Well, what does Josh think?" I interjected before we could get further derailed.

"He's totally on board," English said with that dreamy smile she had every time she talked about her husband. "He's spending the summer in London, shooting his next movie. It's this really intense action film, and he's trying to do his own stunts. So, he's super buff right now. He can't eat anything I make at home, but damn, it might even be worth it."

"Pictures, or it didn't happen," Whitley said eagerly.

I swatted at her. "Shut up."

"What? You were thinking it. I just said it."

"Anyway, he said it's only through November. He'll have some time off after they finish filming. He said we could get a place here before he has to go out to promote."

"See, it's perfect," I insisted.

English smiled briefly. A secret smile I'd seen her use one too many times. She wanted this. But she hadn't quite convinced herself yet.

"Maybe...maybe it is perfect."

"Now, you just have to rock that interview."

Whitley wrapped an arm around English's shoulders. "As if there's any doubt our girl is going to blow everyone away! She's a natural."

"Fingers crossed," English said.

For the first time, she actually looked excited about the prospect of being here again with us, doing something more worthwhile than what she'd been doing in LA. And god, I just hoped she really did blow Leslie away. Because selfishly, I needed her here too.

"So, how did it go?" I asked English the next day when she stepped into my office.

"Great!" she gushed. Then her smile faltered. "I mean...I think."

"If you think it went great, then it did. You know you interview well."

"I haven't interviewed like this in years though," English reminded me. "I interview potential clients, but that's different. Gah, if I do this, I'll have to talk to Margery and figure out what to do with my existing clients. Some of them don't need much, and I can manage them remotely. One or two are kind of a nightmare, and I was going to cut them loose anyway. But there are a few who I think want more from me than I would be able to give from here."

"You'll figure it out," I assured her.

"Yeah. I mean...if I get the job anyway."

"If you do, then you know it'll be right."

English nodded. But I could tell she'd gone from rocking confidence to nerves in a matter of seconds.

She just shook her head. "I think I'm going to go grab some lunch. I barely ate today. Do you want anything?"

"I'm good. I had a bagel."

"All day?" she asked skeptically.

"Uh, no, I think I had a few of those sour Life Savers gummies. Have you had them before? They're incredible."

"Seriously?" She sighed heavily. "Maybe *you* need a handler too. That's not enough food for how much you work. I'm going to rummage around in that break room and find you a snack. And then I'll bring you back real food later. Pho sound good?"

"Divine," I admitted, my stomach gurgling on command.

She was gone for a few minutes before returning with an assortment of snack food—peanut butter crackers, a chocolate chip granola bar, and some sort of raspberry fig bar. I tore into the granola bar.

She shrugged. "Not that many options. Good thing *Sam* was there though," she said with raised eyebrows. "He reminded me that you're allergic to strawberries."

A flush suffused my face. "Ah. Well, good. I don't have an EpiPen on me. Try not to kill me before the election is over. Okay, English?"

"Sooo," she said with a look of one who delighted in gossip, "what's going on with him?"

"Girlfriend, remember?"

"Yeah. Ugh! You just seem...okay about each other now. I didn't know if something else had happened."

"We have to work together," I said helplessly. "We're either friends or something like it or we don't make it through the election. The latter isn't an option for me. So...I put it behind me."

"Whatever, liar," English said with a laugh.

"Okay, fine," I grumbled. "When Court was arrested, I had,

like...a panic attack. I called Sam, thinking he could help get Court out of the situation."

"Uh-huh."

"And well, he didn't need to because Leslie had it handled. But then he kind of...took care of me." I shivered at the memory. "Talked me down and took care of some work stuff. Then he walked me back to my apartment. We decided...we were friends."

"Right. I mean, I'd leave my apartment at one in the morning to rescue you, but I've known you for almost a decade. For a coworker?" English made a face that said her colleagues were SOL. "Seems like...there might be more there."

"Are you encouraging or discouraging me?" I asked her. "Because this sounds like encouragement, and I thought you were against him."

"I'm way against this," English confirmed. "Just trying to make you see where your head is really at. Are you and Sam just friends?"

I bit my lip. "We have to be."

English tapped the raspberry fig bar. "All right. I'll leave you to mull over your non-strawberry snacks while I go eat some food."

"I love you." Then I muttered under my breath, "Asshole."

English snorted. As she walked toward the door, she flipped me off. I burst into laughter, watching her ass disappear around the corner. She was the best.

I returned to my work, prepared to get a deep dive into the new field positions we were looking to bring on for the summer to help with outreach leading up to the August primary. Then my office phone buzzed. I pressed the intercom button.

"Lark, I have a call with the mayor on line one," Aspen said.

"Great. I got it."

I lifted the receiver to my ear and pressed the line to Leslie. "Hello, Leslie. It's Lark. How can I help you?"

"Lark, would you mind coming into the conference room for a few minutes? We just finished up the first round of interviews for Court's publicist, and I wanted to go over something with you."

"Of course. I'll be there right away."

Leslie hung up the phone, and I hastily stuffed the rest of the granola bar in my mouth as I stood to go meet her. I wondered what this was about. I didn't normally talk to her about hiring. In fact, Kelly from HR usually did most of the hiring. The fact that Leslie was involved at all meant that she was taking Court's situation seriously.

I brushed a crumb off of my black skirt and pulled on my matching blazer before heading down the hallway to the conference room where Leslie and Kelly were holding interviews. But when I stepped inside, Leslie was all alone, staring down at what appeared to be three résumés.

"Shut the door, would you?" Leslie asked.

I did as she'd instructed and then stepped up to the table. "How did the interviews go?"

"Surprisingly well," Leslie said. She rubbed her forehead. "I wish I didn't have to sacrifice an afternoon for this. I really need to be at City Hall right now. Which means I have to make this decision today."

"Of course. Your time is important."

"It is," she agreed. She smiled kindly at me. "I want to hire Anna."

"She'd be wonderful for the job," I said, beaming.

"She would. But have you met my son?" Leslie asked with a raised eyebrow.

"Of...of course."

"She's too pretty."

I guffawed at the explanation. I hadn't been expecting that. "What?"

"Court is a known womanizer. She's gorgeous. She looks like a supermodel. And he'll eat her for breakfast."

I shook my head, barely suppressing a laugh. "There is no way. For one, English...uh, Anna is a complete professional. She didn't get into this business to sleep with her clients. And two, she's married."

Leslie waved her hand. "That doesn't matter."

"She's married to Josh Hutch," I finished.

Her mouth popped open. Now, I'd surprised her. "The movie star? He's talented."

"He is," I agreed. "He's also probably the most-sought-after man in Hollywood. I don't think English has any interest in another man when she has *that* to go home to."

"I really enjoyed his latest Bourne remake," Leslie admitted. "He's a sight. That's for sure."

"She is immune to Court's charm. Just...give her a trial run. Let me go with her and see how she handles Court. I can report back, and you know that I'll always be honest with you."

"You will," Leslie conceded. "You've never failed me."

"If you think she's the most qualified, then I think it'd be worth it."

Leslie nodded. "Okay. We'll start with a trial this weekend. If Court doesn't manage to seduce her"—she rolled her eyes skyward—"then she has the job."

15

LARK

"A trial run?" English groaned later as we took a cab north.

"I know. I knew you wouldn't be happy about that."

"It just...doesn't make any sense. I have the credentials. I've been doing this for years. I'm at the top of my game. Why wouldn't she want me?"

I'd been debating on telling English what Leslie had said. I still didn't know if I should. Leslie had called English back into the conference room and offered her a trial to see how she worked with Court. Of course, she'd acted like she was thrilled for the opportunity. Until she got in the cab and was allowed to be frustrated by it.

"Like, what's the deal? Does she want someone with more experience with all you Upper East Siders?"

I sighed. She wasn't going to let it go.

"No, it has nothing to do with you and everything to do with Court."

"Please, I've dealt with plenty of entitled assholes."

"No...it's more that...you're beautiful."

Her eyebrows rose. "So?"

"She thinks he's going to try to seduce you."

"Oh, gross. Who would ever hook up with their client? You

know everything about them, and they do so much disgusting behavior. You're the one who has to clean up after them and make sure no one finds out about the strippers and the cocaine and the gambling." She crinkled her nose. "There is *no* way."

"Yeah, but Court is hot and charming. It's how it goes."

English held up her hand. "I have both of those things back home. Court might be hot and charming, but it's not going to work on *me*."

"That's what I told Leslie."

"All right, all right. Trial run it is then." English pushed her shoulders back and put on her game face. "We can conquer this. It'll be fine."

"I love how you really want this job now."

She shot me a cutting look. "I like a challenge."

"Well, Court should be that at least," I said as we pulled up in front of his building on the Upper East.

We hopped out of the car and passed a surprising number of paparazzi who were still camped out in front of his place. I would have thought they'd be gone by now. But I guessed putting him under house arrest was making his picture more valuable. No one had seen him since the night coming out of the police station. And everyone wanted to hear his side. Not just his mother's canned answer. They were probably all expecting him to come out drunk and rant about what had actually happened. God, he needed English.

We took the elevator up to the penthouse. I glanced at English to get her reaction to his insane apartment. But she was all business. She might gush over my place, which wasn't even this nice, but not here. Not when she had a job to do. She was a total babe when she got serious.

Court was sprawled out across the couch with a bottle of gin and a tome cracked open to the middle. He glanced over at us when we came in and then returned to the book. "I have to finish this chapter."

My eyes widened. I'd never seen Court Kensington with a book in his hand. I'd thought the only things he cared about were girls, alcohol, drugs, and having as much illicit fun with those things as possible.

English just crossed her arms and assessed the room. I saw what she saw. The maid must not have been here this week. Another precaution, but it made his living situation look like even more of a mess. There were empty beer bottles, a few wine bottles, and a half-dozen liquor bottles lining the kitchen counter and the bar. It appeared the only thing he'd done all week was get shit-faced. Typical.

Eventually, he stuffed a receipt into the book and shut it. I could see that it was a fantasy novel—*The Shadow Rising* by Robert Jordan. He rose to his feet and ran a hand through his mussed, dark hair. At least he was dressed decently in slightly rumpled khakis and a button-up that he'd rolled to his elbows. It almost looked like he'd thought about leaving earlier and changed his mind. Maybe he was too drunk.

"Larkin St. Vincent and the illustrious Anna English," he said with a charming smile. "What can I do for you two? A drink? I have...gin." He reached down and grabbed the bottle off the table. "I probably have olives. Martinis?"

"No, thank you," I said. "That's not why we're here."

"Ah, right. You're here for Mommy dearest," he said, stepping into the kitchen.

We stepped farther into his apartment. I could see him making another drink. From my perspective, it looked like straight gin. Maybe a hint of olive juice. No olives.

"We're here because English has been hired to work as your publicist. She's going to be handling the aftermath of your arrest and what that entails for the campaign through November," I explained.

He walked back into the living room. He didn't stumble or slur. His tolerance was too high for that. But I could see he was teetering on a precipice, and any minute, he might fall off of it into oblivion.

But he glanced at English. He looked her up and down with a flick of his eyes. And then a dangerous smile crossed his face.

"So, you'd work for me?" he asked English.

"Incorrect," English said. "I would be an employee of your mother. I would report to her."

He stepped closer. A wave of charisma seemed to wrap around him. Or perhaps that was just the gin. "And would you have to tell her *everything*?"

She narrowed her eyes at him. "No. That's not how my business relationships work. I am hired to fix problems. You are a problem. So, we'll spend the next couple months trying to *fix* you."

"That's not exactly what I had in mind," he said, sipping on his martini.

"Court," I groaned. "It's not a romantic relationship. It's business."

He waved his hand at me. "Sure thing. You know all about keeping business and personal separate."

His eyes met mine with a gleam that said he knew exactly what was going on with me and Sam. My cheeks flushed. God, I was *not* letting a Kensington get under my skin.

But before I could respond, English stepped forward. "Look, this is how it is. You need me," she told him—straightforward, no bullshit. "You need me more than you even know. Because right now, I'm staring at a husk of a man. One who was brought to his knees by a liar and a fraud. And I don't know if you knew what she did or not. I'm not here for answers. I'm not here to babysit you. I'm here to make people believe that you've turned over a new leaf, that you want to repent for your actions, and make you the fucking golden boy of the Upper East Side."

Court snorted. "Good luck with that."

She took another step toward him. She looked fierce as hell. "*That* is what I'm good at. And it's what I'm going to do for you. You're going to stop trying to think we'll sleep together because that is *never*, ever going to happen. You're a client. That's it." She shrugged nonchalantly. "You have two options: you can put your drink down and listen to how I'm going to turn your life around, or you can stay in this apartment until you drink yourself to death. It wouldn't be the first time I've seen it."

She crossed her arms and waited.

"Maybe I'd like the latter," he said. But something had shaken loose. He didn't have the same rich-boy confidence when he spoke.

"No, you wouldn't."

"Don't you think this is all just going to blow over anyway?"

English held her hands out. "That's what I do for a living. I make these things blow over. I make them go away before they even hit the press. And you're going to need someone to do that. Because the arrest might disappear after a week or two. The charges might not have ever been filed against you. But what about when Jane goes to trial?"

He winced at those words.

"What about when her face is in every newspaper in the country for fraud? What if they publish a book about her? What if they make her crimes into a blockbuster movie? You think you're just going to disappear through all of that? Especially if you're still the bad-boy prince, drunk and high and fucking anyone who will sell your pictures or sex tapes to the tabloids?"

Court frowned. Even I frowned. I hadn't thought that far ahead. My life was to think about the campaign and how this would affect us through November. English was thinking long-term. Past the election. To how all of this would go down in the press. And it looked bloody from my perspective.

"Do you want to be the sympathetic ex or the accomplice?" English asked. "Because how we react and shape the narrative determines how Hollywood portrays you years down the road."

"Fine," Court spat. "Whatever."

"Good," English said with a satisfied grin. "I thought so. We'll start in the morning."

Court laughed and downed his drink. "I don't wake up before noon."

English seemed undeterred. "Noon it is. Most creatives I work with aren't morning people anyway. Plus, I'm still on West Coast time."

"Are we finished?" Court asked. "I'd like to go back to getting shit-faced. Thanks."

I frowned at him. He was such a mess. Jane's betrayal had really fucked him up. I knew that English would help. That she was the best at this and she'd get him back on track. But right now, I actually...pitied him. I wished there were more that I could do. But I could see that he just wanted us to leave.

"Thanks for hearing us out," I said.

Court waved me off, and I followed English to the elevator. We were silent as we headed back to the ground floor. I could see that the wheels were working in English's head. That she wanted to get back to the apartment right away, so she could get started with all of her ideas. I just wanted to give Court a hug and ask how he'd gone such a different direction than his brother. Sometimes, it amazed me that they were related.

The elevator opened on the bottom floor, and I nearly walked right into the person trying to enter before we were out.

I stopped in surprise. "Sam?"

He glanced up, and I could see that something was off about him. His hair was standing on end as if he'd been pulling it. His eyes looked lost. His shoulders were slumped forward. I didn't know if I'd ever seen him look like that.

He frowned when he saw me and English. "Hey." Then he stepped back to let us pass and entered the elevator.

"Going to see Court?"

"Yep," he said tersely.

"Try to get him sober for us?"

He shook his head and shrugged. "Court does what he wants."

I tilted my head in confusion. What was his deal?

"Are you done?" he asked, nodding toward where I was still holding the door open. I hadn't even realized.

"Uh, yeah. Are you okay?"

"Fine. Just a long week."

"Oh...okay."

Then the elevator door slowly closed in my face.

"Well, that was...something," English said, sounding pissed.

"Yeah, something."

"He was a total ass. I thought you'd said you two were friends."

"I thought so too," I said, stepping away from the elevator and following her toward the exit.

"See, this is what I'm saying," English said. "You need to let Sam stay in the past. He's a colleague and nothing more. All he does is make you miserable, guessing at his reactions."

"I suppose."

"One minute, he's all concerned about your strawberry allergy, and the next, he's all but pushing you out of the elevator to get away from you. You can do better."

Everyone kept saying that.

And still, I hadn't found anyone. Wasn't sure I ever would.

16

SAM

"I think that's everything," Claire said from the bedroom.

I set down the carving knife on the table. I'd been whittling a piece of wood all week. It still looked indistinct to the casual observer, but I knew it was being shaped into a small, bushy owl. It just took time to get there.

"You're finished packing?" I asked.

"Yeah." She tipped her suitcase up onto its wheels and rolled it into the living room. "Nothing like waiting until the last minute, huh?"

"You have everything in that one suitcase?"

This from the same girl who couldn't go to visit her parents without a giant suitcase filled with shoes.

She shrugged. "I figure I'll mostly be wearing work clothes. And the director said that we'll do laundry while we're there, so we don't need as much as if we were on vacation."

"I still can't believe you're leaving for twelve weeks." I stood and stretched out my shoulders. "I feel like you auditioned for this so long ago that it just might never happen."

She laughed softly, but the smile didn't reach her eyes. She'd been...weird all week. Distant. As if preparing herself to leave for Europe for twelve long weeks.

"Yeah. I can't believe it's here either," she said.

"I wish I could go with you," I told her. Even though it wasn't true.

I wanted to go to Europe again. I'd backpacked with my brother the summer after college for a month, sleeping in hostels and living off of scraps. That had been a different time. Now, I couldn't even think of Jake.

The truth was, I didn't want to leave my job. I'd liked what I'd been doing back in North Carolina, and then the firm here had been...fine. But campaign work. It was a whole other beast. And I wasn't prepared to give it up to follow Claire around with her ensemble. I'd already moved to New York for her. And now, she was leaving again.

"Me too," she said a minute later.

"It's going to be so strange, being here without you."

She nodded and then looked away from me. "I kind of, um... wanted to talk to you about that."

"About what?" I asked warily.

This wasn't normal Claire behavior. She didn't try to hide herself from me. She had no amount of subterfuge in her body. It was part of what had drawn me to her. She wasn't like girls I'd dated before her. It was simple and uncomplicated. Something casual that had turned into more without interference or objection. It was what I'd wanted after Melissa.

But now...she didn't seem like the Claire I knew at all.

"Well, I'm going to be gone for three months. I've never been to Europe before. It's a once-in-a-lifetime opportunity here. And I, uh...just think that maybe we should, um, take-some-time-apart," she said in a rush.

I froze at her nearly indistinguishable words. She'd slurred them together so fast that I almost convinced myself that I hadn't heard her right. "Wait...what?"

"I'm just going to be so busy, Sam," Claire all but whispered. "I'll...I'll hold you back. I won't be there for you. Not like you deserve."

"Are you breaking up with me?" I asked more harshly than I'd intended.

"No!" she gushed. Then she bit her baby-pink-lip-gloss-coated lip. "Maybe. I don't know."

"You don't know," I repeated.

"I just think we need a break."

"I know what a break means, Claire," I growled at her. "It means, this is over."

"That's not what I mean," she said in earnest.

I almost believed her.

"I just...I just want to give you the space you need. I'm going to be gone. We can decide what we're doing when I get back."

"So...a breakup," I said, taking a step away from her in shock and horror. "So that you can go date other people."

"It's not like that," she said. Tears came to her eyes. "That's not what this is at all. I just think we need space to figure out what's best for each other. And we're already going to be apart. This is the time we should take."

"*You* need the time," I spat at her. "You never even asked me what I wanted. You already made up your mind."

"Maybe I did," she said through her sniffles. "We've been together for over two years, Sam. Where are we going? Do you want to spend the rest of your life with me? Do you want to marry me?"

I hesitated. Did people *know* these things? Was I supposed to?

Claire sighed, swiping at her eyes. "That's what I thought. That's the whole point. You don't know. I don't know. And I think we should at this point."

"So, this is it? You're breaking up with me because I won't... marry you?" I asked in confusion.

She covered her eyes and shook her head. "That's not it at all. I don't even know if this is a breakup. I just think...we should figure out while I'm gone if this is what we really want. It's just...space."

"Fine," I spat. I brushed past her and headed into the bedroom. I grabbed a backpack out of the closet, stuffed work clothes in it, and then slung it over my back.

"What are you doing?" she gasped.

"You think I'm going to stay here another minute?"

"Sam!"

I just kept walking. She was the one who wanted this. She had to know there were consequences to her actions. It wasn't all just *fine* because she wanted it to be.

"Please," she said, tugging on my arm. "It's my last night. You're just going to leave?"

"Yes."

"But...please, please stay. I have to go to the airport in the morning."

I pulled my arm free and met her gaze. "This is what you want, Claire. I'm just respecting your wishes. Here's your *break*."

Tears fell freely from her eyes again. She choked on them and buried her face in her hands. And I sympathized with her. I didn't like to see her cry. But she'd chosen this. I wasn't going to stick around and wait for her to walk out of my life.

"Have fun in Europe," I muttered as I yanked the door open and strode out of the apartment.

I had nowhere to go. I could probably get a hotel somewhere nearby, but I was too on edge to do that. Plus, I didn't really want to waste the money. Who even knew what the living situation would be like after this? Would Claire pay for her half of the rent? Was I on the hook for the whole thing?

"Fuck," I spat into the black night sky.

I pulled out my phone. My first thought was to text Lark. It'd be so easy to rush over there and tell her Claire had left. To stay with her. To rebound so hard that we'd both miss work the next morning.

I blinked away that daydream. Because Lark didn't deserve that. I didn't know what I wanted. But casually fucking my boss probably wasn't the answer.

I ran a hand across my face and then sent a text to Court.

Remember how my girlfriend was leaving for Europe in the morning?
Well, she just dumped me. Any chance you have a free guest room?

It felt too soon to ask Court for something like that. Plus, he was dealing with so much shit himself. But he was the only friend I had in the city.

His response came almost immediately.

Fuck, man. I have liquor. Come on over.

I sighed with a semblance of relief as I trotted into the subway and headed back into town. It took a half hour to get to Court's place. I spent the entire time ignoring Claire's ever-increasingly desperate text messages and tugging on my hair at the root. I was physically and mentally exhausted. And irritated. And I felt like I wanted to put my fist through something.

None of these were good feelings to have and then talk to Claire. Especially about our supposed "break." Everyone knew that was just code so that she could go and fuck other dudes in Europe. It had nothing to do with anything else. And I couldn't deal with it. I didn't want to deal with any of it.

I just wanted to get to Court's place and get fucked up with him. Misery loved company.

I slipped past the lingering reporters and pressed the button for Court's penthouse elevator. Finally, the thing dinged open. I stepped toward it, only to find two people standing in the elevator.

I froze with a frown on my face. The very last person I wanted to see right now was there. I couldn't deal with that complication at the moment.

"Hey," I forced out, stepping back to let them get out of the elevator.

"Going to see Court?" she asked with pep in her voice.

"Yep." I darted into the elevator.

"Try to get him sober for us?" She smiled brightly at me.

And I just did a combination of shaking my head and shrugging. Court sober was the opposite of what I wanted right now. I just wanted oblivion.

"Court does what he wants."

She looked at me like I had just stepped on a land mine and it might explode any second.

I nodded at her hand still holding the door open. "Are you done?"

Because, god, I needed this to be over.

"Uh, yeah. Are you okay?" Her voice was laced with concern. I couldn't handle it.

"Fine," I said, jamming the up button. "Just a long week."

"Oh...okay."

Then mercifully, the elevator door closed in her face. I slumped back against the metal container, feeling like a total fucking jackass. Lark probably thought I was crazy. But right now, it was hard to care. Hard to care about anything.

My girlfriend of two years had just dumped me. Something I'd never dreamed would happen. Claire had been so...dependable. But here I was, being forced to face reality. I'd moved to New York for a girl who was taking off at the first opportunity. Now, I had to stay until November, and I had no idea what I wanted anymore.

PART III

THE HIGH ROAD

17

LARK

The campaign office finally quieted down over the next couple of weeks.

English had officially taken the position to work with Court and moved into my guest bedroom for the time being. She spent most of her time dealing with Court, but having her in town was infinitely better than having her clear across the country.

The city was in flux as well. By Memorial Day weekend, the city had emptied of my friends and family as everyone migrated to the Hamptons or Paris for the season. While I was stuck here with the tourists. It was one thing I missed about my old life—getting to jet off to exotic locales whenever I liked. I was basically stuck in the city until November.

Stuck here, dealing with Sam being...strange.

I'd confronted him after how he acted at Court's apartment, but he'd just smiled and shrugged it off. As if nothing out of the ordinary had happened. If English hadn't been there, I would have thought I'd made the whole thing up.

Even though I knew that I hadn't. I couldn't possibly have invented the way he had been acting toward me since that night.

I wouldn't say he had been avoiding me at work because it seemed impossible. The office was too small for that. We had to see each other. My job was to work with all of the head of departments, which meant I worked with Gibbs from legal. Not that it had stopped Sam and I from talking before. But suddenly, all my communication went through Gibbs alone. As if Sam could no longer contact me at all. I'd even asked Gibbs if he'd tightened the reins on intra-office communication.

Negative.

It was just Sam.

"Lark!" Demi said, sashaying past Aspen's desk to enter my office. "I know you normally stay another couple hours. But one, it's Memorial Day. So, we shouldn't even be working at all. And two, a new bar just opened down the street. Which means we must emancipate you from this square box and take you out for drinks."

She had clearly come prepared with a speech. She thought she had to convince me. But the truth was that after what had happened with Court, my life had been hell. I needed to take a few hours off early today. I should have cajoled Shawn into giving everyone today off. Though...he'd claimed we'd have a day off soon—probably the day after the Fourth of July.

"Come on," Demi groaned. "Shawn already left to deal with some field issue. Please tell me you'll come. We're dying to get you out of here."

"All right, I'm in."

"Really?" she gasped.

"Yeah. We should have taken today off anyway."

"Oh my god, I'm so excited. Let me tell Aspen. She's going to flip."

I laughed and nodded. "Who else is coming? I think I'll tell everyone to take the rest of the day off."

"You're the best!" She stepped out of my office and up to Aspen's desk. "The rest of the day off!"

Aspen slapped her hand in a loud high five. I just shook my head and closed everything up. My head hurt, and I needed to get out of here. Even if I would have preferred to head home and chill with English, this was good for my team.

Especially since word was stewing that the mayor might get a primary challenge. It wasn't uncommon for some nobody to enter against the incumbent, just hoping to get their name out there. But after Court's debacle, I feared that someone from her own party would try to make a splash and actually attempt to get the nomination. And I feared even more that they might have a chance.

I didn't want to think about it. Instead, I walked around the office and told everyone to go home. We were done for the day.

I told myself that I wasn't purposely leaving Sam's office for last. But...

"Hey," I said, peeking my head inside.

His office looked like a bomb had just gone off in it. I'd shared an office with Sam for months before I needed my own, and he'd been meticulously tidy. This was...crazy.

He glanced up once and then returned his gaze to his computer. "Hey. Can I help you?"

"Actually, we're done for the day. Memorial Day and all."

"Oh."

"Also, some of us are checking out a bar that just opened. Any interest in heading over with us?"

He shook his head. "I really can't. I'm so bogged down here."

I could see that he was. "Oh, okay. You know, it's crazy for *me* to say this, but it's all going to be there in the morning."

"Yeah," he said. His face was grave. "I just want to get ahead. See if I can get through this paperwork. You know how it is."

"Sure." I ran a hand back through my unruly red hair, trying to tame it into a ponytail. "Well, if you change your mind, text me."

"Okay. Have fun." But he didn't look up when he said it.

And I was pretty sure he wasn't leaving.

"You ready?" Demi asked as I left Sam's office behind.

"Yeah," I said, trying for cheer.

"Great. Let's go, girlfriend."

Then I followed them out, trying to wrap my head around what had just happened in Sam's office.

It was another week later before I ventured back into Sam's office. The announcement had just come through. Ronald Reyes, the owner of one of the biggest tech conglomerates, had just announced that he was going to challenge Leslie in the mayoral primary.

I was sick about it. Even though we'd guessed that it was coming, it was harder to hear it. Even harder to know that he looked like a favorable candidate. He had a fortune to rival the Kensington name. He was a rather attractive Hispanic man in his early fifties and still happily married to his wife of almost thirty years. As far as we knew, he didn't have any scandals or children who were going to try to ruin his campaign.

But if he did, we'd find it. We had opposition researchers for a reason.

I had one hand on my aching stomach when I knocked on Sam's door. I'd felt sick all day once the news broke. I'd taken medicine, and nothing helped. The stress was gnawing at me.

"Come in," Sam called.

I stepped into the office. I knew I was pale and shaky. I was determined that we'd still win this, but the first wave of anxiety never suited me.

He glanced up at me and then frowned. "Hey, are you all right?"

"Uh, you know, just the announcement about Reyes."

"Yeah. That's shitty. But we'll get through it."

I nodded, trying to find relief in his words. It was the first thing we'd said to each other that wasn't stilted in weeks.

"You're probably right. I think I just need to get out of the office. English said she'd meet me for lunch. Any interest?"

He opened his mouth as if he was going to say yes and then shook his head. As if his brain and body were out of alignment.

"I think I'm needed here," he said. "Plus, I brought a lunch."

"Oh."

Another rejection. Even worse than when he hadn't wanted to go out for drinks last week. I'd thought we were friends. Friends did these sorts of things. We had normal conversations. We got lunch together. Had something changed?

"Next time," he assured me.

But I didn't believe him. I didn't think he had any intention of going out with me again.

"Okay...yeah, next time."

I waved good-bye and then left the office, meeting English at a seafood place that boasted the best scallops in the city.

"No Sam?" she asked as we were seated against the window looking out onto the New York City street.

"Nope. He wanted to stay and work."

"So...do you think he's purposely brushing you off? Do you think this has something to do with Claire?"

"Could be. Maybe she found out we'd dated in the past?" I suggested. "I mean...I don't know how she'd find out unless he told her. And it didn't seem like he was interested in letting her know about that."

"Yeah. If he wasn't up-front with her about it before the banquet, then I can't see him bringing it up now."

I shrugged, at a loss. "Maybe all that stuff about being friends was bullshit. He could have decided I wasn't worth the hassle."

English rolled her eyes. "What I think is that you need to get *over* Sam. Get over him, Lark." She said it as if it were that easy. "Who are you bringing to Court's charity event? It's coming up, and you need a date."

I frowned. "I wasn't planning on bringing a date. I thought we were just all going together to support Court and his donation."

"Katherine and Camden have both confirmed they're coming."

"Which is strange since they're not even *living* together right now," I grumbled. "I can't believe that douche made her move out."

English sighed. "Yeah. That's...out of my wheel house. I fix people who want—or at least, desperately need—to be fixed. They're so far gone. I don't know what will put them together."

"Yeah. It's sad."

"It is. But they'll be there. I guess they're trying to keep up appearances. Whitley said she's bringing a plus-one but hasn't narrowed it down between her three choices yet."

"Typical."

"Gavin said he's bringing a date." She pulled her phone up and scrolled through a list of names. "Charlotte Warren. Why does that sound familiar?"

I guffawed. "You remember my friend Lewis? He's part of my high school crew?"

English nodded. "Sure. I've met him before. Tall, super-hot, black guy? Impeccable taste in suits?"

"That's him," I said with a laugh. "Well, Charlotte is his *much* younger sister. She's a model for Elizabeth Cunningham and a junior at Harvard. She must be back for the summer."

"Is she...a problem?"

"No, she's actually wonderful. Though I hear she plays the field."

English shrugged, unconcerned. "That's fine. As long as she can handle herself."

"Oh, she can," I assured her.

"Great. So, you need a date." English switched to another list and passed it toward me. "I'm not saying that I made a list of eligible bachelors in the city, but..."

I snatched the phone up and scrolled through the list of guys she'd put together for me. It wasn't just names either. It included photos, current job, hobbies, and even, in some cases...net worth.

"How the hell did you get this information?"

She winked at me. "It's part of my job. Now, look at this guy..."

"No way. I already went through this with my parents. I don't want to date a guy that someone else picks out for me. I don't want to blind-date anyone. I want no part of it. I am *too* busy to take anyone serious right now. It would just end so poorly."

"I thought you might say that. So, I took the liberty of inviting them all. That way, you can mingle and meet them as you go. And then you can decide if you like any of them!"

I rolled my eyes to the ceiling. "You're as bad as my mother. You know that, right?"

"Honey, Hope St. Vincent has got nothing on me."

I snorted and then raised my hand for a waiter, done with this conversation. Having a bunch of eligible bachelors waiting to meet me sounded like a dream. Except that it was really a nightmare. One I already wanted to wake up from.

18

SAM

I hadn't seen Lark since she invited me to lunch. Almost as if... she was purposely avoiding me. Well, I'd been avoiding her. So, maybe it was Karma.

The problem was, I didn't know how to tell her about Claire.

Not just her. Anyone.

I'd told Court. And that was only because I'd been desperate and pissed off and needed someone with no judgments to get shit-faced with me. It had worked until I'd walked into work the next day, hungover as fuck and irritable.

But I hadn't told anyone else.

Not my parents, who loved Claire but hated that she'd moved me eight hours north.

Not my new friends at work.

Certainly not Lark.

At first, I hadn't wanted it to be true. I'd moved for Claire. I'd sacrificed for her. I'd wanted it to work. Just not enough to *propose* when she wanted me to.

Then I'd stupidly tried to convince myself that maybe it *was* just a break. She really *did* just need space. Which meant... we were still together. We were still dating but without having to talk all the time. She'd come back in twelve weeks, and we'd work it out. Things might not be fine now, but they'd get there.

Denial.

Straight into anger.

Anger at Claire mostly. For leaving me like that. For waiting until the last possible second to tell me how she had been feeling. For moving me here and then leaving.

It didn't matter that she had been *right*. That I hadn't been into it...us...her. That a certain redhead had started taking up residence in my brain again. That I'd wanted to be at work instead of with Claire at home. That I loved New York City and my new job despite all its problems.

And now...I was pushing Lark away.

There were a million reasons to do it. But none of them felt sufficient when I saw her disappointed face as I brushed her off for lunch...again.

Fuck, I was going to have to tell her.

We were friends. Or we had at least been working toward that before I completely cut her and everyone but Court out of my life. And friends...shared information about their relationships. They explained why they had been acting like a douche for three weeks.

I was not looking forward to this.

Not a bit.

But I drafted the email anyway.

Lark,

I didn't bring my lunch today. Any interest in going to Buns? I'd kill for a burger right now.

Best,
    Sam

I hovered over the Send button. What could go wrong? Aside from everything?

I pressed Enter.

I didn't know why I expected an immediate answer. When we'd previously had email conversations, she had been almost instantaneous in her responses. But a half hour passed and then another, and still, I heard nothing.

I was halfway out of my chair to go to her damn office and demand an answer when it finally came.

Sam,

A burger sounds nice. Meet in twenty?

—Lark

Good. That was easier than demanding she go to lunch with me. Even if I knew that her hesitancy held weighted meaning.

Twenty minutes later, almost exactly on the dot, Lark was waiting at the front of the office. She stared down at her cell phone, ignoring me and the rest of the world. I could tell by the set of her shoulders that she had likely almost talked herself out of coming.

"Hey," I said, striding toward her.

She glanced up from her phone. "Oh good. Are you ready to go?"

"Sure. You still want Buns?"

She typed away on her phone, pressed a button, and then shoved it in her bag. "Yeah. I'm always game for burgers."

"Great. Me too."

We stepped out of the office and into the busy New York afternoon. She brushed her long red hair off of her shoulders and cursed as she dug around in her bag.

"Ugh, I don't think I have a hair tie. Why is it so hot already?"

"Because it's the beginning of June."

She sighed. "Yeah. And it's just the start of this." She fidgeted as we crossed the street. "If I wasn't on campaign, I'd be lounging at the Hamptons right now."

"Such a hard life."

"I chose the hard life."

"Why did you do it?" I asked curiously. "I know you said you didn't like working for your parents, but you don't even *need* to work, right? Definitely not a hundred-plus-hour weeks. When we were in Madison, you said you did it because you wanted to try to be someone else. But you're not here. You're still Larkin St. Vincent while working the campaign job."

"You can't escape who you are," she told me. "But you shouldn't ignore who you want to become either."

"Insightful."

She smiled hesitantly up at me. "After what happened with us...and the person I was at the end of our relationship, I decided I didn't want to be that person anymore." She laughed softly. "I gave her a name actually—Bad Lark."

I raised an eyebrow. "Bad Lark? Really?"

She nodded. "She's the person I was before I gave up the Upper East Side persona. When I decided that I couldn't be the person I was if I wanted to be the person I was meant to become."

"Well, I guess I'm glad to meet Good Lark. Is that what you call yourself?"

She shook her head and nudged me. "No. Don't be silly. Bad Lark is who I was before. Now, I'm just Lark. So, while I might like to be in the Hamptons, relaxing with a drink in hand—who wouldn't, right?—I want to elect Leslie more."

I held the door open for Lark as we entered Buns and put in our order. I thought about all she'd said and how it aligned with what I'd seen of her the last couple of weeks that we'd been working together. I'd spent so long blaming her for what she'd done in the past that I hadn't seen until just then how much she'd changed. Purposely changed to get beyond the person she'd been at the time. The person I'd thought she'd been with me all along. But now, she wasn't pretending. There was nothing nefarious about our interactions. She was just...Lark.

I grabbed my burger and sank into our booth in the back corner. She grabbed the seat across from me and dug into her fries.

"God, these are so good," she groaned. "Greasy and delicious."

"The best."

"You know, I'm surprised that you wanted to get lunch," she said, peering up into my eyes. "I thought you were avoiding me."

"Oh. I mean, I wasn't avoiding you." *Lie.* "I've just been busy."

"I'm the queen of busy, but things have been weird. I thought we were friends, then we weren't and now, we are?" she asked tentatively, hopefully.

"Yes," I said automatically. "We're friends."

"And you're going to stop avoiding me? Because it's kind of awkward at the office."

"I am," I agreed.

I had to tell her. Jesus, I needed to tell her.

"Okay," she said slowly. "And you're coming to Court's charity thing, right?"

"Yes. He told me to get a tuxedo, and so I'm renting one."

"Wait," she asked with wide eyes, "you're *renting* a tuxedo."

I shrugged. "What else am I supposed to do?"

She shook her head. "I'll figure it out. You'll probably have to go get measured this afternoon if we're going to get it in time."

"Are you making me Upper East Side?" I asked with an arched eyebrow.

"You're going to one of our events. I wouldn't do this if it was a work thing. But you'll want to blend in."

"Is it really that different for guys?"

Her eyes widened again. "If you have to ask that question, then you'll definitely need my help."

I laughed and conceded. "Fine. Tell me where to go, and I'll get measured for a tux."

"Great. English can thank me later. Oh, also, are you coming in the limo?"

"Court mentioned something about a limo. I didn't ask questions."

She rolled her eyes. "Guys. Okay, look, just meet at my place, and you can get the pick-up with me." She froze as the words left her mouth. "I mean...unless you want to go to Court's place. Or if you're...bringing someone."

She didn't say Claire's name. But we both knew that was what she meant.

It was my opening. It was the moment that I should say something.

But what could I even say? *Claire and I broke up, and I didn't want to tell you because I didn't want you to be a rebound?* Was that presumptuous? What if she didn't even want that to happen?

Fuck. I'd thought this would be difficult...but not impossible.

Especially with her gorgeous green eyes staring up at me with questions dancing in her irises. If I told her now, it would make the whole event awkward. We were just *finally* on solid ground in our friendship. Just finally putting the past behind us at work. Able to have a nice, normal lunch together like colleagues.

And if I told her, I'd ruin this all in some way. If wanting more...would ruin everything. I didn't even know if it was arrogant to think she even wanted something back.

Fuck.

"Uh...no, no one is coming with me."

"Oh. Okay," she said.

"And meeting at your place sounds great."

"Great. I'll get you directions for the suit and find out what time the limo will show up."

"That sounds good."

She smiled up at me, and I released the tension from my shoulders. I'd tell her after the event. No matter what, I'd tell her. I couldn't keep it secret forever. And I didn't even want to. But just not yet. When I knew whether or not this was even something she was interested in again...then I'd tell her.

19

LARK

There was a knock on the door.

I froze from my pacing, checked my reflection in the mirror one more time, and then hastened to open it. I reminded myself for the hundredth time today that this wasn't a date. There was no risk to my heart. It was just friends getting together to support another friend.

Then I opened the door.

And saw Sam standing in the doorframe in a tailored tuxedo. My mouth went suddenly dry. Cognizant thought fled my brain. I just stared at him.

There was a reason designer clothing was so expensive. It just molded to the body in a way nothing else could. It was the details. The hand-sewn glossy buttons, the shape of those broad shoulders, the silk bow tie. It was everything and nothing. It was the suit that looked so spectacular on him. And also...just Sam. The swipe of his dark hair and easy smile. Something in his eyes that said he'd eat me for dinner and again for breakfast if I was lucky.

"Wow," he breathed, seemingly unconscious of my blatant ogle.

"Wow is right," I agreed softly.

"You look beautiful."

"Oh." He must have been doing the same thing to me. "Thank you."

I adjusted the fit of my dark blue silk ballgown. I'd been eating like shit at work, and the gown was just a touch tight on the hips. But it fit like a glove otherwise and made me look like I actually had cleavage. Which was...a total deception.

"You look great too. Tom Ford never does me wrong," I said with a small smile.

He shook his head. "I still can't believe you got me this tux. It was like the cost of rent for the month."

Oh, right. I'd forgotten about that sort of thing. I didn't dip into my trust fund all that often, but I knew it was a privilege that I didn't have to worry, even when things got tight. I hadn't thought twice about helping Sam out for the event.

"Don't mention it," I said with a wave of my hand. "It looks too good anyway."

"You know, I always wondered how celebrities pulled off the staggering confidence and effortless good looks. But I kind of get it in this suit. It changes something."

I grinned. "I know just what you mean. However, I think you had that before the tux."

Our eyes met, and for a second, I thought maybe I'd said too much. That it was going to get uncomfortable and he was going to step back. But he didn't.

I needed to keep reminding myself that he had a girlfriend. I'd met her. She was nice. I didn't know why she wasn't here with him tonight, but I wasn't going to second-guess it. I would enjoy the evening regardless.

"Shall we?" I asked. "The limo should be here soon."

"Yes. Let's."

I grabbed my black clutch and then followed Sam back toward the elevators. We took it down to the first floor. By the time we made it across the foyer, the limo appeared.

The driver came around to open the door for us.

"After you," Sam said.

I peered into the limo with a smile to see so many of my

friends here all at once. That not everyone had disappeared off to the Hamptons. I sank into the seat next to English and Whitley in the back while Sam ducked in and took the seat against the long bench next to Court and Gavin.

"Hey, babe," English said.

"Hey."

Whitley winked at me. "You look hot."

She'd already dyed over her pink ombre so that the whole thing was a medium blonde with highlights that suggested she was going to try to get to English's platinum color.

I laughed. "Thanks. So do you."

She brushed her shoulder off. "Obvs. You remember my date, Keri, from Sparks?"

I glanced at the girl sitting next to her and realized I *did* remember her. She had been the waitress at the bar a couple of weeks ago. I wouldn't have thought that Whitley would still be talking to her. She was notoriously bad with relationships.

"Hey. Nice to see you again."

Keri flushed. "You too."

But it was the beautiful black woman at the very front of the limo who caught my attention. She was in a skintight black dress with legs for days. Her natural hair was in coils, and her eyes were coated in gold. She looked like a celestial goddess.

"Charlie!" I exclaimed.

Gavin shot Charlotte a look. "You go by Charlie?"

She laughed. "By people I've known my whole life. Lark, I'll come give you a hug when we get there."

"You'd better."

"How exactly do you know each other?" Gavin asked, slinging an arm around Charlie's shoulders.

"She's, like, best friends with my brother," Charlotte explained. "Lewis Warren."

"Ah, yes, I've heard all about him."

Charlie frowned. The investigation into Warren Enterprise had been a blow. I doubted she wanted to talk about that.

I turned my attention to English to allow them some privacy. She was giving me a look. I knew that look.

She lowered her voice and asked, "Why did you show up with Sam?"

"We didn't show up together. He lives in Brooklyn, and I thought it'd be easier than having one more stop."

"And he couldn't meet us at Court's?"

I shrugged. "Guess not."

"Don't think that I don't know your game. Has Bad Lark come back out to play?"

"No," I insisted. "Seriously...we're just friends."

"No guy with eyeballs wants to just be friends with you in that dress. You're basically wearing lingerie."

I rolled my eyes. "I am not."

"Fucking hot lingerie, but still..."

"Then I'll have no trouble attracting the attention of all the eligible bachelors you took the liberty of inviting."

English smiled devilishly. "Excellent."

I couldn't stop from laughing, but it was soon after we arrived at the venue that I realized that English had been dead serious. She got Court all set up, grabbed drinks, and then ushered me across the room. Far, far away from Sam.

"Okay, so...the first guy is Caleb Hendricks. He's a professional baseball player. He's actually making a donation alongside Court tonight. He grew up in LA but moved here about a decade ago to play ball."

"What do I have in common with a baseball player?" I asked with wide eyes.

"He has a nice butt. Who cares?"

"English..."

"Look, this is just for fun. There are no strings and none of your parents' stipulations attached. Just talk to him and get to know him. It's all low stakes."

I sighed and then nodded. "Fine. I'll meet Caleb."

English pulled me over, introduced us, and then slithered away like the snake she was.

I halfheartedly smiled up at him before taking a sip of my champagne. "So, you play baseball?"

"Yeah. Are you a fan?"

I laughed and then shook my head. "Not really. I don't have time for sports with my job, and mostly, we had northeastern prep school sports, growing up on the Upper East."

He raised his eyebrows. "Oh, so you grew up here?"

"Yeah, I did."

"Wait, Lark...St. Vincent?"

I frowned at the way he'd said my last name. Like there were dollar signs attached. "Uh...yeah."

"Like St. Vincent's Resorts?"

"Yes," I ground out. "That's my parents' company. But I don't work for them. I run the mayor's reelection."

He crinkled his nose. "Eh. I've never really liked her. She seems kind of like a stuck-up bitch, don't you think?"

I froze in place. Yeah, we could mark him off the list.

"I probably wouldn't be working for her if I agreed with your assessment."

"Hey, no hard feelings."

"No, of course not." I glanced around and saw my lifeline. Katherine was striding into the building for the event. "Excuse me. I just saw a friend."

"Oh, uh...okay. Did you want me to..."

"No, that's okay. Thanks."

Then, I hurried away from him as fast as humanly possible. Between the dollar signs at my name and calling Leslie a bitch, there was no way he could recover from that. No matter if he had a nice ass in baseball pants or not.

"Thank god you're here," I said to Katherine as soon as I reached her.

She arched a perfectly manicured eyebrow at me. She looked stunning, but there was something else underneath. Like she had on more makeup than normal to hide the circles under her eyes. She must not have been sleeping. Plus, she looked thinner than usual. Thinner for her was *not* good. Katherine self-medicated with food...lack of food.

"Larkin," she said, kissing my cheeks as if we were in Paris and not stuck in the city all summer. "You look like you're flourishing."

"How have you been?"

"Wonderful, of course." Katherine shrugged. She didn't have to say what she was really thinking. Penn and Natalie staying in Paris for the summer made it easier for her to stay on top of her social life. But her falling-out with Camden was making her fall back into all of her dirty habits. If there were a separate entity that was Bad Katherine...she was coming out this summer.

"Of course," I said softly. "I've missed you. Sucks not having the crew all together."

Katherine glanced around at our fledgling, new group. "Looks like you've found a sort of replacement."

I laughed. "Nothing replaces the crew."

She frowned. "Maybe it should."

I didn't even know what to say to that. We'd been together through it all. I'd never wanted something different. But it was true that things were different. And this new group might just help make that okay.

"Oh god," Katherine said under her breath, barely audible.

"What?" I asked and then saw why she'd said it.

Camden had arrived. And on his arm was Fiona Berkshire.

"I cannot believe that he would show up with her," I ground out.

Katherine just tilted her head up higher. She was the queen. Nothing bothered her. Except I knew it was all a lie.

Camden approached then. He released Fiona and pulled Katherine toward him. He pressed a possessive kiss to her lips. "My beautiful wife."

"Hello, Camden."

I didn't know how she kept the break from her voice.

"Hi, Katherine," Fiona said with a knowing smile.

Katherine said nothing to her. Didn't even acknowledge her. It might as well have been the wind.

"I hope your bed has been as warm as mine," Camden said like a taunt.

Katherine's expression never wavered. "I would expect yours to be frigid. All things considered."

Then, she glanced at Fiona. Just once. Just briefly.

A challenge.

Damn. She was good. I was ready to punch them both for acting like this. But still...I could recognize good game when I saw it.

"Hey!" Fiona gasped.

"Come. We should be photographed together," Camden said. "Wouldn't want anyone to think anything was wrong with the Wicked Witch of the Upper East Side."

I wanted her to say no. But if I knew anything about her, it was that appearances mattered more than reality.

"Tell your pet to heel," Katherine said.

A strange look crossed Camden's features. It wasn't anger. It was hunger. Like a predator trapping its prey. And then he took her arm in his hand and guided her away from Fiona, who promptly pouted.

I whirled away from her as quickly as possible to avoid having to have an uncomfortable conversation. As far as I was concerned, Fiona had gotten everything that was coming to her.

"Hey, it didn't work out with Caleb?" English said, materializing as if out of thin air.

I shook my head. "He called Leslie a bitch."

English's eyes widened. "Uh, yeah, that wasn't in his profile. Guy number two?"

My eyes flicked to Sam, who was laughing with Court and Gavin. It'd be so much easier to just see him. But then again, it would also be slow torture as well.

"All right, one more guy," I agreed.

"Excellent. This is Danny Park. He owns a pharmaceutical company. Every year, he donates millions of dollars to help the poor combat medical expenses. He's, like, the opposite of every greedy Big Pharma company you can probably name off the top of your head. Also, he went to Brown. So, yay!"

"Brown, huh," I said in surprise. "Normally, these types went to one of the big three Ivy's. Okay...Danny."

English made the introduction again, but this time, I tried to be more open-minded. Danny was cuter than Caleb. He looked like the lead from *Crazy Rich Asians*, if only he had the British accent.

It wasn't until I realized that I was on my third drink with Danny that I was feeling a bit tipsy. I'd even given him my number. What the hell? It was so unlike me. I had no time to date. Giving out my number made no sense.

"I'll get us another round. Champagne still?" Danny asked with his award-winning smile.

"Yes. That'd be great."

He stepped away to grab a drink from a passing waiter, and then suddenly, Court Kensington was there.

I jolted in surprise. "Hey, Court!"

"What are you doing?" he asked.

"Um...just talking to Danny. Do you know Danny Park?"

"No," Court said, "I don't. Why are you talking to him?"

My brows furrowed. "English introduced us."

"What I mean is...are you purposely trying to make him jealous?"

This time, my eyebrows rose to the ceiling. "Make *who* jealous?"

He stared into my eyes with all the Upper East Side flooding through him. "Seriously, Lark?"

"I don't know what you're talking about."

"You're one of us. You have to realize what you're doing. I've seen you take down my brother," he said evenly. "This is classic Lark behavior. Talk to multiple guys, laugh and flirt and smile, flip your hair, overtly give out your number. It's textbook."

My good mood deflated. "Wait...you think that I'm trying to make someone jealous? On purpose?"

His eyes bored into mine, and I froze as I realized what he was saying. Ice water sloshed down my back as it all came together. He was saying...Sam was jealous of me talking to Caleb and then Danny.

"You know about me and Sam," I whispered.

He arched an eyebrow. "It was obvious the first time I saw you two together."

"And you think I'm making him jealous?"

"Insanely," he said just as Danny returned.

"Here you go, Lark," he said, passing me another glass of champagne.

Court raised an eyebrow. "Do what you will with that information."

Then he promptly disappeared.

"What was that about?"

I took a sip of my drink and shook my head in confusion. "I have no idea."

Why would Sam be jealous?

Unless...he'd told Court something he hadn't told me.

20

LARK

I found the first excuse I could to get away from Danny. He seemed like a nice guy, but Court had ruined some of the charm. As if I'd been under a spell, and now, I was back to reality.

The organizer of the charity event tapped on the microphone. She spoke about the intercity sports charity that the donations from the event would benefit. It included more than a dozen sports with boys and girls ranging from three to eighteen. And how they were hoping that the older kids would get off of the streets and into scholarship sports, thanks to the money donated today.

Court and English were standing off to the side, waiting for his moment to walk onstage. But I meandered toward the rest of my friends. Gavin, Charlotte, Whitley, Keri, and Sam were standing in front of the stage. Katherine and Camden had just stepped up to the side. I watched Camden nod at Court, and Court grinned at his oldest friend. Their friendship still confused me, but I had the crew, so...maybe it was the same in its own way.

Finally, I stepped up to Sam's side. He glanced sideways at me. His expression was unreadable. For once, I had no clue what was going on up there. Was he jealous? Why was he jealous? What had he told Court that made him reveal that he was jealous? And why had it made me want to immediately abandon a perfectly nice guy to find out?

"Make a new friend?" Sam asked, tossing back the rest of his drink.

"Yeah, actually, I did. English has this insane idea that I'll have time to date on the campaign. So, she's making it her mission to try to set me up," I told him, carefully watching him. "Isn't that crazy?"

"Crazy that you're being set up or that you'd have time?"

"Both."

He seemed to contemplate that. "We don't have time. That's for sure. Not for anyone who isn't working on the campaign."

My heart pounded at the way he'd said it. As if...he meant I wouldn't have time for anyone but him.

"That's true," I agreed slowly.

"But not crazy that she'd set you up." He brushed a stray lock of my hair out of my face. "I can't even believe you're single."

I swallowed. "Bad luck, I guess."

"Is that what you'd call it?"

I had no answer to that. Because it wasn't what I'd call it. I didn't like any of the guys my parents threw my way. I didn't want to date someone on the campaign for convenience. And I didn't know how to *meet* people that didn't involve a dating app, which was so *risky*. I had no way of trusting those people, and it made me uncomfortable. The few times I'd even made a profile, I'd had to lie about who I was, which, from experience, was not a great way to start out.

Luckily, I didn't have to respond because Court was walking onto the stage with Caleb and some other guy that I'd never seen before. English pushed a giant check into a volunteer's hand, and it was handed off to one of the charity organizers.

"We'd just like to thank all three of these gentleman for being so generous with their donations to our recreation departments. Caleb Hendricks has given a quarter million dollars to help our youth baseball program. Jessi Ramirez has donated another quarter million dollars to assist in our youth soccer program. And the wonderful Court Kensington has been so kind to give a full million dollars to help with our lacrosse, field hockey, tennis, sailing, and crew programs. Court, would you like to say a few words?"

My eyes widened. Court had given a million dollars? Holy shit. English must have really talked him into this. I didn't think he'd ever donated before in his life.

Court stepped forward, looking every inch the golden boy that English wanted him to be. "Thank you so much, Linda." He touched her shoulder and gave her the charming smile that won over every woman he came in contact with. "It's my pleasure to be here today. As many of you know, I played lacrosse, growing up, and even played collegiate lacrosse for Harvard. It's a sport that I love and believe in. And I don't think that it should be reserved for the privileged few when it could be enjoyed by all." He smiled dazzlingly. "That's why I'm pleased to be here today with Caleb and Jessi to donate to improve these programs. And if you're so inclined, I suggest you donate today as well. Thank you."

The crowd applauded for him. Even I did. It was a good speech. I bet English had written it. She certainly looked pleased with herself.

Court shook hands and took pictures before striding offstage toward English. They exchanged a few tense words before Court brushed past her in what appeared to be frustration. A determined look crossed her face. I'd seen that before. She used it with other celebrities when she needed to whip them into shape. And she was trying so hard with Court.

"That was quite a speech," Sam muttered. "I can't believe he can just donate a million dollars like that."

"What's a million dollars to someone with a nine-digit trust fund?" I muttered, my mind still following Court and English's interaction.

"I can't imagine that either."

I laughed it off. "I don't think many people can."

"You're so different than you were five years ago."

"Yes, I am. But not because of the money. Money doesn't buy happiness. In fact, most of the people I know who have it are pretty miserable. And I was the happiest on campaign when I was pretending to have next to nothing. So, I don't think trust funds make a damn difference, except that they can cover up fuckups like Court."

"It wasn't a complaint," he said evenly.

I noticed English coming toward me out of the corner of my eye. I knew what that meant. "Oh god."

"What?" he asked, seeing where I was looking.

"English is like...a used car salesman tonight."

"Have you ever *been* in a used car lot?"

I frowned. "Well, no, but it's an expression."

He laughed softly at my dismay. "I see."

"Save me," I pleaded.

Our eyes met. I begged him for his help in that look. I knew that I had agreed to go along with English's plan...sort of. But now, I was tired. I did small talk all day at work. And though I'd had a good time with Danny, I was more curious about what Court had said about Sam. If it was true and what it meant and whether or not I should ever think about it again.

"Please," I whispered.

Finally, he nodded. "Act drunk."

I obliged, finishing off my drink and stumbling a little into him with a giggle. "Sorry."

He put a hand out to steady me with an amused look on his face. "Looks like someone has had one too many."

"Lark, hey," English said when she approached us. "Oh my god, did you get wasted?"

I fluttered my eyelashes at her. "I think...Danny might have given me one too many drinks. I lost count."

She sighed. "Well, shit."

"Yeah, but...I'm fine," I insisted.

"You're not fine. We should probably get you home and sober. But I have to stay here with Court for a little longer." She bit her lip.

"I can get her home," Sam told her.

"Oh no..."

"It's not a problem. We have work tomorrow anyway. I should probably get going or else I'll be dead in the morning."

"Are you sure?" English clearly disapproved but couldn't say what she was really feeling in front of Sam.

"Completely."

"All right," she said on a sigh. "Thanks. I'll owe you one."

"Don't mention it," he said as he slipped his hand around my elbow and directed me toward the exit.

"Bye, English," I called out to her.

She waved with another pointed shake of her head.

Once we exited the main ballroom, I straightened up with a laugh. "Worked like a charm."

"Yeah, I didn't know if you wanted to leave, but we really do have to get to work in the morning."

"This is fine with me," I told him honestly.

We hailed a cab to drive us back to my apartment. We were strangely silent on the drive. Not uncomfortable, but just...silent. As if whatever was said next would cause a ripple, and neither of us was willing to be the first one to dip our toe in the water.

Finally, we stopped outside of my place. I paid the cab, and Sam followed me out.

"Oh, you can take this one if you want," I told him.

He shrugged. "Nah. I'll just take the subway."

"Are you sure? In that suit?" I reached forward and ran a hand down the front of the tuxedo. It was perfection.

"Oh yeah. I guess I didn't think about that," he said with a laugh. He didn't pull back from my hand. "Not used to clothes this nice. I can grab an Uber or something."

"All right." I hesitated on the threshold to my apartment building. I'd had just enough to drink to feel bold. My hand was still on his suit. I should pull it back. I should walk away. I didn't. "Can I ask you something?"

"Sure."

"Were you jealous tonight?" I whispered, looking up at him with a flush on my pale cheeks.

He froze at the words. And I thought I'd pushed him too far.

Asked the wrong question in the middle of our fine evening. But I couldn't get Court's words out of my head.

"Yes," he said in surrender.

"Because I was talking to other guys?"

He nodded once. My fingers curled in on his suit. I shouldn't. Bad Lark would. She would drag him inside right then and there. But I couldn't. I had to resist.

"Why?" I asked, forcing my fingers to release his suit and fall back to my side.

"You know why."

I raised an eyebrow. "I don't think that I do."

He opened his mouth to answer and then closed it. I didn't think he'd answer at all. He'd just turn around and walk away. But he didn't.

Instead, his hands came to my hips. Those long, callous dug into the silk of my dress. A peep escaped me at the feel of him touching me. Really touching me. Like he hadn't done in so, so long.

I could barely think, let alone speak, as he walked me two steps backward. My back hit the brick wall of my building. My chest heaved as I glanced up into those depthless eyes. And I saw my mirror in them. Our bodies were pressed tight together. The scrape of the brick against my back was the only thing that reminded me that this wasn't a dream.

"Sam," I breathed. Not sure if I was telling him to stop or not.

But he didn't say a word. Not one. As his lips crashed down onto mine.

I gasped in shock and want and desperation. So much need. My lips parted. His tongue devoured. And every movement, every touch, said, *Yes, yes, yes.* He tasted like whiskey and smelled like leather and new books and fresh soap. He was pure eroticism to my starved body.

My hands buried into his dark hair, dragging him closer, kissing him harder. Tasting him, wanting him, needing him. Our bodies knew this dance. We'd performed it many, many times back in Madison. It was like remembered choreography, achingly familiar and full of passion.

Then, the world crashed back down on me.

I brought my hands down to his chest and pushed him back from me. Just an inch. Just enough to breathe.

"I can't," I gasped out. "I can't. It's not...it's not fair."

Sam dropped his head backward. A sigh escaped his lips, and he closed his eyes as if he was in pain. "Fuck."

"Yeah," I breathed.

Then he looked at me again. And there was something else there. "Claire and I broke up."

I froze. "Excuse me? When...when did this happen?"

"You remember when I passed you in the elevator, going to Court's place?"

My mind reeled before it caught up. "That was *weeks* ago!"

"I know."

"Why didn't you tell me?" I demanded. "Is this why you've been acting so strangely at work?"

"Yes. I wasn't in a great place after it happened. She went on tour in Europe for twelve weeks and broke up with me the night before she left."

"Fuck," I said. "Harsh."

"Yeah. And then...I don't know. I didn't...want you to be a rebound. And then it sounded insane and presumptuous in my head that you'd want to be with me. Then we were friends after Buns the other day. I didn't want to ruin that or the event. So, I promised I'd tell you after the event."

"Wait...that's why you invited me to burgers?"

"Yeah. I was going to tell you. And then you were so happy and animated. And...I just couldn't."

I stepped away from the wall and held my hand up. There was something like fury coursing through my veins. If he'd come to me when it first happened, I would have been there as a friend. I wouldn't have expected anything. But this...this was duplicitous. He'd held it back on purpose. He'd made me suffer those weeks, wondering what the hell had happened with us. And he was only telling me now because he had to.

"Lark," he muttered.

"I think you still need time to figure this all out."

"That's not what—"

"No," I said, cutting him off. "I don't want to be used by you to figure out your problems. I won't ever be that girl. And you shouldn't treat me that way."

"That isn't what I meant."

"Yeah, well, that's how it feels."

Then I took a deep breath and walked away.

It wasn't easy. I wanted Sam to tell me how he was wrong, how he should have told me, and how we could fix this. But I didn't want to hear it. Not tonight. Not after being made to feel like I was the crazy one the last couple of weeks. Or that I was the bad guy, somehow making him jealous when he was perfectly single and couldn't even let me know.

I was done playing games.

21

LARK

I was still mad the next day.
  And the day after that.
And the day after that.

Anyone who knew me could probably see that I wasn't myself. I was just as dedicated, just as on top of things. But there was a fury to my pace. A lack of calm that I'd always exuded, even when I was at my highest anxiety point.

Demi nodded in front of me. "Got it. I will get right on that."

"Great. Thanks."

"Hey, Lark, is everything all right?"

"Peachy," I said with no enthusiasm as I continued to type away on my computer.

"You seem a little...intense."

"Aren't I always?"

"Well, yeah. And I mean, you have an crazy job. I just wanted to check on you."

I managed a smile that was a bit more like baring my teeth. "I'm fine. Thanks, Demi."

It was a dismissal, and I saw her take it with a worried expression on her face. I continued my assault on my keyboard before finally finishing off the memo I needed to send out. I sighed heavily and leaned back in my chair. What the hell was wrong with me? I needed to figure out how to let this go. At least, to let it go at work.

The problem was...I hadn't even told English.

She was living with me, seeing my anxiety-ridden madness, and I couldn't bring myself to tell her she was right. She'd been right all along. Sam was a bad idea. And if I kept this up, then he'd break my heart like he had the first time.

"Lark," Aspen said on the intercom. "Call for you on line one."

"Did they say who it was?"

"Danny Park? Does that sound familiar?"

In fact, it did.

I'd completely forgotten that I'd given him my number. I'd been a bit preoccupied with what had happened after I left the party.

"I got it," I told Aspen and then pressed the button for line one. "Lark St. Vincent speaking."

"Lark," Danny said with his cool, crisp voice. "It's Danny...from the party last weekend."

"Right. It's good to hear from you." *Is it?*

"I tried to get your cell, but it kept going to voicemail, and then the voicemail was full."

I hit myself in the forehead. I'd forgotten about that. I avoided telemarketer calls like the plague and never answered a number I didn't recognize. I'd been telling myself that they'd leave a voicemail if it was important. Except...he hadn't been able to.

"Sorry about that. How did you track down my office number?"

"You mentioned that you worked for the mayoral campaign. So, I just called and asked for you. They redirected me to your office."

Oh. Obviously.

"Makes sense. I hate to cut this short, but I am actually heading into a meeting."

"Oh, yeah. No problem. How about I call you tonight, and we can talk?"

"Sure."

I could practically feel his smile through the phone. "Great! Well, if you get a call from a 212 number, that's me."

"Got it. I'll make sure to answer this time," I said with a breathy laugh.

"Looking forward to it."

We said our good-byes, and then I hung up.

Except...I had no pressing meeting. I'd just been flushed and flustered that he'd managed to track me down after I didn't answer. I pulled out my cell and scrolled through the list of missed calls. There did in fact seem to be a handful of missed calls from the same 212 number. I quickly cleared out my voice-mail and made a mental note to talk to English about this later. I had a feeling I knew what she'd say. But I needed to lay it all out there.

By the time eight rolled around, I was exhausted and ready to head out. Aspen had left two hours ago on some kind of errand. I stepped out of my office and almost made it out of the building when I saw him.

"Hey," Sam said, appearing out of the shadows.

I took a deep breath and let it out. "Hi."

"Can we talk?"

"I really don't want to talk right now."

"We can't just avoid this."

I shuffled the papers under my arm and hiked up my purse. "That's rich, coming from you."

He winced. *Good.* "I deserve that. But if we could just talk..."

"No," I said. "I'm not ready to talk. And you can wait until I'm ready."

"Do you know when that will be?"

"Nope. I don't."

I took a step away from him. Part of me wanted to fling myself into his arms. The other part was too conflicted to even know what it wanted. It was great that Sam was single. It was not great that he hadn't been honest with me. Not exactly a foundation to start a relationship on.

"I just need time," I told him honestly.

Then with a pang in my chest, I pushed through the open door and walked out into the windy New York city street beyond.

"Oh my god, stop! Josh, stop! I can't," English called into the phone as I entered my apartment.

A giant smile was on her face, and she was using her biggest, girliest voice. The one that said she was so disgustingly in love that she was going to burst at the seams.

Any other day, it would be music to my ears. Right now, it was grating. And I dodged into my room as fast as possible.

English and Josh were a fucking icon. The most adorable couple in Hollywood. It had to be hard for her to be away from him for this long. For both of them.

I yawned and stretched my arms over head and then frowned. "What the fuck?"

There was a stack of Bergdorf Goodman bags in the corner of my room.

"Where the hell did you come from?"

I headed over to the stack and found a purple card resting on top.

Lark, darling, you looked so good in that Badgley Mischka dress that I took the liberty of purchasing you a few new things for the season. In particular, the Elizabeth Cunningham dress will be perfect for the St. Vincent's company dinner over Fourth of July weekend.

—HSV

My mother. I swear.

I needed to find a way to steal my key back from her. Because I was not cool with her just barging in whenever she wanted and depositing clothes in my fucking room. It was an invasion of privacy. Not to mention another way she was attempting to control me. The gifts she let were only an excuse to get me to a company dinner. I had no plans to run the company. And anyway, I would be working that weekend.

I just shook my head and shoved the bags into a corner before stripping out of my work clothes. I threw on a black nightgown that was perfect for this heat since it was more of a slip than anything. I tossed my hair up a topknot and then walked back out into the living room.

English had blessedly finished her call. Though she was still in the afterglow of the conversation.

She frowned when she saw my expression. "Bad day?"

"Emergency ice cream," I told her as I yanked open the freezer and removed a container of chocolate chip cookie dough.

"Oh dear."

I grabbed a spoon and settled on the couch.

She followed, tucking her legs up underneath her, prepared to hear me out. "So, I'm finally going to find out why you've been walking around the apartment like a hurricane."

"Sam and I kissed."

English's mouth popped open. "Lark!"

"Yep. And *then* he told me that he and Claire had broken up."

"Wait, what?"

"Yep. And *then* he gave all these bullshit excuses for why he hadn't told me they'd broken up *weeks* ago. That day when we went to Court's for the trial run."

"Oh geez."

"So, anyway, I told him I didn't want to be used and to leave me alone while he had shit to figure out."

"Damn," English said. "No wonder you've been so pissed."

"Yeah. Well, he tried to talk to me at work today. But I blew him off. I don't know what to say to him. And Danny called, and I think he's supposed to call sometime tonight. I don't even know what to say to him."

"Okay, slow down. Too much at once," English said. She snatched my spoon from me and dug into the ice cream. "So, Sam is single. He wants to talk to you. And he kissed you."

"Correct."

"But Danny also called and presumably wants to go on a date."

"Also, yes."

"Hmm…"

I took my spoon back and dug in for another bite of the ice cream. "I don't know what to do."

"You don't know, or you don't want to admit it?" she asked intuitively.

"In a perfect world?"

She nodded.

I took a deep breath and continued, "I'd try it out with Sam again."

"I see."

"I know that you don't like him."

"I never said that," English said. "What I said was that I didn't like what had happened in the past. That he'd broken your heart. I didn't want to see you get hurt again."

I shrugged and had more ice cream. Maybe there were answers in the cookie dough.

"You don't want to date Danny," English decided.

"Not really. He was nice. I mean, I gave him my number. But he just wasn't…it." I sighed. "I know I'm still messed up from Thomas. It's just hard to let go."

"But you can with Sam?"

I nodded reluctantly. Because I could. Even though things were screwed up with Sam now. It had been so perfect and easy when we were first together. There was so much history there that it'd felt like we were drawn together. Before I'd known about Claire, it was as if we were magnets. Even after, I'd be lying to say that we'd just been friends. That was a clever lie we'd been telling each other. Because that kiss had said it all.

"Okay"—English shifted to face me—"I've been against Sam from the start. But I think you need to give this another chance."

"What?" I gasped through a mouthful of ice cream.

"Hear me out. Sam was always that guy for you. No matter how broken you were or how mad you were at him…you still wanted him. You still wanted to make it right. And you've changed *so* much since I first knew you. Maybe he has too. I think you should go for it. Because if you don't, you'll always wonder, *What if*...You'll compare every guy to him. Wonder if he's waiting on every street corner. You need to find out if he's really the guy you want. Even if it means putting your heart on the line."

"I don't know, English. How do I put myself out there again? That level of vulnerability"—I shuddered—"it feels like a risk."

"A calculated risk. You look at the odds and decide if the pros outweigh the cons. You know what the chance of failure is. You've already seen failure in this. It's not an election. You don't have to plan out all the moves. You don't have to decide a year out what the first Tuesday in November will look like. You just...try."

"That easy, huh?" I asked my friend who knew all about jumping, talking to the girl who had never taken a risk...let alone with her heart.

"The easiest and hardest thing you'll ever do. Let go. Live."

I sighed and bit my lip. "Maybe I will."

22

SAM

I hefted a box into my arms and tossed it onto the top of the stack I'd made in the one spare corner of my apartment.

"That's the last of it," I said to my now-empty apartment.

After how hard I'd fucked up with Lark, I'd come home to my apartment and seen Claire staring back at me from every available space. She wouldn't be back until the end of the summer, when we'd have to decide what to do about our shared place. But I couldn't keep having her stuff in my face.

If I was going to live here for another couple of months, I couldn't see her every day. Not like this. Not if I was going to move on.

Even though it had been nearly two in the morning, I'd started packing. And I'd kept packing all week in the time I had after I got home from work.

And that was the last of it.

It meant the walls were blank, the side tables and coffee table were free of miscellaneous junk, her set of drawers and half of the tiny closet were empty. I'd had to go get new sheets and a comforter. I'd placed my wood carvings around the room to try to make it look like Claire wasn't the only one who decorated. But it was still bare.

All that mattered was that it no longer felt like Claire.

After the day I'd had, the confrontation with Lark, and packing, the last thing I wanted to do was go to Camden Percy's penthouse and play poker. But Court had insisted that I had to show up for their monthly game.

I'd tried to argue that I couldn't show because I didn't have the ten-thousand-dollar buy-in. Of course, Court had agreed to spot me the money. Not like I could ever pay him back if I lost it all. Which I thought was unlikely since my brother, Jake, and I had grown up, playing poker. But still...

I ran a hand back through my hair and then hopped into a quick shower. I changed into slacks and a button-up, and then I took the subway into Manhattan. I'd never been to Camden's place before. He lived on the top floor of Percy Tower, and it was very easy to locate.

It was still disorienting to think that I was even being invited to the top floor of Percy Tower. Me, a nobody who had done construction work for most of my life in rural North Carolina. Even three years at Duke Law hadn't prepared me for taking an elevator that opened up into someone's house.

But that was exactly what I did.

And I tried to pick my jaw up off the floor when I entered Camden's residence. It looked like I'd just entered a palace. Like I was on my way to visit the king. Everything was lavish and lush and extravagant. The living room opened up to a vaulted ceiling, which I had no idea how that was even possible from an architectural standpoint. I'd built a lot of houses in my life, but this was something else entirely.

It had a wraparound staircase that led to a second floor. Paintings taller than my person on the walls. Gilded place settings on a dining room table in its own separate room. And just so much space.

Space was a luxury in New York. To have this much open and emptiness...it was incredible. And terrifying. Because I'd thought Court's place showed wealth. I hadn't realized there was a level above. A level for someone who put his mind to running the Percy hotel company, while Court stayed out of the Kensington business affairs. From the looks of this place, Camden Percy could Scrooge McDuck dive-bomb into his money.

"You're gawking," a voice said as high heels clicked onto the foyer.

I'd expected Katherine and was surprised to find it was English. "Uh, yeah. How could anyone not gawk at this?"

"You get used to it after a while."

I shook my head in disbelief. "I don't see how I could ever get used to this."

"You say that now."

"So, uh, do you know where this poker game is happening?"

She nodded. "I do in fact."

Her expression said that she wasn't prepared to tell me. That she had something else on her mind. It seemed likely that there was only one other thing she would want to discuss. And I doubted it was Court.

"I'm a fixer," English finally said. "I make problems go away."

"I understand. You can make me disappear."

She shook her head. "You misunderstand me. I don't want to have to fix her. She can't sustain another heartbreak."

I tilted my head in confusion. "I don't think that she's in any danger of heartbreak."

"That is yet to be seen."

"She won't even talk to me," I told her. "I tried."

"Well, we'll see," she said and then turned and walked away.

We'll see? What the hell did that mean? That Lark might talk to me now? Why were women so confusing? Why couldn't they just say what they meant?

"Are you coming?" English asked.

I breathed out in exasperation but followed her through the enormous penthouse and into a billiards room with a glossy wooden poker table at its center.

"You made it," Court said, shaking my hand. "Easy enough to find?"

I almost laughed. "Yeah. Very easy."

"See, English," Court said. His eyes narrowed, and his voice sharpened when he talked to her. "Everything is fine. Just the four of us with a friendly game of poker. Some scotch and a few Cubans. You can leave now."

She just blinked at him. "I can see that, Court."

"You don't have to babysit."

"Trust me. I don't want to do anything of the sort. But you are notorious for bad decisions. I'm just going to stay long enough to make sure this isn't one of the many. You might think that the heat is off of you, but the public is vicious. If you turn away for one minute, you'll be on TMZ in a heartbeat."

Court ground his teeth and then ushered me over to the table. I took the seat between Court and Gavin.

"You've played before?" Gavin asked with a grin as he played with his chips.

"Once or twice back home."

"Excellent," Gavin said with a grin. "Blackjack is more my game. But I like a friendly game of poker every now and again."

"You're shit at blackjack," Camden said. He deftly shuffled through the deck once and then twice.

"No way. Remember that time we went to Vegas in college?" Gavin asked. "I won fifty grand."

"You never remember that trip right," Camden said. He arched an eyebrow. "Court and I spotted you a hundred *each*. You came out with fifty *total*. Then you tried to get married to a stripper."

I laughed at the story as Gavin waved it off.

"It would have been annulled anyway. And she was hot!"

"You were wasted," Camden reminded him. "And you have the worst beer goggles."

"Court, come on. Back me up!" Gavin said.

Court just shrugged. "Camden isn't wrong."

"Fuck you both. I'm going to clean up here, and then we'll talk."

Camden looked up at me with a faint grin on his face. "This should be fun."

I smiled back, ready to see just how bad Gavin actually was.

And also surprised to see that Camden was almost…normal. Here, in his own house with just his friends, he didn't have to put on airs. It was almost like what Court had said about how Camden didn't have to pretend for him. They had each other's backs. And now, somehow, I'd been pulled into it.

About an hour into our game, we'd gone through half a bottle of scotch, and Camden had pulled out the cigars. English finally got up from where she'd been seated, typing away on her phone.

"Okay, boys, this is boring as shit. Court was right," she said, stifling a yawn.

"We can make it more fun for you," Gavin said. He patted his knee as if to tell her to sit down.

She raised one eyebrow. "I'll have you know that I have a black belt. I'd reconsider that offer."

Gavin guffawed. "You could probably kick my ass."

"Yes, I could." She turned her attention back to Court. "Let me know if you need me."

"Don't worry. We won't," he said, turning away from her and back to the cards.

She shrugged and then walked out of the room. Gavin followed her ass the whole way out.

"Phew, she's smoking hot," he said.

Court furrowed his brow. "Don't even fucking think about it, dude."

"What? Are you hot for teacher?"

"That doesn't even make sense," Camden said.

"She's a huge pain in the ass," Court ground out. "It doesn't matter if she's hot. Also, she's married."

"Never stopped you before," Gavin said with a shit-eating grin.

"Yeah, well, it's stopping me now."

"And what about you?" Camden asked, diverting attention away from Court. He was looking right at me.

"What about me?"

"You and Lark have it bad."

I shrugged. "Did you tell everyone, Court?"

Court laughed and leaned forward on the table, lighting his cigar. "I didn't tell Camden shit. It's just that fucking obvious."

"Wait...you and Lark?" Gavin asked with wide eyes.

"Except to the most oblivious dude on the planet," Court added.

"So, are you going to do something about it?" Camden asked. His eyes stared pointedly into mine. Like he had his magnetism that made you want to answer. "When you want something, you take it. However you have to."

And for a moment, it felt like he was talking about himself. Not me at all.

"Yeah...maybe I am," I conceded.

"That's right," Court said, clapping me on the back. "You get your girl."

Camden nodded. "Also"—he glanced down at the chips—"did you fucking hustle us?"

My laugh was real this time. I had three times the number of chips as anyone else. Court and Gavin had almost nothing at this point.

"I did say that I played some at home."

Camden's smile grew. "Well done. I don't think anyone has ever beaten me at poker like this before." He brought his cigar to his lips and leaned back in his chair. "Court, you chose well. You're welcome next time."

In that moment, it felt like I'd just been tapped into a secret society. Except this might be even more elite.

And while it felt good to be accepted...my mind was on Lark. Something about what Camden had said struck a chord in me. Now, I needed to figure out how to get what I wanted.

23

LARK

"What the hell?" I groaned.

I opened my bleary, tired eyes and reached for my phone, which was buzzing on the nightstand. Finally, it stopped. I flopped back onto the bed and searched desperately for the dream that I'd been in. But it wouldn't return.

Then suddenly, I heard a banging on the door.

"Ugh," I muttered as I pulled myself out of bed.

I rubbed a hand over my face and hurried through the apartment to the front door. It looked like English was sleeping through this racket. If it was another drunk ass who had the wrong apartment, I was going to fucking kill someone. I could see why my parents wanted me in another apartment. If this kept up, I might actually agree with them. My sleep was too fucking valuable.

I ripped the door open, ready to curse the asshole up and down for waking me. But instead, Sam stood there, taking up the entire doorframe. He was in navy slacks and a white-and-blue button-up with mussed hair and hazy eyes. He smelled like tobacco and bourbon. And my mouth went suddenly dry at the sight of him, as if conjured straight out of my dream.

"What are you doing here?" I blurted out.

"I came to see you," he said, all smooth words and long vowels.

He'd had plenty to drink, enough to make him lean against the doorframe, but he wasn't drunk.

"I said that I wasn't ready to talk to you."

"I don't want to talk," he said.

Then his hands were in my hair, and his lips sensually fitted to mine as if they had always belonged there. His tongue trailed along my bottom lip, asking for permission to enter. A moan broke free at the pure power of him. He stole the breath from my lungs and the thoughts from my mind and power from my body. God, I fucking wanted this and him and everything.

He skimmed my shoulders, my sides, my waist. I shuddered at his touch. At the feel of him and how long I'd waited for it.

"Sam, you...you have things to figure out," I said, gripping his shirt hard in my fists. I wasn't sure if it was to bring him closer or push him further away.

"I figured them out."

"You did?"

"You. I want you." He nibbled along my jawline. "Just you, Lark."

"Oh god," I breathed and then yanked him into the apartment.

He toed the door closed behind him.

Our lips crashed back together, hungry and possessive.

"Yes," he growled against my lips. "*Yes.*"

And I came apart.

"Please," I groaned.

"Anything."

What did I want? I wanted him. I'd just admitted that to English...and to myself. I'd just decided not to go on a date with anyone else. To figure out what was happening here. Even though we'd ended terribly in the past, that didn't mean we had to be history repeating.

It was a fresh start. Turning over a new leaf. A blank slate. All those things and more. It was me and Sam. And in every way, we felt right.

Against the odds, we'd found our way back to each other. It was easier to stay mad at him. To harbor that inner fire that said this couldn't be mended. We'd hurt each other too bad. Irreparable damage had been done. My paper heart had been cut up into little pieces, and no matter how I tried to tape it back together, it would never be the same. But there was hope.

Hope that we could survive what had happened and move on. That he could love that taped-together paper heart again. Find a few scattered pieces and put them back into place the correct way.

It was that hope that had me leading him back to my bedroom. Heedless that English was asleep in the guest bedroom. No protests left his lips.

"God, I missed you," he breathed against me instead. "So fucking much."

My insides melted at his words. "I missed you, too."

"And this...I don't remember you sleeping in this." His hands trailed the bottom of my silk nightie.

I'd completely forgotten I was in this tiny, scandalous thing.

"It was cold in Wisconsin," I reminded him.

"Ah, yes. I'm deeply regretting that we were in a snowy state if this was what I was missing."

His hands dipped under the material, trailing along the tops of my thighs, against my creamy skin, and up to the edge of my panties. My body shuddered at the touch. Sam's long fingers, the coarse, callous texture, the assured way he intimately knew my body. No hesitation. No questions.

"You didn't wear clothes like this either," I said as I began to unbutton his shirt.

He smirked. "What good would I have for a suit when I was out, getting voter registrations and knocking on doors?"

"Well, see...we've both changed," I mused softly.

He tilted my chin up to look into his eyes. "We have."

My hands stilled on his shirt. I swallowed, captivated by that gaze. "Some things haven't."

He grinned as he tugged his shirt over his head and tossed it onto the wooden floor of my bedroom. "How much I want you for instance."

I bit my lip. "Like that first day on the job."

"You were the most beautiful thing I'd ever seen," he said, returning to teasing the bottom of my dress. "In the most ridiculous heels for a Wisconsin winter. I was smitten from then on."

"If I remember correctly, you had no objections to me wearing those heels in bed," I said, flicking the button on his pants.

"None," he confirmed.

Then he lifted the hem of my nightie, and when I didn't stop him, he pulled it over my head where it landed next to his shirt. I was naked, save for my small cheeky panties. My nipples were erect, and he took in my breasts with hunger in his dark eyes.

"There's something else I'd like to see if I remember correctly," he said as he backed me against my bed.

"And what's that?" I breathed.

"If you taste as good as I remember."

My breath hitched.

His hands rand down the back of my thighs and lifted my ass onto my entirely too-tall bed. But it didn't seem to faze him since he was a giant of a man. He just set me down and then gently pressed my back into the comforter.

He slid his fingers over my exposed skin on his way south. Taking his time to flit across my collarbone, over the map of light freckles on my chest, to the curves of my small breasts. I'd stopped being self-conscious of them a long time ago. But the way his hands cupped each of them, tweaking the nipples between his fingers and generally obsessing over them, it reminded me what it was like to be adored.

I squirmed as he slid his tongue over the nipple, sucking it into his mouth.

"Oh god," I breathed. My eyes squeezed shut as my core tightened.

He released the first and moved onto the second. He gently bit down on the sensitive skin, making me cry out in pleasure.

"Fuck, I love the noises you make too," he groaned.

He flicked the nipple once with his tongue, and I whimpered.

He continued lower, dragging his hands down my stomach

and over my round hips. He hooked a finger under the hem of my panties and slipped them off, leaving me bare before him.

"Sam," I pleaded.

He lifted my leg and began to kiss his way inward, starting at the knee. Each kiss supple, luxurious, and excruciating. If I'd thought we were just going to fuck and be done with this, I'd been wrong. This was more...so much more. He was remembering every inch of my body. I shivered again at the thought that he wanted to reacquaint himself with my taste.

"I like when you say my name," he told me, nipping at my inner thigh.

I squeaked. He just moved closer and closer and closer. I thrust my wanton body toward his face. But he just chuckled, breathed against my most-sensitive skin, and then started on the other knee. I was about ready to combust, and he hadn't even gotten to the main event.

He didn't speed up on the left leg either. He took his time as he dragged his lips back toward my core, which was already pulsing with need. And then he was there. An inch away from me. Slowly, ever so slowly, he dragged his finger through the folds of my pussy, slicking his way through the evidence of what he'd done to me.

"Fuck," he ground out. "Fuck, Lark."

"Yes, please."

His thumb moved to my clit and experimentally circled the small nub a few times. I almost jolted off the bed. Fuck, masturbating was nothing compared to this...to the feel of him. And he wasn't even inside me yet. This was just the beginning, the cocktail hour to the main event. And I was the one who was going to be devoured.

Then his tongue replaced his finger, and it felt so fucking good that I might have blacked out. As he licked at my clit, he spread my pussy open for him and slipped a finger inside of me. I clenched as my entire body contracted.

I hadn't realized how close I was already. I was on the brink of orgasm. And I didn't want him to stop. Not at all. I wanted everything he was willing to give.

And he gave it, sliding another finger into me. Then he curled his fingers inward as he began to move them in and out of me. Building me up to a crescendo. The music filled my ears as he licked and sucked on me, drawing out my pleasure.

For a split second, I had enough cognizant thought to open my eyes and look down at him between my legs. And he glanced up at me in that exact moment. A confident, cocky-ass grin split his face. Like he could see on my dazed face and glazed eyes that I was in pure bliss...and it was all because of him.

"Fuck," I moaned.

He continued on, never stopping as I built and built up to that point. And just when I was about to peak, I put my hands down into his dark hair and shoved him down against me. I cried out as everything hit at once. My climax ricocheted through my body. And it wasn't until I stopped screaming that I finally released him.

He was grinning at me like he'd just won a prize. I could see his dick straining against his slacks. But he seemed not to care as he continued to swirl a finger against my pussy while I came down from my orgasm.

"So...sensitive," I bit out. My body shook at his continued ministrations right after my orgasm.

"My favorite time to touch you. You get so jittery that you look like you might explode again already."

I flushed despite what had just happened. That he remembered that about me. That he wanted to do it again.

"And you do taste just as good as I remembered."

I blushed even deeper.

"There's something else I want to remember," he said with a devilish grin.

"What's that?" I managed to get out.

He shucked his pants onto the floor. His black boxer briefs followed, revealing his cock in all its glory. My mouth watered at the sight. Just like all the rest of him, he was...big. He wasn't just huge. He fucking knew what to do with it. And fuck, I wanted more of that.

"Fuck you. I want to remember how it feels to fuck you."

I nodded slowly and then pointed at a nightstand. "Second drawer."

He smirked and then grabbed a condom. I watched him deftly slide it into place. My body shuddered at the sight of him touching himself. Fuck, I wanted to touch him. I wanted him in my mouth. But I wanted him in my pussy more. A lot more. Like, right fucking now.

He came back around to the bed and crawled on top of me, his dick jutting out between us. He moved to his elbows, positioning himself between my aching legs. Then he brushed a stray hair out of my face.

"This what you want?" he asked, seemingly conscious for the first time that he'd just barged in here and not asked me what I wanted. "I don't want to—"

"*Yes*," I told him. And then more calmly, looking into his eyes, I said, "Yes."

That was enough for both of us. *Yes*. He slid himself deep inside of me in one firm thrust, seating himself to the hilt. I breathed out in a half-gasp, half-whimper as he stretched me and stretched me, almost to the point of breaking. And then stretched me just a little more. So effing big.

I tightened my grip around his neck and held him in place, letting my body adjust to the feel of him. The man who took up doorways, filling something else entirely.

He just leaned his head into the crook of my neck and kissed gently, soothingly, up and down. One hand slid under my back, pressing our bare chests together. He bit at the hollow of my neck, and my entire body clenched as goosebumps broke out over my neck.

He grunted. "Fuck...you're so tight."

But then everything settled into perfection. I urged him with my hips to begin to move. He slid out of me with a shudder and then forward.

Once he started to move again, we were both goners. He sat up, gripped my hips in his hands, and thrust deep inside of me. Part of me thought I couldn't take it. Part of me wanted him to go deeper still. And he did somehow. He kept going, driving into me with abandon. I gripped the comforter in my hands, arched my back, and cried out over and over again. I felt sure I was going to wake up everyone in the building. And I didn't give two fucks.

"Lark—"

But he didn't get to finish because he plunged into me one last time, and I saw stars again. I erupted on command just as he came hard and fast inside of me. He shuddered on top of me as we hit our orgasms together. Then, the waves died down, and we crashed onto the shore together, collapsing into nothingness.

We were both panting as he slid out of me and removed the condom. He pulled me tight against his side and kissed my hair. All the fight had left our bodies. Just Jell-O left behind.

"This...feels like a dream," I told him as I nearly fell asleep against his chest.

"And yet, it's real."

"What happens in the morning?"

He ran a hand up and down my back. "I make you breakfast before work."

"What happens at work?"

"You don't overthink this, and everything works out."

I laughed softly and then yawned. "That sounds just like me."

"Don't worry about work. We can be discreet. Now that I have you, I'm not giving you up."

It sounded dangerous to me. But in the moment, I couldn't muster up the energy to care.

"Okay," I said and then pulled him in even closer. "I'm not giving you up either. No matter what."

PART IV

WHO COULD EVER
LEAVE ME?

24

LARK

Sam leaned forward over my desk. "I'm just saying...I want a real date."

I shook my head, but my smile was megawatt. Everyone in the office had to have seen the change in me over the last two weeks. It was like a light had switched. Who knew getting laid would make me a little less insane and intense.

"We don't have time to go out on a real date," I told him. "The primary is a month away."

"Not quite," he said. "And anyway, who said anything about going out?"

I arched an eyebrow. "I'm listening."

He stepped around my desk and came to stand before me. He offered me his hand, and against my better judgment, I let him lift me to my feet. We were mere inches apart. My stomach tightened with excitement and nerves. I didn't know how the campaign would react to us dating, considering I was the deputy campaign manager and he was just legal counsel. But I also...didn't want to find out.

He slid his hand into mine. "This is what I'm thinking. After work tonight, you come over to my place. Dinner, drinks, some Brooklyn magic."

"Brooklyn? You want me to come to your place in Brooklyn?" I asked in surprise.

Two weeks, and he had never once intimated that he wanted me in that space. I feared that it was because it was where he had lived with Claire before she went on tour. Or that...maybe he just didn't want me to see where he lived. After hanging out with me and Court and Camden in our varying levels of fancy Upper East Side apartments, maybe he didn't want to show off what it was like to really live in the city.

"I mean...unless you don't want to."

"No! I do. I would love that."

He arched an eyebrow. "Really? You sounded skeptical."

"Well, I didn't think *you* wanted me there."

"It's been easier to stay at your place," he admitted. "Even with English and her self-satisfied smiles. As if she were the match-maker in all of this."

I laughed softly. "That's English. And...it is easier at my place, but that doesn't mean I only want to stay at mine."

"So, you'll come then? Tonight?"

I opened my mouth to reply, staring up at his lips...so damn close to mine. Wondering if I should just respond with a kiss when the door to my office burst open.

Sam and I jumped away from each other faster than humanly possible. I brushed my hands down my shirt even though it didn't have any wrinkles. Sam stuffed his hands in his pockets. He could have whistled, and he wouldn't have looked more conspicuous.

"Lark!" Shawn cried, walking into the office. Luckily, Shawn was oblivious to most human interaction. "And...Sam, right?"

"Yes, sir."

"Great. I just wanted to pass along a word from Leslie. She said that if we hit our voter registration goal for the Fourth of July, then she is going to give everyone the weekend off. Which means a full Friday, Saturday, *and* Sunday off."

"Wow," I murmured. I couldn't remember the last time I'd had three days off in a row. Campaign life was weird.

"Yeah. So, we're going to need all boots on the ground. Talk to the field team and see what they need," Shawn said enthusiastically. "Give them whatever they ask for. We have less than a week of full prep to get as many people out at as many events as possible to get those voter registrations in."

I shuffled through papers on my desk and found a map of the boroughs. "We already have teams in place for most of the main events," I explained, handing him the paper. "The structure is already there. But we can get everyone on phones the rest of the week to bolster our numbers."

"Excellent," Shawn said with a grin. "Also, I want this office empty on the Fourth. The mayor wants me and Christine to be with her when she's out at events on the Fourth. The rest of you, she wants at each of these events. Boots on the ground. Making things happen."

I gawked. "You want us to be out there?"

"Yep! And posting to social media about it!"

I nodded in surprise. Leslie must be desperate about the Reyes primary challenge if she wanted nearly all of her head campaign staff to actually be out in the field.

"Let everyone know," Shawn said. "Hit our goal on the Fourth, and you all will get the weekend off. Light a fire under them."

"I will let them all know."

"I can always count on you, Lark." He nodded his head at Sam. "Good to see you. Boots on the ground!"

"Yes, sir," he said.

And then Shawn sauntered out.

I sighed. "Well, *this* is going to be interesting."

"To say the least." He grinned. "But hey, we used to do this every single day in Madison. It'll be like old times."

His smile was infectious.

"Maybe. I'd better get back to work if we're going to hit that goal."

"Sounds good, boss." He winked at me as he walked backward toward the door. "Still on for after work?"

I nodded at him. "You convinced me."

"Good. See you then."

As much as I wanted to follow Sam back to his place, I had to run home and get clothes for the next morning. There was zero chance that I'd be coming back. And anyway, Sam had said that he could get dinner ready.

"Going somewhere?" English asked with a raised eyebrow.

"Date with Sam."

"A sleepover?"

I laughed. "Yeah. I finally get to see his apartment."

"Nice. That sounds like it's getting more official."

"I think so. Plus, our boss just said we could take the weekend after the Fourth off. I'm thinking we'll get a whole lot of..."

"Wait, really?" she asked, suddenly excited.

"Uh...yeah. Why?"

"That's when I have to be in the Hamptons for Court's thing." She waved her hand. "He's doing that photo op. Some party. But you should come too! I can get all of us out there. Then I might not kill myself, being there with him alone."

"Oh, the Kensington Cottage?" I said with a grin. "I love that place. I'll ask Sam if he wants to go."

"Thank you. *Thank god*," she said.

"Is it really that horrible, working with Court?"

She shook her head and blew out a breath. "No, he's fine. I just know that he's purposely trying to make my job harder. He can be pleasant. He just isn't."

"Sounds right."

"Well, have a good time," English said. "I'm just waiting for Josh to call."

"Have good phone sex," I called as I headed for the door.

"I will!" she called back with a laugh.

I grabbed an Uber into Brooklyn, and it pulled up in front of a tiny brick apartment building. It was a cute, if not quite trendy, part of the city. This definitely wasn't Williamsburg. I slung my bag over my shoulder and pressed the button for him to buzz me up. There was no elevator. So, I climbed the stairs to the third floor, glad that I'd opted for Nikes.

The door was unlocked, and I stepped into his apartment with wide eyes. All exposed brick and natural light with sparse furniture and a close, comfortable feel. A large stack of boxes took up the front left corner. An open door revealed the darkened bedroom. I was actually surprised how little there was in the space. It seemed the only real decorations, other than the blue curtains, were the little carvings on several surfaces. I knew from personal experience that Sam had a knack for woodworking.

"Hey, you found it," Sam said with a wary smile. "What do you think?"

"It's so adorable." I closed the door behind me and hefted a bottle of red wine in front of me. "I brought wine."

"Great. I have an opener here somewhere."

He began to rummage through the drawers as I dropped my bag onto the couch. He triumphantly pulled out a corkscrew.

"Aha! I knew I hadn't packed them both," he said.

"Why are you all packed up anyway? Does your lease end soon?"

He hadn't mentioned it, but I figured it must be up soon. Maybe by the end of the summer. Since he said he'd been here about a year.

"Oh, no." He took the bottle from me and began to open it. "Well, yes. It is soon. Going to have to figure out what I'm going to do about that. But...I actually packed up all of Claire's stuff." He gestured off to the boxes after he pulled the cork out. "It was everywhere. And I was tired of looking at it. So, I did it after Court's event. Hence..." He gestured around again.

My heart fluttered. He'd packed all of Claire's stuff up. He hadn't told me that before. I'd tried to tell myself that I wasn't worried. But in some way, this felt more real than anything else he could have done. He'd said he had things to figure out...and then he'd actually figured them out. Here was the proof.

"I like it," I told him.

"You're just saying that." He pulled two wineglasses out of a cabinet and poured us each a glass. "It's nothing compared to what you're used to."

"That doesn't mean that I don't like it."

"True," he conceded. "It has charm."

A buzzer sounded from the oven, and he hustled back over. He pulled out garlic bread wrapped in aluminum foil. He set it down on the stove and then began to stir something in a giant pot that smelled amazing.

"Need any help?" I asked.

"Uh, nope. You can take a seat, and I'll dish us up some spaghetti."

"All right." I took my wine to the small table pressed against a wall just big enough for two.

A few minutes later, Sam brought two plates over full of spaghetti with a red sauce and garlic bread. My mouth watered at the sight.

"This smells amazing."

"Thanks. It's my mom's recipe. She seemed surprised that I was making it in the city. I don't remember the last time I had time to cook. Or more specifically, had the energy to cook."

I laughed as I twirled my fork in the pasta. "I feel you. I'm glad that you did it for me."

His smile was magnetic. "Me too."

"So, now that we're getting three days off..."

"Tentatively."

I rolled my eyes. "Leslie will give them to us regardless if we hit the goal. She just wants this to be the big last push before the voter registration window closes. She'll want us to be fresh for the last month before the primary. She'll seem magnanimous. Or at least, it's what I'd do."

"True. It makes sense. Why is Shawn running her campaign and not you anyway?"

My cheeks flushed. "Shawn is more qualified."

"Bullshit. He's a head case."

"A genius strategist and head case."

"Maybe," Sam said. "But you have the heart."

"I mean, I'd love to," I told him. "Honestly, ever since I got on this campaign and realized how much I love it, I've wanted to be a campaign manager."

"You would be already if you went with a candidate for a lower office. A state senator or local mayoral race."

I nodded. "Yeah, I could. But how could I pass up the opportunity for the mayor of New York City? Even at a lower office? What I'd love to do is eventually be a campaign manager for the presidential race."

"That's big time," he said. "Even more work."

"I know."

"You'd be great at it," he said with a smile.

"Yeah?"

"Absolutely. I already think you should replace Shawn."

I laughed and waved my piece of garlic bread at him. "You're a bit biased."

"Just a bit."

"Well, it's only a dream anyway."

"It's not a dream," he said. "It's a goal. One you're already working toward and going to achieve."

"How do you know?"

"Because you're the most determined and hardworking person I know. How could you *not* achieve it? The work is worth it."

A smile tipped my lips. "Sometimes, I think you know me even better than I know myself."

"No, I think you know yourself. I just remind you that you're a badass who is going to take over the world." He took my hand across the table. "Everything else you hear or think is the world saying that you can't do this. You're not good enough. That a guy like Shawn should be in your place. That you didn't earn your spot. That's bullshit. You're here where you are because you deserve to be. You've already shown me that time and time again."

I flushed this time at his words. The words he had no idea how much it meant to hear. I'd been given everything in my life, except this. This was the one thing I'd worked at. The one thing I wouldn't stop for. Not for anyone or anything.

"Thank you. Sometimes, you need to hear that."

He winked at me. "Anytime."

"So, speaking of those three days off," I said after I finished my next bite, "how do you feel about going to the Hamptons?"

"The Hamptons? Really?"

"Well, Court is doing some kind of photo-op thing with English, and she wants us to all go. I think he's giving her a hard time."

"Hmm. I wanted to go home to see my parents, but I wasn't sure how I'd even make that work since it's hardly enough time to fly. Let alone drive."

"Oh, I didn't even think about that. You know...I could get you a ticket...if you wanted to go home."

"No way. I can buy my own ticket if I have to." He started laughing and shook his head. "I mean...I did hustle the guys out of about thirty thousand dollars at poker."

"What?" I sputtered.

"They invited me to play. They didn't ask if I was any good."

"Jesus Christ!"

"Yeah," he said with another laugh. "They insisted I keep the money too. Said that they didn't play for fake stakes."

"Sounds like them."

"Anyway, it's obviously not about the money. It's more about the time."

"Right. I get that."

"I think I'd rather go to the Hamptons with you."

"You're sure?"

He nodded with a glimmer in his dark eyes. "How can I say no to a weekend alone with you in a dream locale?"

I bit my lip, thinking of all the trouble we could get into. "You can't."

"Exactly."

25

LARK

"Have you heard how many we're at?" Sam asked again.

"My phone has been going off *nonstop*," I said, pulling it out of my back pocket. "Reports of how many voter registrations people have at each event around the city and then field updates on totals. Looks like we're close. Maybe a few hundred from our goal."

"Not bad."

It wasn't.

On any normal day, asking for more several thousand voter registrations would be insane. But with so many people out for the Fourth of July and all the festivities around the city, making them easily accessible, it might actually happen.

It was crazy that we were even out here.

"Boots on the ground," as Shawn had said.

This was the kind of work Sam and I had done on the campaign in Madison. Field work was the most tiring and also the most rewarding. Contact with voters made them five times as likely to vote. Any contact. Everyone hated getting phone calls and having their doors knocked on, but every time you had that inter-action, it increased the likelihood of voting. And considering voter turnout generally sucked, getting as many people *out there* to talk to voters helped.

Which was why Sam and I were in Mayor Kensington T-shirts in Prospect Park in Brooklyn, walking around and trying to get as many people registered to vote as possible.

"All of this would be a lot easier if they lowered the cost of voting," Sam grumbled.

"I know," I said with a shrug. "It's costly for so many people to vote. You have to find the time, a way to get the poll, sometimes drive long distances to get to a polling place, maybe take off work, not to mention if you're a single parent you have to arrange child-care or bring them to the polls, wait in long lines, and that's all bare minimum on the *day of.* Voting is a right, but a lot of times it feels like a privilege."

"Preaching to the choir."

"And anyway, registration is the biggest impediment to getting people to the polls. Especially in New York where you have to be registered twenty-five days before election day. For a presidential election, where there's so much media attention, it might make sense. People have it on the brain to register early. But for local elections...primaries, it really hurts us."

"It's worse other places."

I nodded. "Yeah. Everyone is so worried about voter fraud even though it rarely happens. What they should be worried about is how few people actually register and even fewer vote. A lot of elections would look differently if we managed to mobilize the entire population."

"Your real passion—participation."

I winked at him and then pointed toward a large group up ahead. "Participating in the government is the hill that I die on," I confirmed. "I was the asshole who didn't give a shit about partici-pating. I thought that I had everything. That it wouldn't matter what happened. I was young and stupid. Politics are personal. Poli-tics are everything that you do in your life. It's your roads and your health and your children and your air and water. It's not just the controversial stuff that makes the news."

"I'm with you," Sam said. "Once you get bit by the campaign bug, it never goes away. I worked for Senator Maxwell back in North Carolina."

"Wait, the hot one?" I asked.

He rolled his eyes. "Yes, the hot one."

"The one who, like, banged an undergrad?"

"I was an undergrad when all that went down at UNC. It was blown way out of proportion. He's a great guy." I eagerly looked at him for details, and he just shook his head. "Anyway, we worked with so many small races where the margin of victory was literally less than a hundred votes. So few people were voting that just asking your friends to come with you could have changed the tide of the election."

"Right! I mean, it's not exactly the same for the mayoral race here. But I think voting is the least you can do. Calling your representatives, going to a phone bank, knocking on a few doors—it all doesn't take *that* long."

"Or you can be like your parents and just give money."

I snorted. "Or that."

"We need the money," he said with a shrug.

"Yeah. Have to pay everyone."

"Buy the fancy ad spots."

I wrinkled my nose at him and smacked him with my clipboard. "It's the people that make the campaign."

"The people and the community."

"Again, preaching to the choir," I said as we finally came up on the ground. "You or me?"

He shrugged. "I got the last one."

"All right."

I took a deep breath and approached the group with my biggest, most genuine smile. "Hi there! We're out today, doing voter registration and celebrating the Fourth with a little civic duty of our own. Are all of you registered?"

One woman smiled and nodded. "Yep, we are."

"Great!" I said enthusiastically. "I hope that you'll all be out to the primary on August 6th to vote in the mayoral race."

"Wait, Mom, I don't think I'm registered," a college-aged girl said.

"We can do it later."

"Actually, the deadline is next weekend. And it's super easy. Only takes about five minutes of your time. We send it for you and everything."

The girl nodded. "I'll do it."

I handed over the clipboard, and then, like clockwork, a half-dozen other people remembered that they'd moved or that they weren't registered at the right address. Sam and I passed out clipboards and pens and let them fill out the information.

The mom who had first spoken just looked at our shirts and lifted her nose. "I don't even know why you support her. She acts like she's tough on crime, but then her son is such a mess."

"But he's *hot*, Mom," the girl currently filling out the form said with a giggle.

The mom just glared at me as if I were the reason for all of this. But I was prepared. It wasn't my first rodeo.

"I support Mayor Kensington because of the amazing work she's done with wage disparity for women. I'm proud to work for her campaign and say that I make a dollar for every dollar a man makes there. It's competitive, but no one is making less just because we're women and we've been taught not to ask for more," I told her with a smile. "And she's working on doing that everywhere. I can get behind that."

Her scowl vanished into something almost thoughtful. "I suppose that makes sense. At least you have a reason."

I smiled. I wasn't here to change minds. But personal stories were always more effective than yelling about political topics that literally no one could debate civilly. I had no intention of getting into a shouting match. I just wanted people to make informed decisions and vote how they felt best.

We finished up with that group, collecting the seven additional voter registrations, and then walked away.

"I lost count of how many people have bought up Court," I said with a sigh. "I hope what English is doing is helping."

"It'll take time. Especially with both Reyes and Quinn harping on it."

I nodded and pushed my shoulders back. "All right, let's get back to work."

We spent the next several hours walking the park. It was a beautiful, sunny day in the city. And as we got closer to the start of the fireworks on the East River, our numbers swelled.

Sam and I made it back to the mayor's tent in the park and handed over our stack of voter registrations. One of the field workers took it from us with wide eyes.

"This is just from the two of you?" she asked.

"Yep," I said.

"Wow. Can we send you back out? You got more than my last group of volunteers. And there were ten of them."

Sam chuckled. "Old habits die hard."

"Yeah, we're staff. We've done this before."

"Oh wow! That's awesome. You guys rocked it."

"We'd go back out, but I think final tallies should be happening soon."

The girl pointed to the voter registration. "We're working through them now."

"Excellent. Keep up the good work." I gestured for Sam to follow me.

"You don't think we should help?"

"I might have a surprise after the conference call."

"A surprise, huh?"

I nodded. "I think we've earned it. The two of us did more VR than ten volunteers."

He grinned at me, and my heart melted. "All right, you've convinced me."

Once we were out of sight of the tent, I took Sam's hand in mine and directed him out of the park. We walked companionably through the busy streets of Brooklyn and to the marinas on the East River.

Sam stopped when we approached the docks. "What are you doing?"

I couldn't contain my excitement. "Come on. I'll show you."

I pulled him toward a medium-sized yacht on the dock. My friends Lewis and Rowe were already on board along with Rowe's boyfriend, Nicholas, and Lewis's girlfriend, Addie. A dozen other people were already on the yacht, awaiting the time when the Coast Guard would allow vessels into the water for the fireworks.

"Are you serious?" Sam asked with wide eyes.

"Yeah. Lewis invited me, but I didn't plan on joining him. But... I thought you'd like to see the fireworks from the water."

He turned his attention to me completely. "You're amazing. You know that?"

"I mean, we're hitching a ride."

But he didn't let me finish downplaying what I'd done. He placed his hands on either side of my face and crushed our lips together. I stood, momentarily frozen by his enthusiasm. I hadn't thought it was that big of deal, but I'd never really shared this part of myself with him before. I'd spent so much time hiding Larkin St. Vincent, trying to be someone else, that he never saw all of me. And now that he had...he wasn't pulling away. In fact, he seemed to be even more all in.

Whistles came from the boat, and we pulled away with laughs and blushes.

"Okay, okay," I said to Lewis and Addie on the boat.

I grabbed Sam's hand and pulled him on board. I made introductions to the people he'd heard so much about all those years ago. It was still strange to have my crew so disconnected, but with Penn still in Paris and Katherine already in the Hamptons, it was impossible. Not to mention, things were still...rough after Natalie's party earlier this summer.

Almost as soon as we boarded, the yacht began to move out into the East River, and the party really started. I motioned for Sam to follow me to the front of the boat to watch us pull away.

"You have such a crazy life," he admitted.

"No, it's pretty boring ninety-five percent of the time."

"But that five percent is pretty spectacular."

I gazed out across the river and smiled. "I guess it is."

Sam pulled out his phone and called into the conference call for the mayor, putting us on mute to block out background noise.

And then Shawn's voice crackled through the line. "Hey, folks. This is Shawn Trotter here, campaign manager for Mayor Kensington. I'm pleased that we have so many people on the line tonight. The most we've ever had for the Kensington campaign. We've done some amazing work today. And I don't want to keep you all too long since the fireworks should be going off soon, but we have a special guest tonight—Mayor Kensington."

There was a short pause, and then Leslie joined him. Sam and I shot surprised glances at each other. We'd had *a lot* of conference calls, but the mayor was so busy that she rarely was able to get on.

"Yes, thank you, Shawn. It's a pleasure to be with you all tonight. And to be the one to announce that not only did we meet our voter registration goal, but we *exceeded* it by over five hundred registrations. That's all thanks to you. Each of you being out there, working on your holiday to try to make the final push for the campaign. The primary is only a month away, and I've never been more confident with the team that we have in place."

I grinned. She was such a natural. Shawn took over the rest of the call from the mayor. She was probably off to some party for the evening, but he stayed on to congratulate each of the boroughs on how many registrations they'd gotten and how good we'd all looked.

By the end of the call, the sky had darkened. Sam turned to face me in the last rays of the setting sun as yellow turned to blue and then to black. He tipped my chin up with his finger. He didn't have to say a word. It was all conveyed in his eyes.

As his lips fell on mine, the first firework exploded off of the Brooklyn Bridge. And I knew I was falling head over heels for this man all over again.

26

SAM

"You drive a Tesla?" I asked with a shake of my head.

"Yeah, I own a fucking Tesla!" Gavin cried.

"You work for Dorset & King."

"And?"

"It's an oil company," I reminded him, running a hand down the slick navy body of the car.

"Yeah. Just because my family owns an oil company doesn't mean that I don't care about the environment."

I quirked an eyebrow. "That literally makes zero sense."

Gavin just shrugged and popped open the driver's side of the car. "Do you want a ride to the Hamptons or not, dude?"

"I'd like to drive to the Hamptons. This thing is beautiful."

"Yeah. No can do," he said with a laugh. He held his arm out wide. "Ladies, after you."

Lark and Whitley left their suitcases by the trunk and then slipped into the backseat, giggling like schoolgirls. Gavin and I added their two suitcases and our two duffel bags to the trunk. I still had no clue why they needed that much stuff for just a few days at the beach. But I was smart enough not to ask.

Soon enough, we were zipping down the highway out of Manhattan and off to the Hamptons. The weather was perfect on

Friday morning, and luckily, we were beating most of the traffic out of the city. It seemed most tourists were staying through the holiday weekend, which made sense. I was just glad to escape it for a weekend even if my parents had been disappointed that I wasn't coming home. Especially since Jake's birthday was Saturday. Not that I particularly wanted to see my brother.

"So, I'm surprised your girlfriend isn't here with you," I told Gavin.

He sputtered. "What?"

Whitley cackled from the back. "Don't you know? Gavin King doesn't have girlfriends."

Gavin shot her a look in the rearview mirror. "Whatever. Charlie and I just aren't serious."

"Have you ever been serious with anyone?" she asked.

"I like to play the field. You should know *all* about that. Didn't you and Keri just break up?"

Whitley shrugged. "We made it, like, six weeks. That's pretty good."

"I didn't know that you and Keri broke up," Lark said. "Admittedly, I have been a little invested in my own relationship."

"Hey, get all that D while you can," Whitley said.

Lark just shook her head. "Sure."

"And yeah, Keri was nice, but I think she wanted us to put a label on it. Make it official. And she wasn't the one. If I already know that, then what's the point of wasting my time? When the person is the one, then I'll know."

"Will you?" Lark asked. Her eyes flittered up to mine, and she smiled.

"Yeah. Of course I will."

Gavin shrugged. "I'll have no fucking clue. If you're supposed to know, then I think I'm fucked."

Whitley laughed. "Probably."

But I knew. And when Lark looked at me, I could see that she knew too. That we'd both known a long time ago, and shit had just gotten between us. It took work to make it work though.

We finally pulled off of the main road and drove through glittering Southampton. Lark directed us the rest of the way to the Kensington Cottage, which she'd claimed was a beautiful house on the shoreline. I'd only ever heard stories about the Hamptons. That it was where celebrities and rich New Yorkers went to summer. It had always felt too surreal to even consider. Even more surreal to be here.

"This one," Lark said from the back, pointing at a house.

We pulled up in front of what appeared to be an enormous mansion, and my jaw dropped. "I thought you said this was a cottage."

"Don't you know *cottage* is just rich people terminology for mansion?" Gavin said with a laugh as he pulled into the driveway.

The place was three stories high and looked to have dozens of bedrooms. It was sprawled on a giant lot with ample privacy from any neighbors. There was wealthy, and then there was Kensington wealthy, apparently.

"Holy shit," I breathed when I stepped out of the car.

Whitley whistled too. "Yeah, damn. So glad my client wanted to move her breast implants to next weekend. This house is way better."

Lark just beamed at me. "Wait until you see the inside."

Gavin and I grabbed the bags and hauled them up the steps and inside. I dropped my duffel, and my eyes widened. Holy fucking hell. It was like stepping into a magazine spread. I'd only ever dreamed of designing and building something like this. My dad's business tended to do more basic work. Monotonous work with little imagination. But sometimes, we got wealthy Chapel Hill clients who wanted our top-end lines, and we'd have some fun with it. I rarely missed construction work, but looking at this house made me wonder if I should have gone into architecture like my dad had wanted.

"Are you still breathing?" Lark asked with a laugh.

I shook out of my stupor. "Sometimes, the construction eye comes out. This house is...a marvel."

"I know nothing of construction and totally agree. It's probably my favorite house I've ever stayed in. And all my friends and my parents have properties in the Hamptons. Nothing beats the Kensington Cottage."

I could see that.

Then English appeared out of a back doorway. She rushed toward Lark, pulling her into a hug. "Oh my god, I'm so glad you're here. I've been cooped up with him for two days, and it's been..." She trailed off as if she couldn't think of words to describe how awful it was to have been here this long with Court.

"You used to work with rockstars. You've had to pay off prostitutes and keep sex tapes out of the news. You convinced that one guy to have his wife say she was sick to explain her absence and had her agree not to divorce him for sleeping with other men until after his movie premiered."

English sighed. "I regret telling you about my profession."

"Court cannot be worse than that."

"He's not. He's a different kind of terrible." She shrugged. "All of those people *wanted* my help. Court would rather throw his reputation and everything to deal with Jane in a burning building that he'd lit on fire himself."

"You'll get to him," Lark said.

"Come on. I need your help with something before the shoot tomorrow." She looked up at me. "You don't mind if I borrow her, do you?"

"No, that's fine. I'll just go find Court."

"Okay, great! He's out back," English said and then yanked a reluctant Lark down a hallway.

I abandoned the bags, figuring I'd find out where we were sleeping later, and went in search of Court. I walked through the living room, past the dining room, peeked into the fucking insane kitchen, and then stepped through the back door. The view took my breath away. A giant deck with a large pool and hot tub. Past that was the Atlantic Ocean, waves breaking along the beach.

"Wow," I breathed.

"Yeah, it's nicer than the city views right now," Court said.

I turned to find him lounging in a chair with a beer in his hand. He was looking out toward the ocean, his gaze distant.

"Hey," I said. "I can't believe you grew up like this."

He shrugged. "It was a total hardship."

"I can see that," I said sarcastically.

He grinned up at me. There was something of the spark of Court Kensington in that look. "It'll be better when everyone is here for the party tomorrow. This house is made for parties."

"I heard that you're giving English hell," I said as I took the seat next to him.

He raised an eyebrow. "Is that what she said?"

"Just that you don't want the help."

"That at least is true. I don't want it. I don't need it. No one fucking cares what I do. They never have."

I leaned back in my chair and surveyed the pool for a few seconds before responding, "I actually think you do need her help."

"Why is that?" he asked with bite in his voice.

"Look, Lark and I were out yesterday, doing voter registration for the campaign."

"Isn't that beneath you?" Court asked with a laugh.

"It's the backbone of the campaign. It's pretty important. But when we were out there, we talked to a lot of voters. And at least a dozen people brought you up. People know what happened. They don't like how it reflects on your mom, and they don't want to elect her because of it." I took a deep breath before saying, "And we need her."

"Why?" he asked, but the bite was gone.

"Because she makes a difference."

"She's a shit mother," Court quipped.

"She's a great politician."

Court sighed. "I see where you're going with this. I should just do what she says because the city needs her. Even if she's never fucking cared about me."

"She seemed to care the day you were arrested."

Court was silent on that regard.

"I can't speak to it. I have great parents. But...I've been in this feud with my brother. A couple years ago, he did something horrible to me. For a while, I would blame my parents anytime they saw him. I'd refuse to come over if he was there."

"That sounds familiar. Penn and I didn't get along for a long time either."

"Yeah, but I realized I was punishing my parents for what he'd done. So, I stopped. I still see him. We're civil. We're not the same, but it's not my parents' fault that Jake fucked up and that I don't want to see him anymore." I shrugged. "I'm not sure it's your mother's fault that she seems to know what the city needs more than what you need. Especially if you don't tell her."

Court looked off in the distance for a long time without speaking. I thought he might tell me to fuck off or something. But eventually, he just nodded.

"Maybe you're right." He glanced at me. "Is this what people who aren't forced to repress their feelings learn from growing up in stable households?"

I snorted. "Something like that."

Court held his hand out, and I shook it. "Come on. Let's go get you beer. I need to be comfortably buzzed tonight since I have to be stone-cold sober in the morning for this magazine shoot." He rolled his eyes. "If I have to play by English's rules, I'm going to look damn good in that magazine."

I laughed as we stepped back inside and retrieved a beer. Gavin came back over, and we all went back on the deck, laughing and joking while the girls were off doing who knew what.

And I realized that for the first time since moving to New York a year ago, I finally felt like I belonged. In this place. With this group. With Lark.

It all felt right. I just hoped I could hold on to it without it slipping between my fingers.

27

LARK

The house was empty.

Sam had left with Gavin and Camden to go golfing. Whitley had plans to meet a friend for some shopping in town. Katherine had claimed she needed a spa day and would be over before the party tonight.

Any minute now, the camera crew and photographers would be here to take over the house we'd spent all morning getting ready. English had had a cleaning crew come in and make the place spotless the day before, but after we'd partied a little harder than we'd planned the night before, we'd had to buckle down and get it sparkling again.

Now, English was just tapping her foot and waiting for everyone to show up.

"I cannot believe you managed to get Court Kensington into hair and makeup," I told her.

She shrugged. "I can't either. He'd been adamantly against it up until this morning. Then he'd just complied as if he'd put all his energy into irritating me and then flipped on a light switch. I'm not complaining. I'm glad he did it. He's gorgeous, but everyone needs makeup on camera nowadays."

"Gorgeous, huh?" I asked, nudging her.

She rolled her eyes at me. "Not Josh gorgeous. Just objectively a handsome man. Come on. You've slept with a Kensington. You can appreciate them."

"Oh, I can. They're like perfect specimens. But I don't really think of Penn as gorgeous anymore. He's just...Penn."

"Well, Court is just Court too."

The doorbell rang, interrupting us. English straightened her perfect white suit and opened the door. The woman who ran the magazine that Court was going to be featured in gushed over English's outfit, made introductions, and then immediately got to work, figuring out the game plan.

"Where is Court?" the woman, who had introduced herself as Evelyn, asked.

And then Court materialized. He was every inch the gorgeous specimen that we'd been describing before Evelyn's team appeared. He was mouthwateringly hot. The hair and makeup team had only amplified his features. The hollowed cheekbones and chiseled jaw. The piercing blue eyes, cropped and styled dark hair, the full, perfect lips. English had dressed him to look preppy and effortless. Like a prep-school boy, all grown up.

"Hello," Evelyn said after she stared at him in shock for a few seconds. "I'm Evelyn Rothschild. I'll be working here with the team today. We're going to start by having you walk us around the house on camera. Our readers are going to die to see this house on display. When we're done, we'll end with a photoshoot. Shouldn't take more than a few hours."

His eyes shot to English's, as if to say, *A few hours?*

But to Evelyn, he just smiled that charming Kensington smile and said, "Let's begin then."

It took the better half of the day for Evelyn to get everything she wanted from Court. And though I couldn't see what she was looking for, I didn't doubt her talent. English had said she was a genius at what she did. And that she had the kind of reach they were looking for.

"Thank you so much, Evelyn," English said. She removed what I could have sworn looked like a couple hundred-dollar bills and passed them to Evelyn as they shook hands once more. "I cannot wait to see you run the feature on my client."

Evelyn smiled like a Cheshire cat. "Our readers will love him. I can just see this house tour going viral. Who knows? Maybe our readers will want to see a bit *more* of him next time."

English just kept on smiling. "Maybe if they're lucky."

Then Evelyn laughed and left with her camera crew.

English shut the door with a snap and leaned against it.

"Did she just ask to see him without his clothes on?" I asked. "I wasn't misreading that, right?"

"She definitely did," Court said. He ran his hand back through his hair, perfectly mussing the do that had taken a stylist a half hour. And then he unbuttoned his sleeves and began to roll them up to his elbows. "God, does this look better?"

I laughed. "Much. Looks more like you."

"Rumpled?" he asked.

"Just real instead of polished."

English was still leaning her forehead against the door. She slowly straightened. "That went well. I thought she'd ask for him shirtless a lot sooner. A second feature with you shirtless is better after we see the audience reaction to this one."

Court just shook his head. "Your job is strange."

She quirked a smile at him. "Tell me about it."

"But we're done, right?" I asked. "No more photo ops for the weekend?"

"We're done," English confirmed.

Court sighed. "Good. We're all getting fucking drunk tonight at my party."

English smirked at him. "Why wait for the party?"

"Now, you're speaking my language," he said, following her into the kitchen.

"If you can't beat 'em, join 'em."

Which was how the rest of the group found the three of us already nice and drunk, lying out on the back deck in our bathing suits, not at all prepared for a party.

Sam just smirked down at me. "I hope you put sunscreen on."

I turned my head to English. "Did I put sunscreen on?"

"Uh...hours ago. I think."

"Fuck," I muttered and then burst into laughter. "I'm going to be a lobster later."

"Come on. Let's get that pale skin out of the sun." He took my hand and helped me up. "We should probably get ready for the party before anyone else shows up."

English nudged Court. "Hey, party boy. Get your ass dressed."

He snorted and then sent her the most charming, intoxicating Kensington smile. "You get my ass dressed."

English rolled her eyes. "It wouldn't be the first time I'd have to get someone into clothes when they couldn't hold down their alcohol."

I left them bickering and followed Sam back to the room we were staying in. It was a giant room with a canopied bed at the center and a beautiful bay window with a reading cushion. It was probably my favorite room in the house.

I flopped back onto the bed and giggled. "I feel so good."

"Did the magazine thing go this poorly?" he asked, stripping out of the polo he'd worn to the golf course.

"Nope. It went great. English thinks it's going to go viral. And Court miraculously behaved the entire time. He didn't even fight English. I don't know what got into him."

"Huh. I guess that would be me. I talked to him about it last night."

"Really?" I asked, propping myself up on my elbow. "You got Court Kensington to behave? Do you want to be his publicist?"

He laughed. "Negative. Just his friend."

"You look good shirtless."

"Thanks," he said with a half-smile. "How burnt are you going to be?"

I stared down at my body and shrugged. "Mostly my legs, I think."

"Let's get you in a shower and then lather you in aloe before this party."

I slid off of the bed and put my arms around him. "Thanks for taking care of me."

"Always."

I pressed my lips to his, and he deepened it. Then he slipped an arm under my legs and lifted me into his arms. I squeaked in surprise as he carried me into the giant walk-in shower attached to this room. He set me down onto my feet once we were inside and flipped the water on as hot as it would go.

He shucked his khakis and boxers onto the ground outside of the shower and then moved toward me. I bit my lip and stepped back until he pressed me into the stone wall.

His lips covered mine again, fiercely, possessively. His hand slipped behind my back and yanked on the strings of my favorite black bikini. The material hit the ground, leaving me in just my ruched cheeky bottoms. But he wasn't satisfied with that. His thumbs hooked into the hem and slid them over my ass and onto the floor.

I had no words. I loved this unbridled, forceful Sam. The one who saw me in a bikini and carried me into the shower to get to me. I wanted this Sam so fucking bad. And his erection pressing into my stomach said how much he wanted me too.

He lifted one of my legs, hiking it up around his waist. I gasped as he pressed his dick against the space between my thighs. My eyes squeezed shut as warmth rolled through me. I dug my nails into his back, wanting more, needing more.

He obliged by grinding against me in the most delicious and dangerous way imaginable. I scrambled to get more. To feel him take what was his. But he hesitated. I could see the strain it took for him to stop.

"Condom?" he rasped.

"Fuck," I said. "I'm on the pill."

He met my gaze, seeing my confirmation that I wanted this anyway. "Okay. Fuck."

Then without another word, he lifted my leg up and slammed me back against the stone shower wall. I groaned as he aligned our bodies and then thrust up into me. My back bowed off the wall as he filled me completely.

The steam rose up all around us, obscuring everything but Sam in front of me. Making us slippery and wet and sweaty. Heightened everything to the point of desperation. His muscles bulged as he held me against the wall and drove up into me hard and fast . Took me with everything he had.

And it was mere minutes before we were both crying out into the steam of the shower as we hit a wave and raced down it together.

Slowly, ever so slowly, Sam released his grip and set me down on my shaky legs. They immediately collapsed underneath me, and I fell into a heap on the shower floor.

"Wow," I murmured.

"Yeah, fuck," he said. "That was…"

"Amazing."

"Do you need help standing?"

I laughed and nodded. He reached down and helped me up, gently walking me back into the stream and kissing my mouth.

"I missed you, by the way."

"Oh, was that what this was?" I asked with a smile.

"Yes."

"Miss me all the time then."

"If you'd like."

Then he kissed me under the stream of water, and I lost cognizant thought all over again.

English shot us conspiratorial looks when we reemerged in time for the start of the party. Apparently, we had not thought about how loud we were being. But also, I couldn't even be bothered to care. It had been some kind of wonderful.

"Well, you're glowing," Katherine said when she finally made her appearance.

"Glowing?" I asked in surprise, sipping on a glass of champagne Sam had retrieved for me after insisting on several glasses of water first. I looked down at the green sundress I'd brought with me. Another from my mother's Bergdorf purchases. She really had figured out my style. It made me weirdly uncomfortable. But I still wore it.

"Indeed."

"You're as stunning as ever."

And she was in a blush sundress with her magnificent hair piled up on the top of her head. Her lips were tinted a lush pink. She looked like the epitome of summer. When she was clearly a winter flower—prized and rare.

"I make do," Katherine said with a choice smirk.

"How has it been, staying here with Camden?"

Her smile vanished. "Acceptable."

Translation: *horrible.*

"I'm sorry."

Her eyes flashed. "Don't."

"I wasn't," I said instantly. I knew Katherine liked pity as much as a bag of tarantulas being dropped on her head.

"Luckily, Fiona isn't in the Hamptons," she admitted. "It's harder in the city."

I could see that. More options. More ways to hurt one another. I just wished they could talk it out and figure out how to move on. But I didn't see it happening anytime soon.

"I'm going to go find a drink," Katherine said. She leaned in and kissed both of my cheeks. "I'm happy for you."

I beamed. "Thanks. Me too."

"You deserve this." Katherine gave me a sad smile and then disappeared in search of that drink.

My heart ached for my friend. I didn't know how to fix them. It was beyond me. Maybe even beyond English's expertise. I just hoped they didn't do anything else that would irreparably ruin them in the meantime.

Sam reappeared then with a kiss on my lips. "God, you look great."

I laughed and wrinkled my nose at him. "Katherine said I looked like I was glowing."

"Must be the sex."

"Sure, throw me up against a shower wall, and I start to emit low-level radiation."

He snorted. "Is that what's causing me to fall in love with you again?"

My mouth opened and then closed. And then he kissed my lips again.

"Rhetorical question," he amended. Then a few seconds later, "But...I am."

"You are?"

He nodded. "How could I not?"

"Good question."

"Cocky much?"

I grinned and brought his mouth back to mine. "I am too. So... you're lucky."

"I am. Very."

We sipped on our drinks as the party passed by. I was so glad that we'd agreed to come out here. The Hamptons had a lulling effect. As if everything was going to be okay. And the problem with lulling was that it didn't make you stay on your toes. It didn't prepare you for what was coming next.

My back stiffened. My eyes locked on the figure that walked into the house. He was tall and lanky with dark hair and hazel eyes. Nothing too distinct about him, but I'd recognize his gait and mannerisms in a heartbeat.

"What is it?" Sam asked, reading my body language and following my gaze to the front door. "Who is that?"

"That's Thomas." I sighed. "My ex-boyfriend."

28

LARK

"Ugh," I grumbled. "Maybe he won't see me."

"Why? What happened between y'all?" Sam asked.

I shook my head. "Fuck, he just saw me." I shot Sam a pained expression. "I'll tell you about it later. But first, keep me from killing him."

"That serious?"

"Please."

"All right. I'll do my best," he said warily.

I didn't blame him for being wary. Every time I saw Thomas, I felt like I'd been mowed over. And I hadn't seen him in a while. I'd thought it was a sign of good fortune. Then here he was, at the Kensington Cottage. He had to have at least guessed that I might be here. Had he come to purposely torture me?

And there he went...walking toward me. As if he were drawn to the one person who least wanted to see him.

Of course there was a woman on his arm. Or maybe a girl. She looked really fucking young. But since we'd broken up, he'd been going younger and younger. She looked like a model—tall and emaciated with large eyes and intense cheekbones and collarbone.

"Larkin," Thomas said in greeting. "Funny seeing you here."

"Hello, Thomas," I said stiffly, losing any lingering buzz.

He looked the same. And yet so different. When we'd dated, he'd always worn these designer jeans and button-ups that he rolled up. He liked jackets and had several dozen of them—leather, linen, bomber, jean. None of them the preppy suit coat he was wearing today. That was before my parents had hired him to work for St. Vincent's Enterprise. Now, he only wore fancy suits with tie clips and shiny shoes. He'd ditched the easygoing guy I'd met and fallen for and dived headfirst into upper management.

But he'd probably always had that snake of a smile and sinister widow's peak. The calculating smile and fake interest. I just hadn't looked for it. Hadn't wanted to.

"I didn't think you could ever get time off work for these sorts of things," he said casually. As if it wasn't a pointed remark about how I hadn't had time for him.

I just shrugged. No use in feeding the beast. "I normally can't."

"Honey, are you going to introduce me?" the girl said. She leaned her head against his shoulder and fluttered her long eyelashes up at him.

"Sure. Felicity, this is Larkin St. Vincent."

"Oh," she said with wide eyes. "Your mother is a genius. I love her signature Larkin bag." She gasped. "Wait...is that...*you*?"

"Yes," I said with an inward cringe. "That's me."

"Brilliant. Do you work for the company too?"

"No," I said at once.

"Too?" Sam asked, finally interjecting.

Thomas looked him up and down and then dismissed him. "Yes, I work for St. Vincent's."

Sam met my gaze as if he had just figured out a piece of the puzzle. He slipped an arm around me. Thomas finally picked up on it.

"And who are you?"

"Sam," he said, holding his hand out. "Lark's boyfriend."

Thomas shook his hand. "And what do *you* do?"

"Legal counsel for the Kensington campaign."

"Ah...so you two *work* together," Thomas said.

My stomach dropped. I hadn't thought about that fact. Our

friends knew and didn't care. I didn't know what Thomas would do with the information.

I was saved from answering by Court, Camden, and Gavin appearing as if out of thin air. Thomas immediately straightened. He could talk to me like shit. But Camden was his idol. I'd heard him lament it many a days once upon a time. And Court and Gavin had enough sway in the Upper East Side that he'd want to kiss their asses.

"Thomas," Court said, shaking his hand in greeting. "I don't remember inviting you."

Thomas flushed slightly but sidestepped easily. "I was in the area."

So, he *hadn't* even been invited. He'd just fucking shown up and crashed the place. Douche. Opportunistic, social-climbing douche.

Camden held out his hand next. "Saw you on the course today. How did you end up?"

Thomas looked like he'd swallowed a golf ball as he shook Gavin's hand next. He was no golfer. I knew that much.

"Par for the course," he lied through his teeth.

Gavin laughed. "Better than me. I sure didn't hit par. I fucking hate golf, but it's a gentleman's sport."

"Which is why you're so terrible at it," Camden quipped.

"I never claimed to be a gentleman. I don't have to pretend to be anyone I'm not." Gavin shrugged with that big grin on his face. Enjoying himself as they slowly crushed Thomas under their collective boot.

Thomas cleared his throat. "I heard that you all have a poker game going in the city."

Camden's attention focused on that comment. "And where exactly did you hear that?"

"Around," Thomas said vaguely. "I was just mentioning because I have a game myself. It's going to be a full night of gambling and drinking and debauchery." He painted the picture for them. "If it sounds like your kind of event, I could get invites out to you. Very exclusive, of course."

"What do you think, Sam?" Camden asked pointedly. "Think you're ready to get your ass kicked in poker again at Thomas's event?"

I held back my snicker.

Sam just shrugged sheepishly, perfectly playing the role. "I suppose. If I get an invite."

That had not been part of Thomas's plan. A look of irritation flashed across his face. "Of course. Any friend of Camden Percy is a friend of mine."

"Then it's settled. Send the invites to me," Camden insisted. "We'll be there."

Thomas smiled brightly, hearing the dismissal in Camden's voice. "I look forward to it."

He took Felicity by the arm and hastily drew her across the room, away from the lot of us.

I was glad that I was watching Camden's face as Thomas disappeared. Or I wouldn't have seen the flash of rage settle across his features.

"I really hate that guy," he growled before returning to his cool Upper East Side mask of neutrality and boredom.

The end of the confrontation left me in jitters. Seeing Thomas always did this. No matter how much I'd put him behind me, he still made me so infuriatingly angry and near-to-tears upset. He'd manipulated me, and I should have known better. Seen it coming. But I'd been blindsided all the same. And it hit me fresh every time.

"Thanks for that," I said to the guys. "I just need some air."

Then I pushed past them all, through the back door, out to the deck, and then continued until my feet were in the sand. The beach was still relatively sparse this time of night. And it gave me the peace and quiet I needed.

I tipped my head back to stare up at the nearly full moon and breathed in the salty air. I wasn't alone for long though. After a few minutes, Sam plodded down onto the beach next to me. I met his gaze, lit only by the moon and the brightening stars overhead.

"Sorry," I said automatically.

"So, your ex is a total dick. I don't blame you for wanting a minute."

I laughed in a self-deprecating manner. "Yeah. I really knew how to pick 'em."

"What happened? Why is he like that?"

I ran a hand back through the tamed loose curls that framed my face. "Well, Thomas and I dated for just over a year. I thought things were perfect. He moved into my apartment. My parents got him a job with the company. I was pretty sure I was going to get married and all that.

"Then this girl who used to work for the mayor was telling everyone about the hot date she'd had the night before with a guy on Tinder. She showed everyone the picture...and it was Thomas."

"What?" Sam asked, wide-eyed.

"Yeah. He was picking up people on Tinder and taking them back to *my* apartment to have sex with them."

"What the fuck? Why?"

I shrugged. "Narcissistic personality disorder?"

"How about a giant fucking entitled douche bag?"

"That too. Well, I confronted him, but he denied it all. Said he wouldn't move out, wouldn't leave the company, wouldn't let me break up with him."

"What the fuck?"

"I'd made it too easy on him. I'd brought him into this world," I told him. "He didn't want to let it go. Penn and Lewis packed all of his shit up one day and threw it out into the hallway, had all the locks changed, and were there to threaten him if he came near me again. But the job with the company...my parents took his side. They didn't believe me. Thought I was exaggerating because I just couldn't be happy."

"God, I'm so sorry. That's horrible."

"It was a really rough couple of months. Between the shit with Thomas and you leaving me for Melissa, I just kind of figured I was done with relationships."

"Wait," Sam said, holding a hand up, "I didn't *leave you* for Melissa."

I raised my eyebrows. "What else would you call it?"

"That isn't what happened at all. You hacked into her computer and made up a bunch of fake emails between her and a nonexistent guy. Then you *paid* someone to pretend to be him. He showed up in Madison and proclaimed his love for her. It was next-level manipulative!"

I took a step back. "You *still* believe all of that? I sent the email. I told him that she was in Madison and to come see her. That was Bad Lark. I admit it. Melissa was just the latest casualty in my warpath," I said in frustration. "But I did *not* invent this guy. Those emails had already been there. She was talking to him. You just refused to listen to me."

"Then how did she have receipts of you paying him?" he asked.

"God, I can't believe we even have to go over this again," I said with a shake of my head. "I paid for his flight to come out to see her. That's the receipt she had. It was wrong. I owned up to that. I spent the next five years trying to not turn into that manipulative person again. But I was not the only one in the wrong that day. Melissa started it all."

He paused and took a deep breath. "Sorry. I don't want to fight about this. I just...I guess I still don't really know what happened."

"Here's what happened," I said with a resigned sigh. "You invited your ex-girlfriend to stay at your place and help with the campaign the last three weeks we were there. You and I were dating, and then there was another girl—your ex—living in your apartment."

"Yeah, that wasn't my best move. But...it was platonic."

"For you," I countered. "The first night I met Melissa, she told me she was going to win you back. I told her, if she tried, I'd ruin her life."

Sam cringed. "Jesus."

"Yeah, and I was...well, me back then. I'd ruined many many lives before hers. I meant what I said. Doing little shitty things to each other. Then my picture appeared in the tabloids: Upper East Side princess in the dirt. She told me she did it, Sam," I reminded him. "But you didn't believe precious, sweet Melissa could do that.

So, I retaliated. I wanted you to see what she was capable of. But of course, as it went down, you only saw what *I* was capable of."

He nodded. "Hindsight is twenty-twenty."

"Yeah, it sure is. So, you can see how, to me, it looked like you had broken up with me for Melissa."

"Yeah, I can see that. Even if that wasn't my intention. We didn't get back together until after Christmas."

"I didn't know that," I whispered. "I thought you were back together before the campaign was even over."

He shook his head. "No, I was a fucking wreck after you."

"Me too," I whispered.

He laughed once, short and painful. "Want to hear how Karma repaid me for not believing you?"

I arched an eyebrow. "What do you mean?"

"Melissa slept with Jake."

"What?" I gasped. "She slept with your *brother*?"

"Yeah. I don't know how long it happened, but it wasn't just one time. Jake and I have never been the same since."

"Fuck. What a *bitch*."

"She really is." He breathed out heavily. "You know, I've been so angry for so long about what happened with us, what happened with Melissa. I was dating Claire because she was the safe choice, the easy choice. But now that I'm looking at you, now that I have you back, I think I've just been mourning the loss of you. No one could ever replace you."

I swallowed back tears. "I'm so sorry about the past. How we acted and treated each other. It was so shitty. I wish I could take back my part in it."

He pulled me into his arms. "I know. But we're here now. And I think it's well past time to let the past be in the past."

As I breathed in his scent with my feet in the sand and the moon shining bright on the both of us, I felt like I might finally be able to come to terms with my past. I was tired of carrying it around with me like Sisyphus pushing the boulder up the mountain for all of eternity. I was ready to let the boulder go. And just be here with Sam, looking forward. Only forward from now on.

29

SAM

It felt impossible to go back to work on Monday morning.

Having the entire weekend alone with Lark had felt like a dream. After dealing with Thomas and our broken past, we were closer than ever before. I still couldn't believe I'd blurted out that I loved her. I hadn't planned to do that. It felt early. Or it had before the weekend we spent together. Now, it just felt right. Like there was no other alternative.

I might be lovesick, but I couldn't contain it. Lark brought out the best in me. It even made work seem better, more vibrant. Despite the fact that we were going into longer hours leading up to the primary. There was so much to do. Never enough time to get it all done. And I still felt like I was in a fucking musical where I was going to break out into song at any moment.

It was ridiculous.

I'd even called my brother to wish him a happy birthday.

He'd been shocked as hell.

I'd been shocked.

But if I was putting the past to rest, then maybe I could put this to rest too. Forgiveness wasn't for the other person. It was grace. And grace wasn't given only to people who deserved it.

I wanted to bury the hatchet. Find a way to truly move on.

Jake had been amenable...as I'd known he would be. He'd been trying to talk to me for years. And I'd finally done it. All because of Lark.

He'd even offered to come up to New York sometime to see me. I still wasn't sure about that, but maybe, just maybe, it might work after the primary was over.

A week passed in a blur of delirious happiness. There was only work and Lark, back to work and then more Lark. I'd thought I'd hate not having anything else in my life. But between the rush of the campaign and the rush of Larkin St. Vincent, I found I needed nothing else in my life.

An email came through on my screen then.

Hey, food after we get off?

—Lark

I smiled. We were always pretty careful about what we said in email or messages through the campaign system. Probably, technically, I shouldn't be dating her. If someone went looking, our messages likely weren't as innocuous as I hoped they were. But the risk felt worth it.

Definitely. Buns in 20?

—Sam

She responded almost immediately.

You're on.

—L

I finished up the memo that I'd been working on for Gibbs. We had to file some campaign finance paperwork this week before we got any closer to the primary. Needed everything to be up to snuff.

I sent off what I had to Gibbs, grabbed my phone, and headed for the door.

Lark wasn't there yet. Just Aspen walked by me.

"Have a good night, Sam," she said with a shit-eating grin on her face.

"Night, Aspen."

I wondered if she knew about us. She was closest to Lark. She'd know if anyone did. I'd have to ask her.

As I waited for Lark to show up, I pulled out my phone to check my social media. I nearly choked when I saw the name on my screen—Claire.

I hadn't heard from her in weeks. She'd messaged me a bunch when she first left for Europe, and then it had all tapered off into silence. It was still three weeks before she was supposed to come home. We had to figure out the living situation. But I'd been putting off getting in contact with her. I didn't want to know what Europe was like, if she was having a good time, and what things would be like when she got back. In fact, I didn't want to talk to her. I just wanted to move out and get my own place and let her figure out what to do with the place in Brooklyn.

With a swipe of my finger, I sent the series of unread messages into the trash. I'd deal with that later.

"Hey, sorry about that. I got caught by Shawn," Lark said, appearing in the hallway. She smiled up at me. "Ready to go?"

"Definitely." I slid the phone back into my pocket and held the door open for her.

"God, Buns has the best burger in the city," Lark said as we got out of the cab and headed up to her apartment.

"You say that every time you go there. And then try to dispute it every time that we debate on going somewhere else."

"True," she conceded. "But it's just so greasy and delicious."

"It is. And their shakes are amazing."

She narrowed her eyes at me as we headed into the building. "I still feel personally victimized that you got a strawberry milkshake."

"It's my favorite!"

"I'm allergic!"

I laughed, dragging her into the elevator. "Are you not going to kiss me then?"

"Maybe not."

"I don't believe you."

She poked me in the stomach and then pressed her lips to mine. "You're insufferable."

"I know."

She tried to pull away, but I just held her closer. Her laugh was infectious as she squirmed against me.

"You're lucky that I like you."

I kissed her again. "I am."

Her smile went all melty at the edges. "Let's get you inside before you're too sweet, and I start taking off your clothes in the elevator."

"I'm not opposed."

She shook her head at me and then dragged me out of the elevator. She was working the key into the door when my phone started buzzing. I took it out of my pocket, wondering who was calling me at this hour. I blinked in surprise. It was Claire. Again. After the text messages.

She was probably in Paris or something right now. So she had a five- or six-hour time difference. Maybe she didn't realize what time it was here.

Wait, or were my time zones backward? If it was midnight here, it'd be like six in the morning there. Why was she up so early?

"Everything all right?" Lark asked.

I hadn't noticed she was holding the door open.

I silenced the phone and let it go to voicemail. I didn't want to know why she was calling me. She'd be back in a matter of weeks. I could deal with her then.

But another text came through right then from Claire.

Why aren't you answering your phone? We need to talk.

I deeply disagreed. We did not need to talk. She'd said everything she needed to say before she left.

"Sorry." I stepped inside after Lark. "Claire just called."

Lark's eyebrows rose. "Really?"

I could see her hackles were up. "Yeah. I don't know why she's calling."

"Do you need to...talk to her?"

"No, I definitely don't. I sent her to voicemail. If it's important, she'll leave a message or something, I guess."

"Oh," she said, walking into the kitchen and grabbing a bottle of wine. She held it up, and I nodded. "Has she called or texted you before?"

"Well, when she first left, she did. But it fell off. I haven't heard from her since before you and I started talking."

She smiled slightly as she popped out the cork and poured us each a glass. "Well, what do you think she wants?"

"I have no idea. I don't really want her to call me at all."

"Yeah." She passed me my glass and took a contemplative sip of hers.

"I mean, we do have to figure out the apartment situation. She's coming back in three weeks, and our lease ends soon after that."

"That makes sense," Lark said. "What are you going to do about that?"

"Well, ideally, I'll find my own place."

She glanced at the ground and nervously toed her foot in a circle. Then her big green eyes met mine. "You could always stay here."

"I already do."

She smiled softly. "I mean...you could move in."

"Really?"

"If you want. If you don't think it's too soon. You're already here a lot, and English told me that Josh found them a place here for when he's done filming. I think they're going to sign on it this week even. So, she'll be moving out. I mean, is it crazy?"

"Maybe a little," I said, clearing the distance between us. "But I want to."

"You do?"

"Yeah, I do. I want to move in with you."

Her only answer was to press her lips against my own and to pull me back into the bedroom. The bedroom that would be *ours* in a matter of weeks.

30

LARK

Something pulled me out of a deep sleep. I squinted up at the ceiling, trying to figure out what the hell had woken me. Then I heard it—the sound of boots on hardwood and something heavy hitting the wall.

"What is happening?" I asked, reaching across the king-size bed to turn on the bedside table lamp.

Sam groaned and rolled over, closer to me. He glanced at his phone. "It's not even seven."

I yawned dramatically and then heard the noise again. "God, I don't know. Do you think someone is breaking into the apartment?"

"Fuck," he grumbled. Then he threw the covers off of himself. "I'll go check it out. You stay here."

He pulled on a pair of joggers and headed out into the living room. But I had no intention of staying here. If someone was breaking into my house, I wanted to make sure Sam was okay and call the cops. I threw on a nightgown and then snatched up my phone as I hurried to catch up.

"Hey!" Sam called. "What the hell are you doing in my apartment? You need to get out before I call the cops."

"*Your* apartment?" a crisp, clear voice asked.

I cringed. Oh no.

I knew that voice.

I dashed into the living room. And there she was. Hope St. Vincent in an Alexander McQueen suit and a St. Vincent's handbag. She was standing firm before Sam as if he were a bug under her shoe.

"Mom?" I gasped.

Sam whipped his head back to me. He shot me a look that said, *This is your mother?*

When I nodded at him, he disappeared back into the bedroom in search of a shirt.

"Larkin dear, I thought you'd be gone by now," my mother said.

"It's seven in the morning."

"Yes, well, perhaps I misjudged the time. I've been up for an hour, and when the furniture company said that the pieces were finished and could be delivered first thing, I didn't even balk."

"Furniture?" I asked in confusion. It was too early for my brain to be able to catch up to this. "What furniture?"

And then I looked around, really noticing my apartment. My couch had been pushed back against the wall. That must have been the banging that woke me. And there in its place was a brand-new white sofa. A rolled-up rug had been set against one wall, and several picture frames were next to it, waiting to be hung.

"Surely I told you about the redecorating I was going to be doing," my mother said.

"Redecorating?" I asked, coming to my senses. "You were going to redecorate my entire apartment without talking to me first?"

"The place needs some sprucing up. And with how busy you are, I thought you'd be glad for the help."

I narrowed my eyes. "No. I don't need the help, and it doesn't need sprucing up. I like the place exactly how it is. I don't know why you thought that I would want this. Why did you go behind my back to do it?"

"Don't be so dramatic," she said, waving her hand. "I'm not

going behind your back. After all, you've been wearing the clothes that I purchased."

"Clothes are one thing, Mother," I snarled. "Sure, I might have needed a cocktail dress or two and not wanted to go shopping, so I went through what you'd purchased and wore it to an occasion. That's annoying that you'd do it and just leave the clothes in my room without telling me. But this? *This* is crossing a line."

"I thought you'd like it."

Was she that delusional? Or did she just not want to admit that this was going too far?

"I don't. I don't like it." I glared back at her. "I am an adult, Mother. I don't need you coming into my life and redecorating without asking me. Would it be so hard to just send me an email about it?"

"You might like what I have planned," she said, undeterred. "You've only seen the couch. It's a whole concept."

"Mother! You're not listening," I spat. "This isn't about the furniture. It's about you interfering in my life. It's about my privacy, which you seem to think I don't need."

"Oh, I see. This is about your new little boyfriend." She waved her hand at Sam, who had just walked back into the living room.

"Don't bring Sam into this," I told her. "He has nothing to do with what you've done here."

"I'm just trying to ask about your life," she said. "I didn't even know you were dating anyone."

"Do you think there's a reason for that?"

My mother just stepped forward and held her hand out. Sam looked at me once before tentatively shaking it.

"I'm Hope St. Vincent. It's a pleasure."

"Uh...Sam Rutherford."

She pursed her lips. "Rutherford. Hmm...are you related to Broderick Rutherford in Connecticut?"

I nearly face-palmed right then and there. She was outrageous. Seriously.

Sam just laughed though. "No. I'm probably not related to

anyone you know. I'm from North Carolina. Outside of Chapel Hill."

"Oh," my mother said, taking a step back. "I see."

"Just stop it," I said, coming between them. "Sam and I are together. I don't need your opinion on the matter."

"I was just curious what his family does."

Sam grinned. "My dad works construction, and my mom works as a receptionist for the local church."

My mother gave him her best pained expression. "How...lovely."

"Oh, get off of your high horse," I muttered.

"You're dating a man whose family does construction," she said in a small voice. "I don't know why you do this, Lark. I swear that you do it on purpose to hurt me. As if not working for the company isn't enough, you have to do campaign work and slum it."

Something within me broke at those words from my mother. I'd already been worked up. Irritated that she had gone behind my back to refurnish my apartment for no fucking reason. Except that it was all likely a hidden agenda to get me back to the company. Because St. Vincent's Enterprise was the only thing that mattered. Nothing else.

And suddenly, I was furious. Beyond furious. I blew a gasket.

"Give me your key," I growled at her.

"What?"

"I said, give me the fucking key to my house. You are no longer welcome."

"Lark—"

"Give me the key and get out. You can't insult me, my job, and my boyfriend, all in the same sentence. We're done."

My mother straightened and lifted her chin. As if she thought that would somehow get her out of this situation. "You're my daughter. I'm looking out for you."

"Then consider me *not* your daughter."

She jolted backward a step. A hand went to her chest. I

thought she was finally getting it. Seeing how upset I was by all this.

"I don't...understand."

"Until you can accept me for who I am, then you don't get to look out for me."

"Lark," she whispered.

A rumble of anger swept through me, and still, I was stuck in place at the weakness in her voice. I knew that I shouldn't let her get to me. That I should stick to my guns. But for a second, I just wanted it all to work out. I wanted my mother to see me, *really* see me for who I was. I just didn't think that was possible. Not when she continued on this way as if my wants and needs and feelings didn't matter.

So, I stuffed the guilt in my back pocket and held my hand out. "The key."

And to my shock, she took out the gold key and placed it in my hand. I closed my hand around it, and it felt like a ten-pound weight. My mother looked sad. But then it cleared away as fast as it had come, and she just returned to indignant.

"If you didn't want me to help with your apartment and wardrobe, you could have just said so," she sneered.

Then, she turned on her four-inch Manolo Blahnik heel and exited my apartment, leaving all the new and old furniture where it was. And two disgruntled movers with two new chairs in the hallway.

Sam took one look at me and closed the door before the movers could come inside. Leaving them to work it out with my mom.

And then I collapsed in on myself. I crumpled into a heap on the hardwood floor, holding my head in my hands and shaking. I couldn't believe that had just happened. I'd always had a volatile relationship with my mother, which had only gotten worse over the years of my defiance. But it had never come to a head like that.

"Hey," Sam said. He sank to the floor, pulling me into his chest. I leaned hard against him, letting his warmth wrap around me. "It's okay."

"Is it?" I whispered.

"It will be."

"I just told my mom to get out of my apartment."

"You were justified," he reminded me.

"I know," I whispered. "But I hate it."

"That seems reasonable. You probably wouldn't be human if you didn't hate what had just happened with your mom."

"I just...had to stand up for myself." I pulled back and looked into his eyes. "I couldn't keep letting her stomp around in my life so carelessly."

"You did the right thing. She crossed the line and was unrepentant."

"I didn't like how she'd talked about you either."

He stroked my hair back. "I don't care what she says about me. I've heard it all before. I know that I don't belong here with a girl like you."

"Hey, don't say that. That's dumb."

"You're so far out of my league that it's not even funny," he said with a self-deprecating laugh.

"You are not."

"Lark, you *are* an Upper East Side princess. I'm a nobody from nowhere, who used to do construction. It's okay for me to admit that. I'm not ashamed. But I'm not giving you up because of any of it. I still love you."

I hiccuped, and a small smile came to my face. "I love you too."

He cupped my jaw and drew me into a kiss. "Now, are you really going to be okay?"

I shrugged. "I'm not sure. I feel like the ball is kind of in her court. But I know my mom. She's not going to try to make amends. She's going to try to pretend like it didn't happen until I give in and make up with her."

"Just give it time. You don't have to do anything about it today."

"I don't need this right now. Not with the primary so close and Thomas's fucking casino party."

"Hey, don't add stress if you don't have to," he said. "We don't have to go to Thomas's party."

I arched an eyebrow. "And miss you taking him for all he's worth? I don't think so."

He laughed. "We'll see how it goes. But really, if it makes you uncomfortable, we could just have a night in."

"No, I think I'd like a night out with our group. I miss having them all together. It was like having a new crew in the Hamptons."

"It was nice to feel like I belong."

I smiled. "This is where you belong."

He pulled me up off of the floor and into a hug. "Yes. Yes, it is."

31

LARK

"You really told her to give you the key back and to get out?" English asked with wide eyes. "And that you were no longer her daughter? Holy shit!"

I laughed softly and shrugged. "Yeah, I was enraged. To put it mildly."

"Jesus Christ! I can't imagine going off like that. I'm not close with my parents, but still!"

"Yeah. I don't know what to do about it. I'm still angry. I just need more time to calm down before I can talk to her again."

"Well, I definitely think this will get your mind off of it," English said as the elevator opened onto the top floor of my apartment building.

"What exactly am I looking at?" I asked her.

English grinned. "This is it."

I stared back at her blankly.

"This is the apartment that Josh and I just closed on!"

"What?" I gushed. "It's so close to my place! Only a few floors up!"

"I know! He knew that I loved your building so much and that I wanted to be close to you, so he bought the penthouse."

"That's insane. I didn't even know it was for sale."

She shook her head with a sly grin. "It wasn't. He contacted the people who were living here and made them an offer they couldn't refuse."

"Holy shit! That had to have cost a fortune!"

"He said nothing was too much for me."

"God, how did you get so lucky?" I asked as I gazed around the gorgeous and *enormous* penthouse suite. It was full of natural light, and I could so easily see English being happy here.

"I really have no idea," she gushed. "But I'm so excited to move in. He bought me a ticket to London to come out to the shoot this weekend. And it's been so long since I've seen him that I've decided to go."

"Oh," I said, my face falling. "This weekend is Thomas's party."

"Yeah, I figure it'll be fine to send Court. Especially since all of you will be there to watch him."

"Sure. I can watch him. I'll just miss you."

"I know. I wanted to go with you all, but it's been so long."

"And you want to get laid," I said with a laugh. "I get it."

"I mean...you're not wrong."

"Gah, I'm having second thoughts about this party. I think it'd be hilarious to see Sam hustle them all at poker, but am I putting myself in a bad position, bringing my ex-boyfriend and current boyfriend together in the same place?"

English put her hand on my shoulder. "It's a reasonable thing to be worried about. But this is Sam we're talking about. It's not like he's going to go rogue boyfriend on you and punch Thomas or anything. I hate to admit I was wrong, but I think Sam is really good for you."

I flushed. "Thanks, English. That means a lot."

"So, just go to this party and have a good time. What could go wrong?"

"Aside from everything?"

She laughed. "Well, I will happily be in a sex coma during it. So, I will be MIA."

"I'm happy for you," I told her with a smile. "This apartment.

You'll have Josh back soon. The job. I'm so glad that you took it so that we could be in the same city again."

"Me too. Best decision of my life."

We hugged like eccentric best friends, and then she dragged me around every single room to show it all off.

Having the most brilliant day on set. So good to be back in Josh's arms. Don't forget to keep your eyes on Court tonight. I'll follow up in the morning. And remember to have fun! I love you!

I groaned as I read English's text. I'd been so bogged down in work that I hadn't seen her message until she was probably already asleep. I hated that Josh was stealing her away for a week. I'd gotten used to having her here in New York. And I really didn't know what I'd do come November when she had to move back to LA. Hopefully, we could work it out, so she could stay.

"All good here, boss," Aspen said, stepping into my office. "Have a good time tonight with Sam."

My head whipped up. "What?"

Aspen froze. "I mean...you are with Sam, right?"

My stomach churned. "That's not...I mean, we're not—"

"Hey, I'm happy for you," she said, holding up her hands.

God, we hadn't been as careful as I'd thought. Did the whole office know? Was someone just waiting to let it slip to Shawn so that it could fuck us up? Because, god, I couldn't risk my job or Sam's job right now. Not this close to the primary. Not when we were both so invested in this.

"Who else knows?" I managed to get out.

"No one. And I haven't told anyone." She bit her lip. "I won't tell anyone. You can trust me."

"Thanks, Aspen. I don't mean for it to be a secret. But it just happened. It has nothing to do with work."

"If anything, you've been *more* productive," Aspen argued. "I think it's great for you."

"I appreciate it."

"So, really...have fun."

I laughed as she tipped her head at me and then dipped out of the office. I powered down my laptop for the night and then quickly changed into the slinky sapphire dress I'd chosen for the party. This one had come from *my* closet. Pointedly not something my mother had picked out.

A minute later, Sam stood in the doorway. He whistled. "Well, hello there."

I smoothed down the front of the dress and then stood in the high heels. "How do I look?"

"The office is empty." He closed the door. "We could...use your desk."

I grinned at him, wishing I could take him up on that offer. "Aspen knows."

"Yeah. I think she's known for a while."

"She said that she wouldn't tell anyone. But I hate that we have to hide it here. And I think we kind of suck at it."

He strode across the room and pulled me in close. "I don't like hiding it either. But we're professionals. Work comes first when we're here, and then, when we're home, who cares?"

"Someone probably cares."

He grinned. "Don't worry about it. What you should be worrying about is the fact that I forgot my suit at home. We're going to have to swing by Brooklyn before the party."

I groaned. "Really? And I already got all dressed up."

"Yes, and I am enjoying that."

I swatted him away.

He laughed. "Let's get going. I'm ready to clean the table tonight."

I followed him to the door. "God, I can't wait to see the look on Thomas's face."

"I'm thanking those long hours with Jake, learning how to play, right about now."

"How are things with you and Jake?"

He shrugged as he hailed a cab and held the door open for me.

He didn't respond until we were zipping along toward Brooklyn. "Same. Better. I don't know. I think he wants to come out after the primary is over." He glanced down and then back up at me. "If he comes, would you want to meet him?"

"Definitely," I said automatically. "I'd love to meet him."

"Cool. We'll see what happens. It's nice that not everything has to be so perilous between us."

"I know it's not the same, but I don't have siblings, so I've always treated my friends like they're family. And I've always tried to hold my crew together. It's all splintered, and I still try to fix it. I think I'm going to make us all hang out when Penn finally gets back at the end of the summer."

"Is he really in Paris all summer? When is he coming back?"

I shrugged. "I haven't really talked to him, but he has to come back to teach at some point."

"Well, I think it's a good idea to get your friends back together. Maybe you could take a weekend away with all of them."

My smile grew. "I like that idea. Though...I also like that we're kind of building a new friend network. Having English around and Whitley and the guys..."

"Me too."

"Sometimes, new is good...healthy."

"It is."

The cab pulled to a stop in front of Sam's apartment, and he paid before helping me out. We took the stairs up to his floor. I was cursing the heels the whole way. I should have stayed in my flats, but I hadn't wanted to bring them with me. The original plan had been to get ready at work and go together to the casino party. Since we had been getting out of work later and later lately, it just made more sense. But we'd have to make do even if it meant we got to the party *really* late tonight because of this detour.

"Sometimes, new is just what you need," he said with a wink at me as he turned the doorknob to his place and pushed it open.

He took a step inside and then froze.

He stopped so abruptly that I nearly ran into him.

"Sam, what..."

But I never finished the sentence.

Because a figure was in the apartment, in the living room, on the couch.

A small blonde figure.

She looked up at us with a tear-streaked face. But she couldn't see me. Or she didn't see me. She only had eyes for Sam.

"Claire?" he rasped.

Then she vaulted off of the couch, dashed across the apartment, and threw herself into his arms. "I'm sorry. I'm sorry. I'm so sorry."

I stood there, shell-shocked, as she pressed her lips to his.

Fuck.

PART V

BUT WHO COULD STAY?

32

LARK

Claire was kissing Sam.

My Sam.

And I just stood there. Because I had no idea how to process this. Like, how the fuck was this even happening? It made no sense. It wasn't...even possible for her to be here. She wasn't supposed to be back for weeks still.

Finally, Sam seemed to come out of his own stupor. He gripped Claire's shoulders and held her at arm's length. She stumbled backward a step, but I could see her red-rimmed eyes and puffy face.

"What are you doing here?" Sam finally asked.

"I-came-home-early-and-everything-is-awful-and-I-missed-you," she said, unintelligibly stringing all her words together with tears springing to her eyes again.

"Wait...wait," he said, gently guiding her back into the apartment. "I can't understand a word you're saying."

"I missed you. I was wrong. I'm so sorry. I shouldn't have left," Claire said, swiping at her cheeks. "I realized that I still love you. I'm still *in* love with you. I came back to make this better."

I stood awkwardly on the threshold between walking into that apartment and staying out here. Because nothing good was going

319

to come from me stepping inside and hearing what the fuck was about to happen. Claire was a mess. And still, I wanted to tell her to fuck off. That she was too late.

The old Lark...Bad Lark...would have done it. The other side of me reared its ugly head. It made my claws come out and my teeth lengthen into fangs and my instincts take over. I wanted her to hurt. She had no right to be here. She'd left Sam. He was *mine*.

But...the other part of me knew I couldn't say any of those things. It hadn't worked last time with Melissa. It certainly wasn't going to work this time with his ex-girlfriend sobbing into his shoulder.

All it would do was make things worse. Make Sam see that I hadn't changed as much as I'd claimed. That deep down, that viper still existed. As much as I tried to charm that snake to sleep inside of me and never come back out, I couldn't escape who I was. I was my mother's daughter. I was Katherine's best friend. I was Upper East Side. There was no denying that. And I could feel it in the vengeance that sprang up when I looked at that crying girl and felt nothing, except that I wanted to make her pay for touching him.

I'd say it was the normal sort of anger. The normal sort of *don't touch my boyfriend*. But it wasn't.

It was the Upper East Side level of *I'll ruin your life, and no one will ever know*. And it terrified me.

Terrified me that it was still in there.

And that somehow...Sam was the only one who brought it back out in me.

I took a step backward. I couldn't walk in there. I didn't know what he'd say or what kind of con Claire was trying to pull. But I knew if I walked in there, the part of me I'd tried so hard to bury would surface. And I had no clue if I could put her back in a box.

"Lark," Sam said, glancing up at me.

Claire seemed to notice me standing there for the first time. "Hey, Lark," she said, sniffling. "I didn't mean for you to see me like this. I just got in from Rome and it's a bitch of a flight and I'm so tired. Such a mess." She glanced down at my swanky outfit.

"Oh god, am I keeping you from something? Do you have a banquet?"

"Uh...yeah," Sam said. "Something like that."

"I'm sorry. I didn't mean to. I came straight here from the airport. We need to talk."

"Yeah, I think we do." He glanced back up at me.

I was halfway out the door like I was ready to sprint in the other direction. I saw his gaze soften for a minute. As if he wanted to say something to appease me, but there was nothing there.

"You want to head to the party? I can meet you."

"You want me to leave?" I asked in surprise. Even though I'd been ready to run, I hadn't thought Sam would send me away.

"Yeah. I mean, Claire and I have some unfinished business. I'll meet you there."

"Oh."

"I'll text you," he said carefully.

I took another step back. "Fine."

"Lark..."

"I'll see you at the party."

And then I turned on my heel and walked out.

My heart pounded the entire drive from Brooklyn to the private location Thomas had booked for his party. I realized when I was almost there that I had both invitations, and you could only get inside with one. Too late now.

I couldn't go back there.

Not to figure out what the hell had happened between Sam and Claire.

Not to see my worst self reappear before my very eyes. Like watching a dark energy seep into my chest and invade my senses.

But I couldn't stanch the rising panic. The rising nausea.

Because in some way, in every way, I should have seen this coming. Claire was going to come home. She would have had her fun in Europe and then realized that Sam—beautiful, wonderful, *stable* Sam—was exactly the person that she needed in her life. Who wouldn't recognize that?

And then it would happen like last time. He claimed that he hadn't left me for Melissa. But he'd invited her to the end of the presidential campaign. She'd stayed in his apartment. He let her infect his mind, and he'd believed her over me. I didn't know Claire. She'd seemed nice the two seconds I met her originally. But I had no doubt that she could do just what Melissa had done.

Sam could leave me. He could go back to being with her. Perfect little Claire and her perfect fucking violin and her nice, normal family that surely didn't barge into his life and insult him.

He might have said that I was out of his league. But maybe that was the problem. Maybe perception and reality were too far skewed. And he'd want someone like Claire again. He hadn't been the one to break it off after all. He spent weeks mourning her departure and not even told me. Hadn't wanted to tell me.

I felt actually sick, thinking of all of this. But my brain wouldn't shut up. It just repeated history and all my darkest fears. Like a broken record, hitting those highlights by scraping across my memories with a needle.

The cab dropped me off in front of what looked like a nondescript office building. I'd never been here before. The street was quiet and empty. Not exactly the place I'd expect a party.

Still, I followed the instructions on the invitation and knocked on the door.

"Invitation?" the man asked when he answered.

I held it out to him. He took it, slipped it into his pocket, and gestured for me to walk down the hallway.

"Last door at the end of the hallway."

"Thanks," I said with a growing sense of unease.

Was this supposed to be like a speakeasy? That didn't seem Thomas's style.

I was regretting coming here. Alone. What if I ran into Thomas again? With my emotions all roiled up inside of me, I didn't put it past myself to give him a taste of the Lark I had been and cut him off at the balls.

With a deep breath, I pulled open the door at the end of the hallway, and my jaw dropped. I didn't know what I'd been expecting. A few card tables and a tiny, smoky room, but this was something else. This was *established*. It certainly wasn't a few tables that he'd thrown together to get this party going. He had been doing this for a while. There were, at quick glance, at least a dozen poker tables. I could see roulette, craps, blackjack, and even a few slot machines against a wall. Music was playing from hidden speakers with a group of girls in micro minidresses dancing at the center. Platforms had been erected between some of the tables, and girls in bras and thongs were dancing atop them.

This wasn't some little poker game he'd put together. This was a full-blown casino in the middle of Manhattan. That I'd never, ever heard about.

My gaze slipped around the room. I found Court at one of the poker tables. Camden was standing nearby with Fiona fluttering her eyelashes up at him. He seemed indifferent to her presence. I found Katherine next, not exactly against a wall—she'd never deign to look like a wallflower—but just far enough apart to make it look purposeful. I didn't see Gavin or Whitley anywhere.

Or Thomas for that matter. Which was just fine by me.

I strode across the room to where Katherine casually sipped champagne. As if her husband wasn't standing nearby with another woman.

"You made it," Katherine said when I appeared before her.

"Barely."

Katherine tilted her head. "What's the matter?"

"Nothing."

"Who do you think I am? I've known you your entire life. I can see when something is wrong with you. You've lost your glow." She inhaled sharply, her eyes narrowing. "Did Sam hurt you?"

God, Katherine was too intuitive for her own good sometimes.

"Yeah. Well, no. I don't know. His ex-girlfriend was waiting for him in his apartment when we showed up. And he decided to stay and talk to her. Told me to go on without him. That he'd be here soon and text me."

Katherine wrinkled her nose. "Text you? After he sent you away?"

I couldn't explain the other part to Katherine. She'd never once grappled with her Upper East Side self. This was just who she was. Take it or leave it.

She'd encourage me to just let go. Find a balance between the two. Or better yet, just let Bad Lark take over for a while and see how much better it could be. How much less I'd have to try. Except that wasn't what I wanted. Right?

"Yeah. And she was blubbering and telling him she still loved him."

"And you didn't break her fucking neck for the audacity?" she asked acidly.

"That's rich, Ren." I gestured to her husband.

"That is different," she said icily. "And you know it. Camden and I were arranged. You and Sam chose each other."

"You're right. I shouldn't have made the comparison. I'm sure Fiona makes you want to rake your nails down her face."

"I've considered it," she said with a small frown before the emotion disappeared. "But it wouldn't be worth the satisfaction it would give him."

"We're both so fucked."

Despite myself, I checked my phone one more time. Waited for that text message from Sam. But nothing was there. Just as empty as before.

Katherine placed her palm against my phone. "Stop looking for him. It'll only make you more stressed."

"Yeah," I said, stuffing it back into my purse.

But when I looked back up, I saw the very last person I wanted to see right now. Well, perhaps Thomas was actually the second after Claire this particular night. Not that I wanted him beelining for me either.

"Oh no," I murmured.

Katherine looked up and narrowed her eyes. "I can handle Thomas."

"Hello, ladies," Thomas said with a dangerous glint in his eyes. "Enjoying the party?"

"It's something," Katherine said, taking another sip of her champagne.

That clearly wasn't what Thomas had wanted to hear. His nostrils flared at her dismissal.

"And you, Lark? Where's that boyfriend of yours?"

"I don't think that's any of your business," Katherine interjected smoothly.

"I heard he liked to play poker. I figured you'd be together," he said, baring his teeth in an imitation of a smile.

Something rose up in me. All that anger that I'd wanted to spew on Claire hit me fresh. And I couldn't stand that slimy grin on his face another second.

I took a step past Katherine's indifference and right into my Upper East Side persona.

"I don't care one iota that you expected Sam to be here with me. All I care about," I said crisply, evenly, "is that you get the fuck out of my presence. I'm here to hang out with my friends. And you are not one of them. You haven't been one of them since you started stuffing your dick in every girl on Tinder just because you could get away with it. I'm glad to be rid of your unremarkable dick, and I don't need you crowding around me. Unless you want this little operation brought up to my parents, I suggest you move along."

Thomas sputtered in shock at my outburst. Even all these years later, I'd never stood up to him. I'd cried and grieved and mourned the loss of a bullshit relationship. I'd put Bad Lark to rest, and I'd gotten walked all over. But I was done letting some dickwad wannabe take up any more of my time or energy.

Katherine just burst into laughter—real laughter. She fluttered her fingers at him. "You heard her. Be gone, snake."

And to my amazement, Thomas actually turned tail and hurried away from us.

Katherine turned to me and wrapped me in a quick hug. "That

was the best Larkin St. Vincent I've seen in years. Where have you been hiding her?"

"Apparently, I just needed to come to terms with both sides of who I am. I'm still Upper East Side, right?"

"Always," she agreed. She snapped her fingers at a passing waiter. She plucked two fresh glasses of champagne off of the tray. "Keep them coming." The man nodded and fell back into the crowd. Katherine handed me a glass and then held hers aloft. "I propose a toast. To Lark, the Upper East Side, and how we stop putting up with men who ruin the entire fucking world."

"I'll drink to that."

I clinked my glass against hers, and then we both tipped back our champagne. And even though my insides were squirming as I wondered what exactly was happening with Sam and Claire back at his apartment in Brooklyn, I felt like a new me.

Lark 3.0.

Not all good. Not all bad. Just me.

33

LARK

Two hours later, and I still hadn't heard from Sam. Not a call. Not a text. And he damn sure hadn't shown up to Thomas's party. Not that he could have even gotten in without the fucking invitation that I had. But he would have had to call me for that. And he hadn't done that. Which meant...he was still at his place...with Claire.

I didn't know what the fuck they needed to talk about for two hours, but I was drunk and murderous. Half-ready to catch a cab and drive back over there to demand answers. But I knew that I wouldn't do it. Even though I'd unleashed something within myself, I wasn't ready to go that far. He'd said he'd text. Until he did, I'd get drunk as a skunk and let my anger simmer.

"Can't we just go dance?" Whitley asked, holding out her whiskey. "You both need to let loose a little more."

"You can go dance," Katherine said. "You've been dancing all night. Why would you need us?"

"It's more fun with my friends."

"You make friends everywhere," I reminded her.

"Well, yeah...but you two are the hottest."

"Obviously," Katherine said with a quirk of her lips.

"And I'm pretty sure Gavin already left with that brunette

chick." She pushed her currently blonde-highlighted hair off her shoulders.

"Are you jealous?" Katherine asked evenly.

"Of what?"

"Gavin being with someone else?" I added.

Whitley snorted. "No. Why would I be?"

"Because you like him," Katherine said.

"You have it all wrong. Gavin King and I are oil and water. We don't mix. We just have a lot of fun dancing and drinking. He's a good wingman."

"Please." Katherine rolled her eyes.

"I'll admit, he's good to look at," Whitley said with a shrug. "But there are so, so many more men *and* women who are pretty to look at."

"If you say so," I said with a smirk.

"Whatever. So...you won't go dance with me?"

"I think we're good here," I told her.

Katherine's attention suddenly shifted, and I saw immediately why. Fiona hadn't left Camden's side all night. She'd been hanging on to him for dear life. He was mostly ambivalent about her presence. As if she were more prop than person.

But now, he was walking away from the table that he'd been playing poker at and leaving Fiona behind. He was coming straight toward us.

Whitley and I fell silent, waiting for the incoming bomb to explode.

"Hello, Camden," Katherine said evenly. As if she were hardly interested in his presence.

But he brushed right past her indifference and took her arm. "We need to grab Court and get you home and safe."

Her eyes rounded only slightly. "Home? You want me to leave?"

"No, you're coming with me. Where you belong."

We all gaped at him. Ever since the party, they'd been living apart. As far as I knew...they weren't even speaking, except at public events where they would be photographed together. Their secret was out about the arranged marriage and his mistress. So, they kept up appearances to a certain extent. But this was altogether different.

"I don't understand," Katherine said softly. Honest confusion in her voice.

"I just got a tip from a detective that I know. He said that if I was at this party, then I needed to get out now," Camden said. "This place is about to blow up."

I gasped. "A raid?"

He nodded once, not taking his eyes from Katherine's face. "I need to get you out of here."

I could see everything roil through her. He was worried about her. About Katherine and not Fiona. Was this a gimmick? Or real?

We didn't have time to worry about it. If a police raid was about to hit the party, we needed to get the hell out of here.

"I'm going to get Court," I gasped.

Fuck, English was going to kill me. This wasn't supposed to happen while she was a thousand miles across the ocean.

I dashed into the crowd, heading toward the table where Court had planted his ass in front of the entire night. He had a sizable number of chips in front of him. He was *not* going to like having to move. I could already tell that he was drunk. Just by the set of his shoulders. Sometimes, he was so like Penn that it was scary.

"Court, we have to go," I said, grabbing his arm.

He didn't even glance at me. He just brushed me aside with the grin of someone who was beating the odds. "Can't leave. I'm on a roll."

"Camden said now," I growled. "Right now."

"Camden can fucking shove it," he said with a lackadaisical attitude.

I got right up in his face, obscuring his view of the cards. "Now, Court."

"Lark, what's the big fucking deal?"

I leaned in, speaking softly into his ear, "Camden got a tip that the place is about to be raided. We need to get you out of here now, or we might all get arrested."

Court reeled back, losing some of his cool. "Fuck. Can I cash my chips in?"

I shook my head, glancing uneasily over my shoulder. I grabbed his arm again and tried to all but drag him out of his seat. "Come on."

"Fine, fine." He lovingly stared down at the chips. "I'm out, boys. Duty calls. Free-for-all on my chips."

The guys laughed, clearly thinking I was dragging him away for nefarious purposes, but I couldn't even care. We needed to go. The last thing that could happen was Court Kensington getting arrested. It would spell defeat for Leslie and the campaign and me and English...and *everything* I'd been working toward. I felt suddenly very sober at the prospect.

As soon as Court and I were away from the table, Camden began to lead Katherine and Whitley away. I followed him, guiding an incredibly, stupidly drunk Court toward them. They must have been pumping him full of alcohol for him to barely be able to keep his feet under him. I didn't know how he'd been fucking winning while he was this intoxicated. Unless the game was stacked in his favor to get him to keep coming back. That sounded like something Thomas would do. Get the big dogs to win a lot on their first night and then start clearing them out.

I shook my head. I'd probably never know. And right now, I had bigger things to deal with.

"Where are we going?" I asked when I finally caught up to the others.

"Camden knows a back way out," Katherine said.

"How?"

Katherine shrugged one shoulder. "He's Camden Percy."

Yeah, that was answer enough, I supposed.

I felt chased by an invisible force. As if, at any moment, the police would burst in through all of the doors and put handcuffs on us. Everything would go down in flames. My stomach was in knots, the buzz I'd had vanished, and I just half-dragged, half-hustled Court toward the alternate exit that Camden was leading us toward.

No one stopped us. No one asked why we were all leaving, where we were all going in the first place. And still, anxiety warred through me.

The anticipation kicking into overdrive.

This wasn't who I was. Not anymore.

I'd done enough in high school to warrant running away from the cops. We'd snuck out and gotten drunk and high and skinny-dipped and on and on. Enough that was horrible. Enough that was just stupid. I hadn't missed this feeling. Like I was in a free fall, and soon enough, I would get caught.

Wasn't this half the reason I'd given up Bad Lark before? I might have come to terms with her today when I was taking down Thomas, but I didn't want this to be my life. I didn't want that anxiety of wondering if...*when* I was going to get caught. It had poisoned my relationship with Sam the first time around. I didn't want to do it again. And yet, he was doing enough bad all on his own.

I'd been so happy since we'd been together. Jumped the gun and used the L-word, even asked him to move in with me. Stupid.

I should have expected the worst. Should have thought the bottom would fall out. Like it always did.

Because I was the girl who was out of everyone's league. Who could ever leave me? Except everyone.

Fuck.

My fears were really ramping up as we hurried out of the back exit and into a deserted alley. I couldn't focus on Sam right now. I just needed to get us away and find a way for us to get home.

That was when I heard the sirens.

"Fuck," I gasped.

Camden seemed unperturbed. "This way."

He led us down the alleyway and out onto the main street. I had no idea where we were. I didn't know this area of town like I did the Upper East or Midtown or even SoHo. I swallowed as our group hurried and yet tried to look casual, moving down the street in cocktail dresses and thousand-dollar suits.

The sirens were getting louder. I glanced over my shoulder

once, just once, and saw the cars zooming toward us. I wanted to pick up my pace but worried it'd look suspicious. They were coming for the party, not us.

Camden finally stopped. "This is far enough."

He gestured at a brightly lit diner with a sign that simply read *Waffles*. The inside looked like a typical sixties-era diner with red booths along the walls, a diner bar at the back, and cheap tables along the middle. A jukebox played music. I could see a collection of framed photos declaring them the best waffles in the city for the last three years. I wondered who had actually voted in that.

Katherine wrinkled her nose. "You expect me to go in there?"

"This is as good of a place to wait until I can get my driver out of that mess to pick us up," Camden said. He yanked the door open and held it for her.

To my surprise, Katherine just walked right inside. I'd never seen her in a diner before. She didn't do food with calories very often.

Whitley barreled after her. "I could go for some fucking hash browns. I've never met a potato that I didn't like."

Court grinned down at me. Not at all concerned that we'd just had to escape a police raid. "Fuck, I want a waffle."

I shook my head at him as he ambled drunkenly into Waffles and joined Katherine and Whitley at a red plastic booth against the wall.

"Thank you," I finally said to Camden now that I was coming down...a little at least from what had just happened.

He shrugged. "Don't want any of my people to get caught there."

"What about Fiona?" I asked, realizing for the first time he'd just abandoned her.

His eyes flicked to Katherine. "Like I said, *my* people."

Then he walked inside. A small smile touched my features. Maybe Katherine wouldn't realize what had happened until later, but I bet she would put it all together. That he'd immediately ditched Fiona. That Katherine was his people. His to take care of.

I wished that I could join them. Sit down in that seedy little diner and overdose on carbs with my friends after escaping something horrible. But my job wasn't over. Other people needed to know about this.

I sighed and then pulled my phone out. I paused for a heartbeat, waiting for that text message from Sam. The one he'd promised hours ago. The one he'd never delivered.

It wasn't there.

I ground my teeth as I pulled up English's number and dialed. It'd be super fucking early in London. Like, six in the morning. But she was used to living weird hours as a celebrity publicist. She didn't sleep like a normal human being. It wasn't out of the norm to see her doing tai chi in the living room at four in the morning. Her brain was just wired differently.

The phone rang once and then went straight to voicemail. What the hell? I tried again. Same thing. Her phone must have been off. It was the only explanation. Except that English never turned her phone off. It was her job to have her phone on at all times. You never knew when you'd have to be ready to deal with something.

I glared at my phone. I needed English. She'd know what to do and how to handle this. But she wasn't answering.

Then another thought hit me, and my stomach turned. What if Sam showed up at the party? Admittedly, it'd be weird for him to do so without first calling me. But maybe he'd forgotten about the invitation.

I knew that I was grasping at straws for reasons to call him. To find out what the fuck he was doing. But I didn't want him to show up there. And if he was already in a cab, as unlikely as that seemed, then I'd rather him just head here.

Maybe I was rationalizing, but I sighed heavily and called him anyway. Damn the consequences.

34

SAM

I tapped my index finger against the side of my phone as the taxi veered precipitously through traffic. I was still trying to craft the text to Lark. What the hell should I say? It was one in the morning. She'd left hours ago. I should just say fuck it. It'd be easier to explain to her when I saw her. But still, I stared at my screen, wondering how not to sound like a total dick.

Then to my surprise, my phone started buzzing in my hand.

I answered on the first ring, "Lark?"

"Sam"—she sounded all business—"where are you?"

"I'm sorry about before."

"I don't care about that right now. Where *are* you? Are you still in Brooklyn?"

I frowned. She sounded super pissed. Understandably so after I'd sent her away and then disappeared. I just needed to get through to her.

"No, I'm almost to the poker party. I know that this wasn't how I wanted our night to go."

She sighed. "The party is already over. It was busted up by a police raid."

"What?" I gasped. The cab driver looked back at me through the rearview mirror with disdain. "Are you okay? Is everyone okay?

Did anyone get arrested? Do you need my help? Should I call someone?"

"We got out. Camden got a tip from a detective or someone he knew. So, we're at a local diner called Waffles, waiting it out. You shouldn't go to the party."

"Right. Of course. I'm glad you're safe and you got out. I'll come to you. The place is Waffles?"

"Yes."

I pulled the phone away for a moment. "Change of plans. Can you take me to Waffles? I think it's nearby."

"Sure thing," the cab driver said, taking the next left.

"Sam, are you still there?" Lark asked.

"Yes. Sorry. Giving the cab driver directions. I'll be there in ten, maybe fifteen minutes, depending on traffic."

"Okay," she said slowly.

"Lark...I'm sorry."

"I can't right now," she said softly. "I'll see you when you show up."

"Okay."

Then she hung up.

I threw my head back into the headrest with a muttered curse. Oh, she was pissed off. A hundred percent. This was going to suck so bad.

It was a solid fifteen before the cab came to a stop in front of Waffles. It looked like some kind of seedy diner, which probably meant that it had the best food in the world. On any other night, I would have loved to discover this kind of place with Lark. A new adventure and good food. This wasn't how I wanted to find it. Not tonight.

I paid the cab driver and asked him to wait.

"I'll have to charge you for the wait time."

I waved my hand at him. I didn't care. There was only one thing that mattered right now, and her shock of red hair appeared at the entrance to the diner.

"Hey," I said with a worried smile. "How are you doing?"

She shrugged. "Everyone is a little shaken up and hiding it

with greasy food."

"I think...we need to talk," I said.

But then she straightened, and there was something different about her. This was business Lark. The woman who ran a campaign without breaking a sweat. I could see it come over her. And I didn't like what that meant for us.

"What I need is for you to take Court home," she said.

"Uh...okay."

"He's drunk and eating waffles. And if his mother finds out what happened here tonight..." She trailed off with a shake of her head. "Fuck, what could have happened."

"Yeah. If you all had been arrested."

"I really don't want to think about it," she said with a shudder. "I just want this nightmare to be over."

And when she finally met my stare, I didn't know if she meant this night or us.

"I can deal with Court. That's no problem. But Lark, what happened tonight...it's not what you think."

She arched an eyebrow as if she didn't believe me. "Please don't. Not tonight."

"Come on," I said, reaching for her.

But she pulled back.

"No, You got to choose when we talked after Claire left. And... and I get to choose now that she's home. Which is not right now. I waited at the party with radio silence from you for hours, and I just escaped a police raid at what was an illegal, underground gambling ring. I'm in no mood."

End of discussion.

That was written all over her as she turned and walked back into Waffles.

She was only gone a minute before she was all but dragging a drunk Court out toward me. "Here. Please just take him home."

"Lark, please. If you'd just let me explain..."

Court stepped forward and put his hand on my shoulder. "Hey bro, even I know that's not something you should ever say to a woman."

Lark raised her eyebrows as if to say to listen to him. "I'm sure you have your reasons. And they all sound perfectly valid to you. But I assure you, anything that you say to me tonight won't sound valid to me. All it feels like is history repeating itself. Nothing you say will change my mind about that. So...just deal with Court. Do that for me, and we'll just...figure it out later."

Figure it out later sounded like a death sentence. Like the end. And this couldn't be the end.

As she slipped back into Waffles, I stepped forward to go after her. As if apologizing again would fix it. Tell her what had happened and how wrong she was. That it wasn't what she thought. This wasn't Melissa again.

But Court stopped me. "I'd let the lady be. It only gets worse from here."

"It can't get any worse than this," I told him, feeling myself fall into a bottomless black pit as Lark walked away from me.

Court sighed. "Here's some Kensington wisdom: it can always get worse."

And I feared he was right.

35

LARK

Camden's limo was finally able to extract itself from the onslaught and whisk us all back uptown. I stumbled upstairs to my empty apartment, prepared to sleep away the nightmare of this weekend. But sleep never came.

All I did was toss and turn and replay Claire throwing herself at Sam. The way she'd cried so prettily and how he had taken care of her as he did. Nausea swept over me, and nothing dispelled it.

At some point, I must have fallen into some kind of comatose sleep on the couch because I was abruptly ripped from it when the front door opened.

"Sam?" I asked before I could stop myself.

But it wasn't Sam.

My vision cleared. "English?"

She sniffled and wiped at her eyes. "Hey, Lark."

I sat up with my fuzzy, sleep-deprived brain. "What are you doing here? You're supposed to be in London for another week."

She swallowed hard, pushed her carry-on into the living room, and closed the door. "Yeah, I was."

"What happened?"

Then English burst into tears. I jumped to my feet, forgetting all my woes of the night before and pulled my friend into a hug.

"Shh," I whispered against her hair.

I maneuvered her back to the couch. She plopped down next to me, completely inconsolable.

It was several minutes before she could even speak.

"I went to the set to see Josh. At first, it was all great. And then...and then I overheard some members of the cast talking about how Josh and his coworker Celeste—you know, the, like, Bond girl of the film—were together. How they weren't even good at hiding it. How they...they felt bad for me."

"No!" I gasped. "But Josh is...he's head over heels for you!"

She shrugged helplessly. "I thought so too. We talk every day. He bought me that apartment. He was so supportive of this job. He was even going to move here before he went on his promotional tour."

"Did you confront him?"

"Yeah," she whispered. "Yeah, I did. He denied it. So, I told him that I'd ask Celeste. Get her take on it. Then it all spilled out of him. He said that he didn't care for her. He didn't love her. It was just a"—she choked on the next words—"publicity stunt."

"He did *not* say that to you. To *you* of all people."

She nodded, tears flowing freely down her cheeks again. "He did. The bastard. He said it was to sell the last movie. He actually had the audacity to say that it worked for *Mr. & Mrs. Smith*."

"No fucking way!" I cried. "That's...I have no words."

"Yeah. I didn't either."

"Oh god."

"I couldn't stay another second. I packed all my shit up, bought the most expensive first-class ticket on his credit card, and came right back."

"No wonder you weren't answering your phone last night. You were over the Atlantic."

"Answer my phone? Why were you calling me last night?" she asked, scrubbing at her cheeks.

I took a deep breath. "There was a raid on the party last night."

"What?" she gasped, sitting up perfectly straight with wide eyes. "Were you arrested? Was *Court* arrested? Fuck!"

"No, no one was arrested. Well, not our friends. Camden knew someone, and they tipped us off. We got out ahead of the police. I don't know what happened to everyone else."

English sank back. "Thank fuck. I couldn't imagine. I'd lose my fucking job over that."

"I know. I had the same thought."

"But why was there a raid on a poker game? It was just for fun. Nothing to try to crack down on with a police raid."

I sighed. "It wasn't what we'd thought it was. It was a built establishment. At least a dozen poker tables. Plus, blackjack, craps, roulette, and slots. There were platforms for dancers and everything. This place had been in operation for a while."

"You have got to be kidding me."

"None of us knew it was going to be like that. It was a nightmare."

"I'd hate to be the publicist for whoever has to deal with the fallout," English said.

"That person doesn't need a publicist. They need an attorney."

"You'd be shocked at how often those two things go hand in hand."

I managed a laugh. "And...something else happened last night."

English arched an eyebrow.

"Claire came back and declared her love for Sam."

"Oh shit. What did he do? Tell her to fuck off?"

I shook my head. "No, she was blubbering about how much she'd messed up. He...decided to talk to her. Told me to go to the party. He'd text me and meet me there. But he didn't...he never texted, and he only showed up two hours later after the party was raided. I made him take Court home and told him I'd talk to him tomorrow. Well, now, today."

"Fuck that shit! Two hours later!" English seethed. "What is with men? Why are they all so awful? I just...I thought Sam was good for you. I was the one who convinced you to see this through. Now, look at the bullshit he pulled. Look at the bullshit Josh pulled," she finished in a whisper as her anger died down to grief.

"When I saw Claire, I wanted to break her into pieces. But I don't know what to think about Sam."

English laughed. "Bad Lark came out to play."

"More or less. And I don't want to be that person. I just want to be me and *also* not get stepped all over. Like, how hard is it to send a text message?"

English shrugged. "How hard is it not to fuck someone else?"

"I'm sorry."

"It's not your fault. And this isn't your fault either. I'm anti-men right now. So, I'm all *cut off his balls and feed them to him*."

I chuckled. "I don't think that's an option."

"It could be!" she proclaimed. "But maybe just talk to him? Pray it doesn't go as poorly as my talk with Josh?"

"Oh yeah, that's really promising."

"What's the worst that could happen?"

I bit my lip. "He decides to get back together with Claire, just like he did with Melissa the last time around."

"And what would you do if that were the case?"

"I don't know," I whispered, bracing myself. "Cry? Eat ice cream?"

"Survive," English said softly. "Just like me. Talk to him."

I sighed heavily, but I knew she was right. I was just putting off the inevitable because I was afraid that during those two hours, he'd decided he'd made a mistake. That he wanted Claire after all. That they hadn't even been broken up and I was the other woman in all of this. A million worst-case scenarios ran through my head, but the only way to know was to talk to him.

"All right. I have to head to work anyway. Are you going to be okay?" I asked as I stood up.

She gave me a noncommittal half-shrug, half-wave. "I know what I have to do next. And that's go to talk to fucking Court Kensington."

"That sounds...pleasant in your state."

She rose to her feet. "I have had a very bad weekend. My husband cheated on me, I flew back and forth across the Atlantic in the span of two days, and now, I get here and find out he jeopardized everything. Again. Yeah, I think he deserves a piece of my mind."

"Go easy on him."

"Oh no, everyone goes easy on Court. That is *not* my job. My job is to whip his ass into shape and craft him into something the public can love—or at least, fucking sympathize with. Nothing in that says that I have to be nice. And nothing in that says that he should be in a position to almost get arrested again!"

"Okay, okay. Give the boy some tough love. I'll be at work, trying not to die and waiting for the rug pull."

"I love you," English said. "Thanks for being here for me."

"Always."

"Good luck with Sam. Text me when you talk to him."

"Will do."

Even though I was really fucking dreading what was about to happen.

I made it to work only a handful of minutes late after my conversation with English. I'd desperately needed a shower to clear my head and nearly fallen asleep under the stream. Today was going to suck. No buts about it.

I yawned as I walked through the door, wishing I'd had time to stop at Coffee Grounds before coming in. But I was already late, I had a meeting with Shawn and the team leads, *and* I needed to see Sam before I could hope to get anything done.

"Morning, Lark," Aspen said with a smile.

"Hey. Could you get me the largest coffee that we have in the break room? I didn't sleep, and I have that huge meeting."

"Sure thing. Oh, also, Shawn came by and said that he needed to see you before the meeting."

I nodded and waved her off. "Will do. I'll go see him."

Right after I talked to Sam.

With a giant sigh and another yawn, I walked across the room, knocked on Sam's office door twice, and then opened it, uninvited.

"Hey, I know that we need to..."

But the rest of my sentence died on my lips.

"What are you doing?" I gasped.

He looked around the office he'd worked in all summer and shrugged. "What does it look like?"

"Packing. It looks like you're packing."

And he was. He had a cardboard box open and was filling it with his personal belongings from the office. It was a blank, nearly empty space already.

"Yeah, Shawn just came in here and fired me."

"What?" I snapped. "He fired you? Holy shit! Why?"

Sam shrugged again, dejected. "I guess someone else found out we were dating."

"Oh my god," I whispered in horror. "But...no. This isn't..."

"It is what it is," he said with a sigh.

Finally, he looked up and met my gaze. I could see what this had done to him. He believed in this campaign like I did. He wanted Leslie to win. He hated that it had come to this moment.

I'd gotten him fired. Somehow, someone had found out we were dating...and he'd been sacked because of me. Without anyone even *telling* me.

Shawn.

He'd wanted to talk to me when I got in. Oh god, was he going to get rid of me too? It seemed unbelievable, but so was this moment.

"I'll talk to him. I'll make this right," I told him before marching right back out of his office.

36

LARK

I stormed into Shawn's office like a thundercloud. "What is going on, Shawn?"

"Lark, good. I'm glad that you're here." He gestured to the chair in front of his desk. "Sit down. We should talk."

"You just fired Sam."

"Yes," he said evenly. "I hated to do it. It would have been easier to let HR handle it, but it came from Leslie."

"What?" I gasped, my stomach dropping out. I sank into the seat in front of his desk.

Shawn steepled his fingers before his face. "Why didn't you tell us, Lark? You could have come to us. We could have worked something out."

"I didn't...I don't...I don't know."

I'd known it was a big deal. I was his boss. His boss's boss actually. Even higher up the chain. I'd freaked out when Shawn walked in on us together. I'd asked Aspen to lie for us. I'd known. I just hadn't wanted to think about it.

"Are you letting me go too?" I managed to ask him.

I'd been with the mayor for so long. Almost since day one. Shawn and I had been together on and off for five years.

He just shook his head once. "Thank god, no. Leslie said you were too valuable."

I sagged in my chair in relief. I felt like an asshole, doing it. Since Sam was currently packing up his office and heading out. He'd just been fired, and I was relieved that I hadn't been. It was shitty, but it was real. I loved this campaign. I couldn't imagine losing it. Fuck.

"But Sam...is there any way..."

"No," Shawn said with a stiff shake of his head. "I liked Sam. He was a nice guy, a great dedicated attorney. But we need you, Lark. We need you to keep running this ship. You're irreplaceable this close to the primary. And honestly, I'd argue, period."

"Thank you. I mean, I appreciate you saying that. It means a lot. I just...can't believe Sam isn't going to be working here anymore."

Shawn held his hands up, wrists together. "My hands are tied. It was Leslie's decision."

"Is she in? Can I talk to her?"

"She's not in. She had something to deal with at City Hall. But what would you even say to her? She's made her decision. Just...let it go." He waved his hand at me. "I'm sorry about this. I really am. But the primary is in two weeks. We have work to do. The team meeting is in fifteen minutes. I'll see you there."

I nodded helplessly as stood and I stumbled backward out of his office. I felt like I was in free fall. Sam had been fired. He wasn't working with the campaign anymore. And there was nothing I could do about it.

I needed to go after him.

The thought hit me like a lightning bolt.

My first reaction had been *no*. No, you can't just fire him. No, you can't do this to him. And it made me realize that I wanted to fight for this. Fight for Sam. All the fear and inaction had done nothing but get us to this point. I couldn't handle this uncertainty any longer.

Without a backward glance, I rushed back to Sam's office. But to my dismay, I found it was already empty.

"No," I whispered.

I pulled my phone out and found a text from Sam waiting for me.

I had to leave the building. Call me later.

Fuck. I headed back into my office, mutely taking my coffee from Aspen, and then dialed his number.

"Hey. Sorry. I didn't feel right, hanging around," Sam said when he answered.

"I'm going to come with you. We need to talk. Where are you? I can meet you."

"Lark, no," he said firmly. "As much as I want to talk to you and figure out where we are after last night, I can't have you jeopardizing your job. Not for me or for anything."

"I was just told that I'm irreplaceable. I think I'll be fine."

He sighed. "Do you want to find out? Because I don't think that you do. The campaign is the most important thing in your life. You love it. You love what you do. You believe in Leslie. Hell, I believe in Leslie. I don't want to see her lose because they fired their best after she followed me out the door."

I ground my teeth together. He was right. I knew it. But I hated it.

"Okay. After work?"

"Yeah. I can meet you outside."

I nodded grimly. "All right," I said, feeling like a failure.

"I am sorry," he said softly. "About Claire. About all of it."

"Me too," I muttered. "Me too."

The intercom buzzed on my office phone, and Aspen said, "Lark, Shawn wants to see you again before the meeting."

I checked the time. Still five minutes until the meeting.

"I'll see you later. Go save the world," Sam said before hanging up.

I pressed the button for the intercom. "I'll be right there."

As much as I wanted to figure this all out right this minute, I had a job to do. I couldn't throw it all away. So, I gritted my teeth and went in search of Shawn again.

The meeting was painful.

Aspen found out about Sam after the meeting. She apologized over and over again that Sam was gone. But it wasn't her fault. It was my fault.

The rest of the day was even worse after that. With the primary so close, I was stuck at the office until nearly eleven that night. A full fifteen-hour day. And entirely *not* sustainable. My brain felt like mush. I just wanted to go home, sleep, and start over. But that wasn't possible.

Shawn was still working when I finally left the office. I didn't say good-bye. I just stumbled out, half-drunk on exhaustion.

Sam was waiting there for me. I was glad that I'd texted him to let him know when I'd be leaving.

"Hey," I said, wiping my tired eyes. "What a day, huh?"

"Not my best." He sighed. "Not my worst either."

"Yeah."

"Are you hungry?"

"Honestly, I don't even know. I can't remember if I ate today. Only that I didn't sleep last night, and I basically feel jet-lagged as hell and I haven't even fucking flown anywhere."

"Let's get you some food. That will help," he said, gesturing for us to walk.

I didn't argue. I really didn't even have it in me to argue. I was used to surviving on little sleep, but this was something else. This was physical and mental breakdown. If I wasn't careful, I was going to get sick. Last campaign, I'd gotten pneumonia and tried to work through it. I had to be bedridden for four days. It had been torture. I didn't want that to happen again.

Sam and I stepped into Buns. He pushed me into our regular booth in the back corner and then ordered our burgers. I was half-asleep by the time he brought them over to our table.

"Eat," he said, sliding my basket toward me. "You'll feel a little better."

"Thank you," I told him. "For taking care of me."

"Of course, Lark. Always."

I smiled softly at that. At the way he'd said it. Something sparked in my chest. Hope. It worried me.

But I didn't speak again until I ate my entire greasy burger and every double-battered fry in my basket. Food coma hit me fresh, and it felt great. I must have skipped lunch or second lunch. I couldn't remember. I was starting to fire on a few cylinders again.

"Before you get to talk, I want to say something," I told him, pushing my basket aside. "A few somethings."

He gestured for me to continue. "Go ahead if you think you need to."

"I do. Well, first, I just…I'm sorry about the job," I told him.

"Yeah," he said with a sigh. "But I'm glad it was me and not you. You love it more than me."

"I don't know if that's true. It's just the only thing I've ever had that was mine. That my parents couldn't take away. And…it just sucks. That I ruined it for you."

"You didn't ruin it for me. I had a choice in our relationship, too, you know?"

"Yes, but…" I splayed my hands out. "I mean, I'm the authority figure. I feels different because we dated before this, but I am your boss. I have the power in this situation. Or it looks like it from the outside. Imagine what it would be like if our genders were reversed. People have been taken down for less especially in this climate."

He nodded. "I see what you mean. Though I still don't think you're to blame."

"I don't know this for sure because I wasn't given a reason or able to talk to Leslie, but I think it was a strategic move. If someone else had found out about us, then it would have looked bad for the campaign. Leslie is touting gender equality, equal pay, more women in politics. All of that equates to more power for women. Then here we are…and it would have looked…no, the spin would have been that I was abusing my power. Just like if it was a man dating a one of his employees. We would have been another hindrance to her campaign. It's the only real explanation that I could come up with in the *post-Court getting arrested* phase of Leslie's campaign."

"Fuck," he said, running a hand back through his hair.

"Yeah. And then...unrelated...or sort of...I want to talk about last night." I took a deep breath. "Can you imagine how I felt last night?"

"Yes. I'm sorry about telling you to go on to the party and not calling you."

"It's more than that," I admitted slowly. "When I saw Claire, I wanted to hurt her. Not physically. Not like that. But I felt a shift inside me. I felt Bad Lark surface, and all the things that I had been trying to tamp down in my personality reappeared as if it had never been gone. And I realized that only you make me feel that way."

He frowned. "I make you want to do bad things?"

"Yes," I told him. "It was just like with Melissa. I couldn't think clearly when she said she wanted you back. It was why I stood on the threshold because I didn't want to become that person again."

"I don't want to make you feel like that," he said carefully.

"I know. I've come to terms with it a bit. I thought it was all bad. But I think it's just the part of me that doesn't want to hurt. So, I lash out to protect myself. I don't want to be vulnerable." I bit my lip, searching his face. "I've never felt this way about anyone else before, Sam. Not the way that I feel about you. Which is why I lash out when I feel threatened by that. It's why I did what I did to Melissa and what I wanted to do to Claire."

"That sounds actually pretty normal, Lark. Maybe not to the extent at which you can lash out at people. You have a certain level of experience in that. But a lot of people get mad when they feel threatened."

"I know," I said with a sigh. "And I don't want to justify my behavior. But I want you to understand where I was coming from last night."

"I get it. You were afraid of losing me."

I swallowed. "So...am I losing you?"

His eyes rounded. "You actually think that's where this is heading?"

My hands shook as I clasped them hard together. "I don't want to think so. But what am I supposed to think? You stayed with her for two hours. After the diner, I can only imagine that you went home to her last night."

"I stayed at Court's," he told me.

"You...you did?"

"Yes. I told you it's not what you think. Claire and I aren't back together."

"You're not?" I whispered. Still waiting for that moment where it all fell apart. Still half-fearing this was too good to be true.

"We're not." He reached out and grasped my hands. "How could I ever want anyone but you?"

37

SAM

Lark looked back at me, unconvinced. I'd wanted her to light up like Christmas morning when I told her that. But after all she'd told me and how I'd been an idiot, I didn't blame her for being skeptical.

"If that's true, then why didn't you show up last night?" Lark asked. "What were you *doing* for two hours?"

I sighed and hung my head. "I'm not entirely sure it's my story to tell. They just found out. It's why she rushed home." I met her gaze with a solemn look. "Claire just found out that her mother has breast cancer."

Her mouth popped open, and she immediately covered it with her hand. "Oh god. No. That's horrible."

"Yeah. I really love her mom too. She's a great woman. Very kind, very loving. She bakes constantly and has this perfect Southern vibe." I ran a hand back through my hair. "She's going to beat it, but I think it was hard for Claire to hear. Let alone when she was halfway across the world."

"Fuck. Yeah. I mean, I don't even get along with my mom, and I couldn't imagine finding that out."

"So, she was understandably freaked out. We spent a lot of time talking about it. But the cancer diagnosis made her look at herself. It made her see what she really wanted...or thought she really wanted. And because I was the first person she thought of, she thought that she was still in love with me. That she'd made some grave mistake by breaking up with me and leaving me behind."

Lark cringed. "Well, I see how something that traumatic could do that. Plus, you're pretty amazing."

"I mean, the thing is that...Claire and I were always just...fine," I told her. I didn't know how else to explain it. "We worked. It was simple. Convenient and comfortable. So, Claire didn't realize she was still in love with me. I think she just fell back on what made her feel safe."

"That sounds right."

"Not that you wanted to hear that, but it wasn't what it seemed when I first walked into the apartment. I had every intention of telling her that I'd already packed her shit up and then following you out. But then she slammed me with this, and I just...couldn't leave her," I admitted.

"Jesus," Lark whispered.

"Yeah, it wasn't great. Especially when I told her about you."

Her eyes widened. "You told her?"

"Yeah. The whole truth this time. That we'd dated before on campaign." I winced. "I'd never heard her scream before that."

"She screamed at you?"

I nodded. "She tried to act like we weren't actually broken up. That she'd just said that we were on a break."

"What is this, *Friends*?" Lark asked.

I grinned. "Basically. And it was a lie anyway. She might have said we were on a break, but she made it clear that she was leaving me because we weren't serious enough. I assumed that she was going to Europe to fuck other guys."

"Ugh. That's...rough."

"It was just an excuse that she flung at me when I told her that you and I were together. She wanted to have someone to blame."

"And she blamed you...or me?" she asked carefully.

"Mostly me. Also some you. And really, I don't even know

whose fault it is. If it's anyone's fault. Just a bad situation. She was hurting and needed someone. I was the person she turned to. Then I ruined it by not still wanting her."

"Do you think she was waiting for you while she was gone?"

A laugh burst out of me. "Definitely not. I'm sure she was doing exactly what I thought she went there to do."

Lark sighed and leaned her head back against the booth. Her gaze was above my head. I could see she was deep in thought. Taking in all that I'd told her.

I didn't know where her head was at. If she was still mad at me for what had happened or if she still needed time to think about it. I didn't want to lose her. Not over this. Especially not after I'd just been fired. But I wasn't going to just let her walk away.

"So...you're really not getting back together?" she finally asked.

"No. We're not. It was a long and horrible conversation. Then we parted ways. She's going to see her mom and then moving in with a friend."

"And what are you doing?"

"I think that depends entirely on you," I said, offering her my hand.

And after a few seconds, she placed hers in mine. "I want this."

A smile lit up my features. "I love you."

"I love you too," she said, fighting back a smile. "I can't believe we're really here. Honestly, I felt like the worst was going to happen. That, at any minute, you were going to change your mind. Perhaps I'm a bit traumatized by the past."

I brought her hand to my lips and placed a kiss on it. "I don't want to leave you ever again."

"I think I'd like that." She looked down and then back up at me under her long, full lashes. "So...where are you staying tonight?"

"Well, I planned to stay with Court."

"I'm thinking no," she said, standing up and pulling me out of the booth. "I haven't slept in, like, forty-eight hours. You can stay with me and make me sleep."

"Is that what we're calling it nowadays?"

She laughed and then threw her arms around me and kissed

me. Relief flooded through my body as I held her in this ridiculous greasy burger joint and knew that she was mine. That we weren't so jaded by our pasts to screw up something this incredible. That, despite all odds, we'd found each other again. And we were going to make it work.

We headed out together, taking a cab uptown. I thought she had been kidding when she said that she wanted to sleep, but as soon as we walked in the house, she stripped out of her clothes and nearly face-planted into the bed.

"Did you honestly not sleep at all?" I asked, pulling back the covers and tucking her legs in.

She shook her head. "I was a hot mess. I couldn't seem to shut my brain off. I think I passed out right when English got back."

I grimaced. "Oh yeah. I heard about English being back. She really laid into Court."

Lark yawned dramatically and reached for me. "She's going through something. It'll blow over."

"Sucks."

"Yeah. That's a word for it."

I came around to her side of the bed and crouched down in front of her. "Can I give you something?"

Her green eyes were hooded as she nodded.

Then I retrieved a wrapped gift from my suit pocket. I'd gone back to my place in Brooklyn for it. I'd been planning to give it to her later. After the primary, when we won. A victory gift. But it felt right now.

"What is it?" she said, leaning up on one elbow.

I passed it to her. "A gift for you."

She took it in her hands and slowly peeled back the wrapping paper. It fluttered to the floor, and in her hand was a small, hand-carved, wooden lark.

"Oh wow," she breathed. "When did you have time for this?"

"You find time for things that are important."

"You made me one of these on the presidential campaign."

I nodded. "I did. I figured that one was probably gone. And you might need a replacement."

"Actually," she said softly, "I was waiting to show you..."

She opened up the second drawer of her nightstand and removed an object wrapped in tissue paper. She undid it and showed me the lark that I'd carved for her.

"You kept it all this time?" I asked in surprise.

"I couldn't get rid of it. Even when I got rid of everything else. It felt too...personal." She held the two larks together. "And now, they're a matched set."

"Like us."

She hummed appreciatively and set the two larks down on her nightstand to watch over us. Then she patted the bed next to her. "Sleep."

I laughed. "You really do just want to sleep."

Her eyes were half-glazed over. "The stress is finally all gone. Well, except for your job. We'll figure that out."

I stripped out of my suit and crawled into bed, carefully tucking her back into my chest. "You sound so confident about that."

"You're good at what you do. We can find something."

"You know, it took weeks for me to get the job on campaign after the other company closed."

She turned in to face me and met my steady gaze. "I'm going to sound Upper East Side here, but you didn't have me before. You didn't have our group of friends. It's different now. And I know that sounds snooty or whatever, but I've kind of come to terms with it. This is who I am. It has some benefits, and we'll use them to get you a job that you enjoy."

I brushed her wild red hair out of her face. "I feel lucky then that you would want to do that for me. I'd never ask."

She pressed her lips to mine. "I know. That's why I'm going to do it."

Something shifted between us in that moment. It wasn't just a soft kiss that bespoke of exhaustion. An exhaustion that we both felt. It was something else altogether. Like our worlds were back on axis, spinning with our own gravity.

Her hands explored my body, and then she was tugging at my

boxers. I eased out of them as she tossed her panties to the ground. She reached for my cock, taking it in her hand and experimentally stroking it a few times. I groaned in the back of my throat. She smiled against my lips.

"I like that," she said. "How you moan when I touch you."

"Fuck, woman," I groaned, grasping her jaw in my hands and crushing our lips together.

It was her turn to make sexy mewling noises against my lips. Then she hiked one leg up and over my body and settled herself on top of me. My hands slipped down to her hips as she aligned our bodies together. I had an unbelievable vision of her naked form on top of me. Her wide hips and the easy roll of her stomach. Her fucking perfect, small breasts. I dug my fingers into her skin as my cock lengthened at that glorious view.

"You're beautiful."

She flushed all over and then slid her pussy down onto my cock. I couldn't contain my own moan as I watched her eyes close and her head tip back.

"Oh god," she said.

Then she started moving. Lifting her hips ever so slowly and then dropping back down onto me. She braced one hand on my chest, working up a rhythm. Her tits bounced as she rocked back and forth.

And soon, I lost the ability to let her continue. It was a fucking sight to watch, but I needed more. She needed more.

I took control back, even as she was on top of me. I grasped her hips harder and began to work them in a rolling motion.

Her eyes widened. "Fuck. Right there."

I thrust up into her as I slammed her back down onto me again and again. Faster and faster, fucking her until we were both gasping for breath, aching all over. My cock grew just a little bit more as I watched her give in and come all over my dick. And then I grunted inelegantly and came behind her.

She collapsed forward over me when she was finished and pressed a kiss to my chest. "I love you."

"I love you too."

Her breathing slowed until she was almost asleep before she went into the bathroom to clean up. I went in after she was done, and by the time I came back out, she was already passed out. I pulled my boxers back on, climbed into bed, and drew her tight against me.

Mine.

She was mine.

38

LARK

"It's just temporary, right?" I asked English the next morning. Her eyes rose when she saw Sam walk into the room and reach for the pot of coffee.

"Oh yeah. We made up."

English snorted. "Go figure."

"But really, you're not moving back to LA, right?"

She sighed and then shook her head. "No, I don't think so. But I do have to go back. I have to finish some stuff off, talk to some people. Lots of decisions to make."

"As long as you come back," I said, pulling her into a hug.

"Well, as much as I hate him, Josh said that I could keep the apartment." She rolled her eyes. "Rather magnanimous of him, don't you think? He got me the apartment out of guilt and is letting me keep it out of guilt."

"I'm just glad you'll be here. But if you hate the apartment, we can sell it and find you something else."

She frowned. "But I want it. And then I feel stupid because I want it and he bought it for me." She shook her head. "I'll have to disentangle some of this."

"You'll get there...just not overnight."

"I know," she said softly. She pushed her carry-on toward the door. "Off through three more time zones. I won't even know my own name, the jet-lag will be so bad. Wish me luck."

"All the luck in the world, friend."

She blew me a kiss and then was gone.

"God, I feel bad for her," I told Sam.

He nodded and offered me coffee. "Me too. I can't believe what Josh did."

"Yeah. Me either. She's such a catch."

"You should be going. Don't want to be late."

"And what will you do all day?" I asked him.

He shrugged. "Start looking at jobs, I guess."

"Well, let me know if you find anything," I told him, giving him a kiss before I headed out to work.

"Lark," Aspen said on the intercom sometime after lunch, "it's Malcolm from the mayor's office on line two."

Malcolm?

That was odd. Leslie's assistant never called over here. We had little crossover between the organizations. For legal reasons, the campaign had to be completely separate from the actual running of politics. So, I'd had to give up the job that I'd had with Leslie at City Hall to come get her reelected. It was all a big ordeal but an important one.

"Got it. Thanks." Then I pressed the line. "Hi, Malcolm. It's Lark. How can I help you?"

"Hey, Lark. The mayor just asked me to have you over at City Hall for a meeting at three o'clock. Does that work for you?"

What the hell? Why?

That was what I wanted to ask. But I had a feeling Malcolm was just the messenger, and Leslie would let me know when I needed to know.

"Sure. Three is fine with me."

"Excellent. See you then."

I was confused. I didn't know what this meant. Yesterday,

Shawn had said that I was irreplaceable. And now, Leslie was calling me into her office at City Hall. Not the one she used when she was here. It couldn't be *good* news. That was for sure.

By two thirty, I told Aspen I'd be gone for the afternoon for the mayor, and I headed to City Hall. My nerves, which had previously calmed down since I talked to Sam, were jittery all over again. I hated this. The not knowing.

I found Malcolm waiting outside the mayor's office. He was a short, round-faced Indian man with dark, curly hair.

He energetically waved at me. "Hey, Lark! It's good to have you back in the building."

I smiled wanly at him. "Sometimes, I miss it."

He rolled his eyes. "Oh, please. You like getting people elected more than you like running a city."

He wasn't wrong.

I just shrugged. "True."

"I think she's ready for you. You can go on in," he said with a warm smile.

I took a deep breath and then pushed the door open. Leslie was sitting behind her imposing desk, writing avidly on a legal pad.

"Hello, Your Honor," I said, forcing a smile.

She glanced up and smiled grimly. "Lark, I feel like we've known each other long enough that you can call me Leslie. Even in here."

"Leslie, what can I do for you today?"

"You can sit. We need to talk."

I gulped. "All right." I sat straight-backed in the chair before her desk. "What do we need to talk about?"

"Court."

I furrowed my brows. That wasn't what I'd been anticipating. I'd thought she'd want to talk about Sam and what had happened.

"What about Court?"

"I don't want to know all the details," she said, crossing her arms on the desk. "Lord knows, I have no interest in knowing what my son is *really* up to. But I heard about the raid. That you got him out."

"Well, it was thanks to Camden."

She smirked. "Thanks to Camden indeed. He was the one who had tipped the police off to begin with."

"Wait...what?" I asked in confusion. "No, he said he knew a police detective who had tipped him off."

"The Percys are not what they seem, Lark. Camden runs practically the entire company. He has significant influence. He likely has a police detective or two in his pocket. But I assure you that he let the police know about what was happening and drew them to the location. There are several men involved, who are currently in custody."

I couldn't figure out why he'd lie about that. How could Camden be the whistleblower? Camden Percy who didn't have a good, just, or righteous bone in his body. It had to have been business. He had disliked Thomas from the start. He must have wanted to get back at him. But I had no idea why he'd go to those lengths for someone like Thomas even if he disliked him.

"That isn't what matters though. What matters is Anna," Leslie said.

"Anna?" Then I realized she meant English. No one ever called her Anna. It always threw me. "Oh, right...Anna."

"I saw what happened with her husband. It's all over the tabloids. She must be going through such a hard time. She wasn't there the night this happened."

"That's not her fault."

"No, but I want to make sure she's not going to be a liability. Is she still on her game?"

God, I didn't even know how to answer that. Any other day, any other situation, I would have jumped at the answer. This was English. She was always on her game. But after what Josh had done, I really didn't know.

"Truthfully, I think she might need a little time. Anyone would in the same circumstance. But I know that she's staying in New

York. She just bought a new place. I think once she comes back, she'll be ready. You won't regret it."

Leslie stared straight through me for a full minute before nodding. "Okay. I'll leave her. She's done a good job. The polling numbers are looking up, especially related to any questions regarding Court. It seems the work she's put in has paid off."

"I agree. The magazine that did the exclusive on the cottage was brilliant. It was everywhere. Who knew we just needed to get him in front of a camera?"

"Lord help us all if we put Court in front of a camera more often," she said with a lighthearted tone. "Let me ask you this, what would you say is Court's main character trait?"

I mused over that. "Charisma?"

She laughed. "Yes, I suppose there is that. It's how he gets away with most of what he does. But I would generally say, selfishness. Whether he is that way because of how I raised him or because of the trauma of his father dying or whatever combination of reasons, Court only thinks of himself."

"I don't think he's that bad. He takes care of his friends."

"And how many of those does he have? How many has he had longer than a year?"

I frowned, trying to think. "Camden."

"Exactly." Leslie leaned forward on her desk. "Anyone who can make Court think of someone other than himself, I think is a valuable person. It's why I've continued to cultivate my relationship with the Percys. Even though...we've not always seen eye to eye, I know that Court sees something worthwhile in Camden."

"Right," I said, unsure of where this was leading.

"And after talking to Court this morning, it seems that he believes Sam Rutherford is another one of these people."

My mouth popped open. "Oh."

"From what I heard, Sam has had a positive influence on Court."

"Yes. I mean, I think he has."

"In fact," she continued, "he insisted that I couldn't fire him."

"What?" I asked in surprise.

"He was quite adamant about it actually."

"But...I thought you fired him because of how it would look to the campaign for him to be dating a superior. I mean, I just assumed that's what it was because it would look bad, considering I was in a position of power."

"I did," she agreed. "I'm glad that you came to the same conclusion."

"Then how..."

"I plan to hire him for the Kensington Corporation." She smiled. "It was Court's suggestion actually."

"Oh my god," I muttered.

"I don't want to let anyone go who is clearly good for my team."

"That would be...amazing."

Leslie stood and smiled. "I'm glad you think so. He's waiting outside right now. Could you do me a favor and pretend to be thoroughly chastised before sending him in?"

I laughed. "You're bad."

"Don't make me lose the element of surprise."

"Okay, okay. I'll do what I can." I reached forward and offered her my hand. "And thank you."

Leslie shook. "I meant what I said to Shawn. That you are irreplaceable. Let's win this thing."

"Yes, ma'am," I said, beaming.

Then I turned back to the exit. I had to force the smile off of my face and slouch my shoulders. I didn't want to oversell it.

I stepped out and found Sam sitting in the waiting area. He looked up when the door opened, and his eyes rounded.

"Lark?" he asked.

"Sam, I didn't know you were going to be here."

"Yeah, I got a call this morning." He glanced to Malcolm. "What were you called in for?"

I sighed. "Leslie wanted to talk about what happened."

"Is everything okay?"

"I don't know. She said to send you in."

He blew out heavily. "Okay. I'll just...I don't know...can you wait for me?"

"Yeah. I'll wait here."

He kissed my forehead and then turned to enter the mayor's office. As soon as he was gone, a smile lit up my face. I had to keep myself from laughing with joy. He was in for the unexpected.

———————

Twenty minutes later, Sam burst out of the mayor's office. He pointed his finger at me with a smile on his beautiful face. "You!"

I laughed and dashed to him. "You got the job!"

"You tricked me."

"I did. It was Leslie's idea."

He shook his head and then scooped me up. He lifted me clear off of my feet and twirled me around in a tight circle. "I can't believe this."

"I couldn't either."

"You know...when you said we should use your connections to get me another job, I thought that you were being abstract."

"I think we both have Court to thank for this. Not my connections. His."

"Yeah. That seems fair. But damn..."

He wrapped an arm around my shoulders and guided me toward the exit. It was a beautiful summer day. The clouds had cleared, and the sun was shining.

"So, can I walk you back to work?"

I laughed and kissed him. "Definitely."

"It's going to be weird, not seeing you in the office every day."

"A little," I agreed. "I liked having you so close."

"Me too. So that my boss could objectify me."

I snorted. "Yeah. Sure. Okay."

"But it's better for the campaign to have this separation."

"It is," I told him. "And anyway, Kensington Corporation isn't that far from the office. We could meet in the middle for burgers."

"You've convinced me," he said.

Then he pressed another kiss onto my lips.

One that meant forever.

39

LARK

The polls were closed.

Ballots were being counted.

We were just waiting on the final numbers.

Everyone stared up at the enormous screen that had been erected inside the grand ballroom of Percy Tower. Newscasters had the tallies up for recorded votes between Kensington and Reyes. It was closer than I'd thought it would be. Closer than any of us had thought it would. We still had so many precincts left to tally, and my nerves were frayed.

Sam put his hand on my shoulder. He had the same edge to him as we waited anxiously to find out whether this was a victory or concession party for the mayor. We'd done all we could for the campaign the last two weeks. We'd laid it all out on the table. If we didn't win the primary, then it was all over. We wouldn't even have the general election to see if we could defeat Quinn.

And then it was time.

I squeezed Sam's hand as hard as I could as the screen put up one name—*Kensington*.

I screamed. But no one noticed. Everyone else was screaming too. Jumping up and down and throwing their arms around each other. Sam and I embraced as tears ran down my face. I'd barely slept in weeks. I had the beginning of a cold. But I was so happy that none of that even mattered.

"You did it," Sam said, brushing my hair out of my face.

"We did it. We all did it."

He smiled. "Don't be modest. You're the heart of this campaign."

I laughed and hugged him again. "I love you."

It was a few minutes before Leslie appeared. I knew she had been making a phone call to Reyes, thanking him for a good, respectable race. It was tradition and classy. But here she was in a sharp black suit. She stepped up to the microphone onstage before her *Kensington for Mayor* banners and the American flag.

"My fellow New Yorkers, it is with great honor that I accept the official nomination for mayor of New York City. You spoke out and said that we need four more years. Four more years to continue to make the changes we have seen all across this great city. The work is just beginning. And I want to be the one to see it through."

I glowed as the mayor continued her prepared victory speech. It was eloquent and energizing. It made me want to get back out there tomorrow and get to work. Of course, I had a few days off and planned to spend them with Sam and his brother, Jake, who was flying in in the morning. He'd never even been to New York. So, I'd play tourist in my hometown. But I was excited to meet part of his family. He promised that, after the election, he'd take me to North Carolina for Thanksgiving, and I could meet everyone. I was looking forward to that too.

"Thank you, and God bless!" the mayor concluded, waving at the array of cameras and the awaiting crowd below.

We cheered our heads off for her as waiters littered the room with champagne to celebrate. The energy in the room felt like New Year's Eve. We grabbed two glasses and sipped on them as our friends swarmed us with congratulations.

"You did it! You're amazing!" English said, pulling me into a hug.

She'd returned from LA, as planned. She hadn't quite been herself, but how could I even blame her? But the weirdest thing was how she was treating Court. Before, she had always been matter-of-fact with him but somehow still easygoing. Like he was business but also a friend. And now, the two glared at each other like they were ready to attack at any minute.

Even as she pulled back, English carefully stepped away from Court and to the other side of me. Court rolled his eyes at the move and downed the rest of his champagne.

"As if I had any doubts," Katherine said with her know-it-all smirk.

"God, I had enough for the rest of us," I said.

Camden actually put his arm around Katherine's waist before he said, "I wouldn't have approved a party like this in my hotel if it wasn't going to be a victory."

He said it as if he'd had something to do with it other than his vote. And god, sometimes, I wondered if he did.

Plus, the way Katherine and Camden had been acting was weird too. They'd actually shown up to the event together. Something I'd never seen happen on purpose. And he was even touching her in public when there weren't cameras. Perhaps, his knight-in-shining-armor routine had worked on Katherine the night of the raid. I'd thought about asking Katherine if she knew that Camden had been the one to call the cops in the first place, but they were happy enough, and I didn't want to be the one to rock the boat.

"Congrats, boss," Aspen said, appearing out of nowhere with her own hug for me.

"The real champion." I gestured to Aspen.

She blushed. "Psh, I just answer calls and keep your schedule."

"You're the best. The very best."

"And cute," Whitley said with a wink.

"Dibs," Gavin said next to her.

I rolled my eyes at the both of them. "Neither of you can corrupt my assistant."

Aspen's eyes were wide as she raised her hand. "I am completely corruptible."

Sam pulled me backward before I could keep that from happening. "I think someone else wants your attention."

I moved my eyes from Aspen talking to my friends and found, to my surprise, my parents standing nearby. They were dressed to the nines. All glitz and glamour.

I took a deep breath, knowing that I would have to talk to them. Even though I didn't want to. But I didn't want to be in this fight forever. I didn't think I needed to apologize. I just wanted new ground rules, so we could be a family again.

I clutched Sam's hand as we traversed the room to stand before them.

"Mother," I said with a head nod and then leaned into a kiss from my father. "Daddy."

"Hey, sweetheart," he said.

"Larkin, darling," my mother said. "It's good to see you."

"And who is this young man?"

I swallowed. "Daddy, this is my boyfriend, Sam Rutherford."

Sam shook my father's hand. "Nice to meet you, sir."

"Nice to meet you too. I've heard quite a bit about you."

I narrowed my eyes at my mother. "I'm sure Mother has been exaggerating."

"I actually heard from Leslie Kensington that he's a fine, upstanding young man. That he's going to be working for Kensington Corporation as an attorney. Impressive."

Sam's eyes shifted to me in surprise before returning to my father. "Thank you, sir."

"We don't want to keep you long from your celebrations," my mother said. "But we wanted to talk to you about Thomas."

I froze at those words. At all the horrors that could come from that comment.

"We fired him," my father said plainly.

"You did?" I gasped.

Thomas had somehow gotten out of the charges leveled against him for the underground gambling ring. Apparently, it hadn't actually been *his* place. He had just been bragging about it. Though others had said that he'd had a bigger part in it than he'd claimed after he was arrested. I thought he'd gotten off with a slap on the wrist, like always. The snake always slithered away.

"We did," my mother said. "You were right about him. We just...we so desperately wanted you to work for us, to be a part of what we have. We thought you would say anything to stay away. We didn't realize the kind of person he really was. And I likely wouldn't have believed it now if you hadn't opened my eyes to our behavior when you confronted me at your apartment."

"And because of that, he is no longer employed with St. Vincent's Enterprise. And he'll receive no letter of recommendation from anyone in the business."

My mouth fell open in surprise. "Wow. I'm so...shocked."

"You shouldn't be," my father said. He pulled me into a hug and kissed the top of my head. "We should have listened to you from the start."

I nearly choked on that. "Wow."

"You know you could be doing amazing things with the company still," my mother said with a grin.

"Mother," I said with a sigh.

"Hope, we talked about this."

My mother chewed on her bottom lip and straightened. "Of course. We see that you're...happy?"

It was more of a question than a statement, but I could see she was trying.

"I am."

"It's not what we would have wanted for you," my father said.

"I know."

"And the door is always open," my mother added hopefully.

"That I am also aware of," I said with a small laugh.

"We could start with brunch?" my mother suggested.

"Great idea. Lark, you should bring Sam over for brunch sometime," my father said and then turned to address Sam. "We'd like to get to know you better."

"Yes, sir," Sam said.

I hugged them both one more time. It was a step in the right direction. Not perfect by any means. But they were my parents.

They'd spent their life expecting me to fall into line, and it would take some time for us to patch this all up. If we ever were able to.

So, I waved good-bye and then they fell back into step with their friends and other big donors. But I just stood there for another moment.

"Did that just happen?" I asked Sam. "I didn't just dream it?"

"Looks like your parents have finally come around."

"Not completely. But maybe just maybe they will eventually."

"You stood up to your mom. She wants to be a part of your life, and you told her there was only one way to do it. So, she did it."

"And I didn't think people could change."

He took my hand and pulled me close. "You've changed me for the better."

"Yes, that's true. And you've changed me for the better."

"Come on. Let's go celebrate your victory."

"Our victory."

And then we walked hand in hand back toward our friends and the future we had created for ourselves. A bright and glorious future.

EPILOGUE

SIX MONTHS LATER -- LARK

"We're still on for dinner, right?" Sam asked. I nodded even though he couldn't see me through the phone. "Yes. Definitely. I'm ready to get out of here to meet you."

He laughed. "Me too. We've been swamped all day today."

"Should I just meet you at Buns later? Or did you want to go together?"

"Meeting me is fine."

"Okay." I glanced at the time. "I have to get going. I have a meeting with Leslie."

"Love you."

"Love you too," I said before hanging up the phone.

The last six months had been a hectic, amazing, brilliant time in my life. Sam had moved in right after the primary. English had moved upstairs to her own place on the same day. I loved having my best friend close and, even more, having Sam with me all the time.

Almost as much as I loved working as Leslie's chief of staff. Shawn had gone to help elect someone else as soon as the campaign was over, and Leslie had asked me to stay on for her top position. It had been an honor to accept.

I hopped out of my chair and knocked on the door that led into the mayor's office. Then before she even had time to answer, I strode in, looking down at my tablet with the list of things we needed to discuss today.

"Hi, Leslie. Everything is prepared for your speech at the charity function tomorrow night. And then the groundbreaking for the new domestic violence facility is coming up..."

"Lark," Leslie said with a small chuckle. "Why don't we sit down?"

I glanced up in surprise to find Leslie walking around her hulking desk and coming around to the couches in front of them. She took the head armchair, and I sank into a blue couch next to her.

"Should I start over with the agenda?"

"Put the agenda away. That's not what this meeting is about."

"Okay," I said as I set the tablet on the seat next to me.

"I need to tell you something. Something I haven't spoken to about with anyone else, except my children," she said evenly.

I frowned. I didn't like where this was going. It couldn't be good. Was she sick? Was she going to have to take a step back? She looked so serious. It made me nervous.

"But I want your honest opinion on this. You're not talking to your boss. You're talking to a friend."

"Okay," I said carefully. "I like to think we're friends."

Leslie smiled candidly. "So do I." Her blue eyes were steady on my face, looking for a reaction. "I am going to put in my bid to run for president."

My jaw dropped open. But my heart soared.

"Leslie! That's...that's incredible. You'd make a great candidate."

"I'm not certain of that," she said with a small sigh. "But I am glad that you think so. I have many things that go against me in the race. Many things that could come out in the election cycle. They would dig through my past, through my finances, my children, my husband, my political career. It would all be on the table."

"And yet, you still think that you should run?"

She nodded once, decisively. "Despite all that, I think that I can make a difference. I think I can do more than just be the mayor of New York City. I could help the nation."

"I think you could too."

"I'm glad," she said. "Because I would like you to run my campaign."

This time, my jaw hit the floor.

My dream.

The one I'd had every day since hearing Governor Woodhouse speak.

The one I'd never thought would be a reality.

It was here.

She was asking me to run her bid for president.

"You're more than qualified," Leslie said. "And I want to put my money where my mouth is. I want as many qualified women in top positions as I can get. I know I can only do this with you at the helm. What do you say?"

"Yes," I said without hesitation. "Yes. Absolutely yes. I'll do it."

"It's going to be tough. We both know it will be. But it will be worth it."

"It will be."

"You can't tell anyone yet, of course."

"Anyone?"

She laughed. "Well, you can tell Sam."

I grinned. "Oh good."

"But we'll have to put together an announcement date and start to get the team back together."

"I'm so happy for you," I told her honestly. "I think we can do this."

"I sure hope so."

We spent the next hour strategizing everything that we could for the presidential election, which would be exponentially bigger than what we'd run in the past. I had pages of notes on my tablet by the end of our conversation. And I felt like I was on cloud nine as I skipped out of the office and headed to Buns to tell Sam.

Sam was waiting for me at our booth in the back of the completely empty burger joint. He stood when I rushed into the place, his eyebrow arched at my enthusiasm.

"What's going on?" he asked.

I grabbed his hand and tried not to jump up and down with excitement. "No one else knows but Court and Penn, but Leslie just told me that she's planning to run for president."

"Holy shit! That's incredible, Lark."

I bounced a little on my toes. "And even more...she wants me to run her campaign."

"Wow. That's a huge responsibility. I can't think of anyone else who would be better for the job."

"I can't even believe this is my life. That I could be this lucky."

"It's not luck. You've put in the work, and now, you're being rewarded for your loyalty and dedication."

"You're right. I know. But it still seems totally out of this world that it's happening."

He grinned down at me. "I guess this might make my news seem a little less exciting."

"Oh?" I asked. "What's your news?"

Slowly, he withdrew a small Tiffany blue box from his pocket. My hands flew to my mouth as he went down on one knee in the middle of our diner and opened the box to reveal a round cut diamond with other diamonds on either side of it on the platinum band.

"Lark, will you marry me?"

"Oh my god," I gasped, tears coming to my eyes. "Yes, yes, so much yes. What is this day? I can't believe this is happening. Of course I'll marry you."

He laughed as I rushed through all of my words. Then he straightened and seized me in a tight hug that made the tears fall down my cheeks. This was happening. We were getting married. I couldn't even breathe.

I pulled back just enough for him to pluck the ring out of the box and slip it onto my ring finger. I held my left hand out to admire the beautiful thing while I brushed the tears off of my cheeks with the other hand.

"I love you so much," I told him.

"I love you too."

The light reflected in his eyes and made them shine. He was beaming, his smile stretching from ear to ear. As if he'd never been happier than in this moment. And I had to admit that finding out I was going to run a presidential campaign had felt amazing. But this moment, here, with Sam, felt even better.

A dream job, an engagement, and burgers, all in one day.

What more could one girl ask for?

THE END

ACKNOWLEDGMENTS

Thank you to everyone who helped make this book a reality especially Kimberly Brower, Rebecca Kimmerling, Staci Hart, Diana Peterfreund, Rebecca Gibson, Anjee Sapp, Amy Vox Libris, Devin McCain, Danielle Sanchez, Jovana Shirley, and my wonderful husband, Joel!

And most importantly, all of you wonderful readers! I hope you loved Lark and Sam as much as I did and fall in love just as hard with Court & English in *Cruel Desire*!

ABOUT THE AUTHOR

K.A. Linde is the *USA Today* best-selling author of more than thirty novels. She has a Masters degree in political science from the University of Georgia, was the head campaign worker for the 2012 presidential campaign at the University of North Carolina at Chapel Hill, and served as the head coach of the Duke University dance team.

She loves reading fantasy novels, lounging poolside, traveling to far off destinations, baking insane desserts, and dancing in her spare time.

She currently lives in Lubbock, Texas, with her husband and two super-adorable puppies.

Visit her online:
www.kalinde.com

Or Facebook, Instagram, Twitter, & Tiktok:
@authorkalinde

For exclusive content, free books,
and giveaways every month.
www.kalinde.com/subscribe

CPSIA information can be obtained
at www.ICGtesting.com
Printed in the USA
BVHW081006140323
660404BV00007B/566